3-29-65

GOD WILLS US FREE

God
Wills Us
Free: THE ORDEAL
OF A SOUTHERN MINISTER

by Robert McNeill

Introduction by Ralph McGill

 HILL AND WANG / NEW YORK

DEDICATION

To the people in my little clan, Jeanne, Janet, Frank, and Walt, whose lives were seriously affected because of my peculiar convictions, but who shared them with me in quiet faith and steadfast love.

Introduction

Observers of the Southern scene across the past quarter century, more especially the past decade, increasingly have noted what came to be designated as the "Agony of the Church." There is almost unanimous agreement that the church and the synagogue have, with a few notable and magnificent exceptions, almost totally failed to come to grips with the most demanding revolutionary, social, and moral problem of our time—the complex one of race. That this was more true of the Southern church, though not exclusively so, was made inevitable by the fact of population and history. A shockingly high percentage of Southern churches was to be found utterly committed to the past and blind not merely to the future but to the present. Even more dismaying was the fact that so large a number of churches were forced to reveal themselves as putting material commitments first. Those who received the fatter pledges were inevitably the most strongly committed to the status quo.

The agony, therefore, was not so much that of the church itself but of those more sensitive ministers and rabbis who sought to present the moral questions and the ethical principles involved, Christian and Judaic, in the nation's race problem. In early 1965, the record revealed that more than twenty-three young ministers had been forced out of Mississippi alone, in the preceding two years. In the same period, pulpits had been emptied in other states in the Deep South. But those ministers who perhaps suffered most were those who early began to try to be literal shepherds of their flock. Some ministers began trying to prepare their congregations well before the May 17, 1954, school decision by the Supreme Court. Others, heartened by this long overdue decision, felt surely their congregations would understand that there was no escape from commitment and that the old ways were done. Almost all these pastors endured shattering experiences.

One of these was Robert B. McNeill. In retrospect, it seems to me that this gentle and sensitive man of equally quiet courage and conviction is perhaps the most revealing symbol of Christian pastoral example that I have seen in a lifetime of looking at the Southern scene. He was, so to speak, born and bred in the briarpatch. He was a typical white Southerner of tradition, descendant of the Scotch-Irish who spilled through the tortured Appalachian passes into what was to become the cotton South. Intelligent, well, educated, stubbornly committed to the principles of his faith, he had attracted attention by his superior performance in small churches. He was called to a large church in the prosperous city of Columbus, Georgia, on the banks of the Chattahoochee River where the descending rapids have for many years turned wheels of commerce. There he spent seven increasingly useful years.

It is almost incredible, in the light of what change has wrought in the Southern scene since the year of 1959, that Robert McNeill was dismissed from his pulpit for the mildest of pleas—that the Southern problem of race be viewed in the light of Christian principles and Christian doctrine. Yet, it did happen. There was, indeed, a sort of crucifixion. There had been weeks of gossip, of abusive, even filthy, phone calls to his family; there had been the coolness of the members of his civic club, the hostility of some of the church members and the determined planning of some of the more influential ones to drive him from the pulpit. Even then it was an incredible action. Time has made it a preposterous one. Many members of that congregation insist that a sense of guilt remains in the church, haunting it as a faithful ghost.

McNeill's travail was just beginning. Shortly after his dismissal he was felled with a severe heart attack. Faithful members of his congregation maintained a vigil at his hospital door, greeting callers, taking messages, and giving word of his condition. The Bream Memorial Presbyterian Church in Charleston, West Virginia, had called him before his illness struck. When he recovered he went there. Slowly but surely Robert McNeill, with his gentle strength of character and commitment, and his fine wife and children have made a substantial place for themselves in that community.

Now he has written a book. It is, without question, a moving and revealing narrative of a man's life, defeats, victories, trials, and triumphs. It is autobiographical, but the reader will understand, as he reads it, that he is reading much more than the details of a dedicated minister's life in times of great disruptive social and political change in the Southern states and in the nation. There is something in this book of Everyman. There is much of Robert McNeill's soul and much about the mystique of the South's commitment to its past. The writing and the style are excellent.

Today, after little more than ten years have passed since the first of the court decisions, it is plain that if the Christian church and the synagogues had moved into a position of quiet leadership, much of the violence, hate, fear, physical assaults, and murders that have strained so many areas in the South might well have been avoided. Robert McNeill is one of the several magnificent exceptions of men who tried to provide that leadership. Almost every one of these men suffered. What it has meant to live through these years in the role of a Christian minister is here told in eloquent simplicity, compassion, and commitment. This is a book which merits wide readership.

RALPH McGILL

Preface

Ordinarily, there are only two classes of people who should write autobiographies: famous persons who owe their memoirs to posterity because they are the chronicle of great historic events, or successful persons who have a formula to offer those who desire a human model.

I fall into neither of these categories. My only excuse for having written about my own life is that I have recorded not what I happened to have done but what happened to me. My story is one that any one of a thousand men could tell today because of the similarity of our experiences. These experiences ought to be recorded while they are still fresh to the memory and while they are being repeated with agonizing regularity.

What happened to me was a gradual emancipation from an attitude of superiority toward another race of people. This attitude spawned prejudice, antipathy, bigotry, condescension, arrogance, and even fear, in varying degrees. My release did not come about as the result of clear-headed reasoning or the hot flash of religious conversion, but through the persuasion of a succession of objective experiences. I submit that this is about the only way that those of my temperament will ever be convinced. I record my experiences, not to argue, but to encourage each person to have his own.

I have said that I have been emancipated but this is not true in the absolute sense. Now and then I discover little tyrannies of prejudice that I thought had been eliminated long ago. Recently, in a panel discussion at one of our local colleges, I admitted that when I watched a boxing match between a white and Negro prizefighter I automatically pulled for the white to beat the other. A Negro professor on the panel exclaimed, "I'm glad you confessed that, because I always pull the other way." We both felt better in the knowledge that we were not alone in our shortcomings and that complete freedom from prejudice was more ultimate than immediate.

Another point about an autobiography—it ought to be written as late in life as possible, thereby giving the author the shortest time to be embarrassed over what he has written. I can't say how late this is for me, but I assure you the embarrassment has already set in. However, if I can initiate an awareness in my people, especially of the South but not exclusively, of what they are doing to themselves in abridging another people's freedom, then perhaps I have my excuse for an autobiography.

ACKNOWLEDGMENTS

My deep appreciation to Mary Perry, church secretary, who typed the manuscript; to Andy and Marian Thomas, Russell and Martha Wehrle, Dolly Sherwood, and Helen Kramer for reading and commenting on the manuscript; and to Jeanne and Janet McNeill, wife and daughter, for proofreading it. I wish to thank the National Council of the Churches of Christ for permission to quote certain passages from the *Revised Standard Version of the Bible,* copyrighted 1946 and 1952. I am also grateful to the publishers, Lawrence Hill and Arthur Wang, not only for encouraging me to write but for patiently tutoring me until I was able to put into writing what I meant to say. I cannot forget, either, that the staff and congregation of Bream Church have been unusually considerate of me and my shortcomings during the time spent in writing this book.

ROBERT MCNEILL

GOD WILLS US FREE

Chapter One

How does a minister face his congregation to which he has just preached his last morning sermon while notice of his dismissal is read from that very same pulpit? Is the occasion like an impeachment, disbarment, court-martial?

I had been notified on the previous Thursday by the chairman of the judicial commission of the presbytery that my relationship to the church was to be dissolved. This forewarned me but didn't prepare me. While the chairman read his statement I could not look at my people nor could they look at me. We listened with downcast eyes, not in shame but mutual sympathy. I did not want to show the wound; they did not want to look upon it.

I had served as minister of the historic First Presbyterian Church of Columbus, Georgia, for nearly seven years. I had come there with my wife and two young children in 1952, young, energetic, and idealistic. The fifties was a decade of much change, portending social revolution. The town people soon identified me with the liberal point of view, both in the church and in society. Though I was not a doctrinaire liberal, my preaching, writing, and conversation revealed a concern for social justice. There was enough of the old guard remaining in the church to resist the implications of this concern, especially regarding race relations. When I recall the ultimate fury of this segment of the congregation I wonder how I lasted as long as I did.

In 1957, two years before my dismissal, a representative of *Look* magazine came into the South looking for a minister who

would write an article on the race issue to counteract the bad
reputation the Southern clergy was getting from the identification of a few wildcat preachers with the Ku Klux Klan. He came
to see me and told me what his magazine wanted, and I agreed to
write my version of a solution to the problem. The article, even
before publication, touched off an explosion. It didn't make any
difference what I had written; I had consorted with the enemy.

I had no peace after that. Tension gripped the congregation.
The people sifted into three groups. There were my bitter antagonists who numbered a few, staunch supporters who numbered a
few more, and middle-minders who made up the vast majority. A
presbytery's commission was called in to investigate the trouble
and settle it if possible. The Presbyterian church does not have
bishops nor are issues of this magnitude settled by congregational
vote. The presbytery consists of churches in a given area, comparable to a Catholic diocese or a Methodist district. Each church
is represented in the meeting of presbytery by its minister and an
elder who is a layman. So a presbytery has ultimate supervision
of each local church within its bounds. The chairman of the
judicial commission who read the report on that fateful Sunday
morning was acting in behalf of the presbytery.

The atmosphere was tense. There was far more drama in the
church than either I or the commission wanted. I would have
preferred to have been fired quietly. Had the commission been
able to anticipate the extent of the national publicity that followed its action it probably would have found some other solution or some other method of severance. Perhaps they were com-
plimenting me by expecting me to remain imperturbable
through it all. I didn't expect that much of myself, but I thought
I could take it in stride. The next day, Monday, our chief elder
wrote the chairman: "I can think of nothing that would destroy
morale and create resentment more quickly than to get a group
together and point out one member of it and tell the group what
a fine fellow and a good worker he is, but you were firing him as
of that instant, and then neglected to say that the real reason for
firing him was that a few in the group did not like him."

Unbeknownst to any of us there were reporters from the *Atlanta
Journal* and the *New York Times* in the congregation. My
antagonists would not believe my denial of responsibility for

their presence, and later, by radio broadcasts, cited this as evidence that I was an egomaniac who espoused the cause of racial justice to gain national recognition. The fact is that I had called a clergyman friend in Atlanta who was under the same pressure to tell him of my impending dismissal and to warn him that his own presbytery would not likely sustain his position. After that, he mentioned to a reporter that something was going to happen in Columbus the next Sunday, just "something." The story would have gone out anyway because the city editor of the *Columbus Ledger* was a member of the church and attended regularly. But the point is that I don't go around inviting people to my own funeral.

When the chairman of the judicial commission stood behind the pulpit to read his report, a good segment of my antagonists filed in and stood against the wall in the back of the sanctuary. They too had been tipped off that "something" was going to happen. Most of them had not been in church in months, even years. But they were there for this spectacle, relishing the possibility that they were going to win out after all these years of bitter struggle. They stood there with unblinking eyes, reminding me of birds of prey waiting for a wounded victim to lose all capacity to fight them off.

And there were my wife, Jeanne, and children, Janet, Frank, and Walt. I had explained as best I could why I was being discharged but, again, how can you prepare your loved ones to watch you take your punishment? How can you explain anything when at that moment right was labeled "indiscreet" and wrong "expedient"? Our ten-year-old son, Frank, had of late made a little ceremony of striding down to the first pew and sitting there by himself. Perhaps this was a way of asserting his independence; perhaps it was a way of advertising to the amused worshipers that he was rather proud of the fact that in this great hall, his daddy did all the talking. Since we televised our services, some of my friends claimed that he held up the idiot cards for me.

But that Sunday morning Frank did not march proudly down to the front pew; he hovered under the arm of his mother where she and our daughter Janet customarily sat, looking brave but inwardly crushed. Henceforth I would agonize over this regular little ceremony of a little boy taking his place directly in front of

me, giving a self-conscious grin and a high sign that all was well
and I could now begin the service. How could I make up for this
failure of mine to him, how explain the love of God as revealed
in Christ which is demonstrated within the community of be-
lievers, when I, the proclaimer of this doctrine, was now about to
be wrenched from my office and from the people who had shared
that love? Judicial commissions have no answer to that.

The sermon I had prepared for that Sunday was the last of a
series on the essential beliefs of the Protestant, entitled "I Believe in the Church." This topic had already been announced in
the bulletin when the chairman called to inform me that I was to
be discharged. I couldn't change now; I had to go through with
it. What a crucible in which to test my emotions—I had to say
what I believed about the church when apparently the church
did not believe in me! The mental torture was the more excruciating because I had to choke back all the anguish of the moment
and write as though nothing was going to happen to me. The
concluding statement in the sermon was a paragraph from the
Look article, which I had believed once and now in this adverse
moment still believed:

Of all the institutions we know, the church is the only one that
possesses the seeds of its own regeneration. The church's weakness
is by reason of its human composition, but its permanence is
because it is God's. Paradoxically, it toughens under persecution,
reverts to strength when it becomes weakest, waxes greater when
it becomes smaller, wanes under the excesses of success, grows
militant when it loves peace, profits as it sacrifices, lives again as
it dies. It is as inevitable as change, as endurable as sin, as ever-
lasting as God. The ebb of complacency produces the flow of
prophecy, the dry rot of sophistication invigorates the seeds of
simplicity, the lull of contentment incites the outcries of dissatisfaction. The church is the conscience of society, the intan-
gible, controlling, and quickening force of it. God willing, in the
church I choose to remain.

When the sermon was over and we had gone off television, I
was required to present the chairman to the congregation and
then sit in a pulpit chair facing the congregation and listen to
my sentence. The chairman began in very complimentary fashion
so that all but myself, family, and staff thought that I was going

to be exonerated and made even more secure in my position. He
read:

The ministry of Mr. McNeill in this church during the past six
and a half years has been noteworthy. His leadership has given to
this congregation a timely dignity. The church has served its
priestly function in the community by ministering to the many
needs of the human family; as a witnessing entity, it has declared
the requirements of the Kingdom of God. . . . In all these
areas of the life of the church, Mr. McNeill has been at the
center. He is to be commended and you are to be congratulated.

In his place here Mr. McNeill has fulfilled a prophetic role
with forthright clarity. His fearless voice has been in the fine
spirit of "Thus saith the Lord." His brilliant sermons, with their
incisive analysis of present-day situations, have attracted comment over a wide radius. His responsibility has been to speak and
yours to hear. His task has been to lead and yours has been to
follow.

But then he came to a judgment that did not logically follow
his previous remarks:

The time has now come when, what has been the voice of the
pulpit, should also become the voice of the people of the church
as a witnessing whole—a strengthening of the sense of divine
mission of all church groups. This leading through united church
groups, calls for a ministry where the emphasis is from a united
church instead of from the pulpit alone. . . .

Here is the action of the commission:

The pastoral relationship between the First Presbyterian
Church of Columbus, Georgia, and the Reverend Robert B. Mc-
Neill is dissolved effective June 7, 1959 [the very day of the
reading], because the Commission believes the interests of religion imperatively demand it. . . .

John Wicklein, the *New York Times* reporter present, sum-
marized the commission's statement as saying "the voice of the
pulpit must be the voice of the pew." This was afterward both
denied and resented by members of the commission. But considering the action taken, he was right.

So I was stripped of my chevrons in front of my people, most of
whom, despite their disagreements with me, would never have
consented if they had had a voice in it. My pastoral relationship
was dissolved as of that day, presumably to prevent my organiz-

ing any schismatic movement while officially connected with the church. I couldn't even clean out my desk on company time. There was so much I wanted to say to the people of the church whom I had grown to love and in whom I had invested the best years of my youth. For the most part they didn't despise me. Many of them, men and women alike, wept openly at the verdict.

The service over, I hurried back to my study, not greeting the people as usual at the front door. This was no time to play a martyrdom role. I felt wooden—not dismayed or resentful or stunned—just wooden. My nervous system had been deadened to the point where I could neither think nor feel. The match was over and I had lost, lost by a knockout. I was now among the lowest of the low, an unemployed clergyman. This didn't bother me so much as the fact that the forces of reaction and bigotry had won the day, and I could not enter the field again for the next encounter. But at that moment I couldn't be bothered much because I couldn't feel much.

I should gladly have foregone the service that night. Another public appearance that day before the congregation, small as it was at the 7:30 service, would have been painful if I could have felt pain. How could I say anything coherent when both head and heart were numb? But I had to; I had to show outward calm and composure, complete freedom from resentment or cynicism. To have called off the evening service would have been an admission that I had cracked or that I was home soaking in self-pity. Or so it would have been interpreted. Few would have granted me the right or the disposition to say, "To hell with it, at least for today." So I put together a few scraps of my thinking at that moment, which I afterward wrote down in orderly form. This last sermon to the congregation was the only one on the race issue exclusively that I had ever preached to these people. And this after the jig was up.

I had not planned that my farewell message to you should be tonight. But my severance from you, the congregation of this church, came abruptly, so I have not had the time to prepare my words as carefully as I should. Neither had I planned to be autobiographical—ever. But the circumstances seem to require that I explain to you why I am as I am. I have been called stubborn and uncompromising concerning the race issue and all of the many side issues that have sprung from it. I have been so called because it has been brought to light from time to time that I have persistently identified myself with this cause of justice instead of dropping it in favor of the more important business of the church. And I should know by now that my unyielding attitude on this issue is a constant source of antagonism to those who ought to be appeased. I do know this and confess to the charge of stubbornness, but I must explain why it is necessary to be so.

When I entered the ministry it was vague to me why I should accept this calling. Now, on this day of my dismissal, when fifteen minutes from now I shall pronounce my last benediction here, not knowing where or whether I shall serve another congregation, I have greater assurance than ever before as to why and how I should serve the church.

In the early years of my ministry I was nagged by a subconscious feeling that I was not fully committed. When this feeling reached the conscious level I tried everything to dissolve it—more prayer, more Bible reading, more "expository" sermons, more frenzied pastoral calling, more mysticism. Much of this was good, but none of it brought the relief I sought. Slowly it dawned on me that there was one pressing human problem that I never faced without first preparing for myself some escape routes. I could not commit myself completely to the doctrine of the brotherhood of man without reservation, the reason being that a substantial minority of mankind living in my area was colored, and I had to make some allowance for the double standard of brotherhood I had always practiced. I wore myself out rationalizing. I came to despise the clichés I was mouthing. Worse still, I learned the bitter lesson that you cannot segregate the problem from all the other phases of the ministry of personal religious living.

You cannot pray as you ought because invariably you will begin with "Our Father," and God is the kind of father Who has but one standard for His sons and daughters. Dare we then have more?

You cannot practice the virtue of humility if at any time you must assume a counter attitude toward another people. George Mason, himself a slaveholder, confessed that the ownership of slaves makes petty tyrants of us all. Either we are humble at all times and before all people or we cannot be humble at all. Humility must be our nature, not our technique.

You cannot honestly extol freedom or democracy if you are not as willing to confer them as to enjoy them. And freedom and democracy brook no exceptions. Free men become slaves once they abridge another's freedom. Democracy means that *all* are rulers and *all* are subjects to their own rule. And I need only to suggest that you review your own aspirations to remind you that shackles to freedom can at once be extremely subtle and painfully strong. Silken cords are as binding as chains of iron.

You cannot read your Bible, even devotionally, without sensing that our long-standing tradition of enforced racial separation is contrary to a way of life given us several thousand years ago. Can we shut our ears to the voice of Amos who cried, "Are you not like the Ethiopians to me, O people of Israel? says the Lord." Have we forgotten that the man who so tenderly lifted Jeremiah out of a muck-filled cistern, even padding the ropes that went under his arms, was an Ethiopian? There were people of several nations and degrees of color in Israel. These wanted to become naturalized and counted as citizens of their covenant. Their great anxiety was that they should not be allowed to become assimilated. Their concern prompted these words: "Let not the foreigner who has joined himself to the Lord say, 'The Lord shall surely separate me from His people . . . and the foreigners who join themselves to the Lord, to minister to Him, to love the name of the Lord, and to be His servants . . . these will I bring to my holy mountain and make them joyful in my house of prayer; . . . for my house shall be called a house of prayer for *all* peoples.' "

What was your reaction to the incident in which Peter began eating with the Gentiles, only to move to a separated table for the Jews when certain important Jewish churchmen arrived? Was he right, or was Paul, who challenged this deportment to his face? With whom did you side when you read it? Remember that an integrated meal was more difficult for the Jews because of ceremonial and dietary differences and their tradition that Gentiles were unworthy of their company.

We have been taught that we cannot compose a standard by which we achieve salvation. By the same token, we cannot frame one by which one person determines that he is of more value than another. Did not Christ reverse every standard of importance man on his own ever set up? Therefore, I can never again look upon any person as being inferior to me. Nor can I ever again require my conscience to consent to a system, legal or traditional, that enforces separation that is in effect subordination and which leads inevitably to alienation. Am I ahead of my time in saying this? Am I not late? The Bible in its present form has been with us at least fifteen hundred years and God has been with us always.

So we cannot pray, become humble, proclaim freedom, refine democracy, read our Bibles; nor can we extend the church, honestly evangelize, practice community charity, rise to face the issues of each day without our racial attitude coloring our every thought and act.

This I had to discover for myself, though the lonely prophets of previous generations patiently warned me that this would be so. At last I have found the integrity of my calling. Would you deprive me of it in order that your consciences be given a temporary reprieve and a fitful rest? Is this what you mean by the peace and unity of the church? Peace and unity are linked to and dependent upon a third quality—purity. Without the purity of the church our peace is but an armistice and our unity is but an uneasy coalition. If I have found the integrity of my calling, could I not serve you better by moving you to throw off this final reservation to your total Christian commitment?

But it is argued that this uncompromising attitude promotes discord that cannot be dispelled as long as it is maintained, that the church suffers irreparable damage from it. We had better ask ourselves which church we mean—the church as an institution, or as that intimate fellowship of the concerned which aspires always to live up to its designation as the Body of Christ? Are we jealous of the structure of the church or its function? In short, what image do we see, Organization Church or the Proclaiming Church?

Organization Church is but the lengthened shadow of Organization Man. A church, like a single individual, can fall for the lures of the present generation. It can prefer security to venturesomeness, group thinking to personal conviction, community consensus to biblical authority, popular mediocrity to contested excellence. The Organization Church has a manager for minister, promoter for pastor, reporter for preacher. Its measurement of success is in terms of enrollment and budget. The caliber of its gospel depends upon the satisfaction of its clientele, and this gospel, though verbally honored, must become subordinate to the institution that holds it in trust. Was this not what the Reformation was about? Any kind of revolutionary spirit, which is essential to the pristine church, is entirely absent from Organization Church. It could not revolutionize life because it would have to revolutionize itself, and that is the very thing it is organized against. Is this the kind of church you want, or is it not so disagreeable to your fearful, immature self as to become a depressant to your soul? Is there not a deep yearning in you for the

Proclaiming Church, that church that above all else speaks forth-rightly the whole gospel and in quiet courage structures its cor-porate life about it?

If my spirit has been uncompromising, it has been so not only for the sake of my fellow child of God in dark skin but for the integrity of the church itself. In our day it must become the agency through which God redeems the time, and it must become the ground upon which humanity becomes reconciled to itself. So if I have been stubborn, uncompromising, relentless, it is not that I should have my own way but that you should have your integrity. For loving you as the people I serve, I knew no greater gift to offer. Amen.

How could I have come to say such things, with my back-ground and in that place? It took forty-four years to come to the point where I could. I'd like to review those years if for no other reason than to come clean with myself, to confess the changes that occurred in me and acknowledge the persons or events that brought them about. The story has its beginning at a place called Dynamite Hill, in a city that has been labeled "the Jim Crowist town in the U.S.A."

Chapter Two

Rounding the crest of Red Mountain at night from the southern side of Birmingham is like entering a cave of a thousand fireflies or seeing the Milky Way reflected in a calm sea. There at your feet is the Magic City, yesterday a hell-for-leather mining camp, today a self-conscious metropolis sprawling up and down the valley as far as you can see. There are cities more beautiful and more carefully arranged, but none offers so stunning a panorama as seen from this balcony under the stars. From a distance above the myriad lights, your senses may be confused by the blend of early summer jasmines from the mountain homes and the acrid smoke of the valley, a commingling of the esthetic with the grimy business of metal making. Sporadically the sky glowers with a hellish red cast as the furnace caldrons spill their molten brew or the open hearths shoot their flames into the air. Hell seems to yawn and pour off her distempered heat in a preview of torment to come.

On top of Red Mountain, presiding over the scene below, stands the statue of Vulcan, Greco-Roman god of the forge. Originally it was installed at the St. Louis World's Fair in 1904 as the symbol of Birmingham, then dismantled and eventually placed on a pedestal on this mountaintop. No statue in America stands higher than this one, save Liberty. Mythology has it that Vulcan, nephew to the ruler of the nether regions, was a pint-sized god with an inferiority complex, too ugly to inhabit Olympus, so he was thrown upon a tiny island where he plied his craft of metal making in a cave, out of sight of the other gods. It was from his forge that Prometheus stole fire and gave it to man, a theft which angered Zeus because of his apprehension that man would eventually use this fire to exterminate himself. This iron god holds aloft in his right hand a spearhead as the symbol of his craft. And there have been no beating of spears into pruning hooks in this volatile, strife-torn city. How pleased Vulcan must be with the thousand forges that burn as an oblation to him and the gaseous incense they waft into his cast-iron nostrils.

My father came to this city in 1898 from a farm in Clay County, Alabama, when he was seventeen and the city only nine years older than he. Nine years later he married my mother, who had come from low-country South Carolina to teach school in southern Alabama. As a boy my father got enough of farming, especially of the cotton-bled land of his family, and hastened to this burgeoning town. He was restless to escape the existence in prospect for him if he didn't move out while he had the vitality and ambition. He became a kind of executive secretary to the town's richest and perhaps most eccentric businessman, having charge of his real estate. He adjusted to this new environment and the new century. I seldom noticed nostalgia in him for former years and places. Occasionally he mentioned the old home place, but usually it was to exhort my brother Walter and me to be more appreciative of our relative leisure and affluence. All he had to say was, "If you don't think you have it easy here, we'll sell out and move back to Clay County," and we hopped to our chores with a little more alacrity than before.

He respected his father but he had no intention of being like him or allowing his boys to be. I remember the old gentleman; he lived with us a while. He was so utterly out of place in the modern generation that there seemed to be a span of a century between him and my father. I think my father must have instinctively understood that—I think that's why he left the farm so early—and yet here I am, holding ninety acres of my grandfather's Godforsaken land that won't grow dirt and bursting with sentiment and reverie every time I walk over it.

My father was outwardly the dominant one of our parents. He was physically and morally strong and was transparently honest. Even when I was a small boy his associates would remark to me, sometimes ruefully, that "you always knew where that tough

Scotsman stood, especially when he was on your neck." He was completely unskilled at deception in any of its forms or degrees. He hated ambiguity and indecision, maybe enough to instill in me that these were the worst of sins. Though he and I were never very close, never as close as both of us wanted to be, I took great pride in his reputation for stark honesty and absolute integrity.

I say he was outwardly the dominant parent. Yet subtly my mother was. She was as strong-willed as he but, typically, she took the feminine role of second lead. From the standpoint of background and education, she had more to offer. My father knew this and did not contest it. In the best sense of the word she was a proud person; it was obvious in her speech and bearing. Being such was a legacy and a calling of her family and her generation. She was a post-Civil War South Carolinian, reared in the low-country plantation town of Lynchburg, consisting of seventeen large families, several of which were her kin. Being a lady or a gentleman was something these people worked at. In many instances in those hard Reconstruction days it was about all they had left.

She did not come out of the Old South—she brought the proud, wounded, indomitable Old South with her. Through her I knew the last decades of the nineteenth century almost as well as I knew her. She lived her three score years in the twentieth century apparently as contemporary as anyone could be. She was modern in her dress, tastes, and reading. She was up to the minute in her knowledge of current events. Younger people marveled at the freshness and versatility of her conversation. What a contemporary person she was, they said. But I knew she never left the nineteenth century. She interpreted everything modern in terms of it. Her sense of values, her social philosophy, her religious views never changed.

Most of us become horse-drawn conservative as we grow older and hold on to our habitual ways and opinions, especially if the younger generation has passed us by. We become so because we lose touch with reality and know of no other way to turn except backward. But this was not the case with my mother. Hers was a doctrinaire philosophy that didn't originate in old age and petulance; it had been carefully molded by a people who considered themselves and their era unique. Their way of life was consid-

ered idyllic if not sacrosanct. This is the Southern mystique, this
is the sectional romanticism that loads our Southern bookshelves.
No other region of our nation has so jealously guarded its mores
or so appreciatively embraced itself. This is a basic point non-
Southerners must perceive if they are to understand the South. So
my mother, broadminded and current though she was, persisted
in measuring everything in the twentieth century by the standards of a never-to-return nineteenth-century South. She indoctrinated her two sons with these criteria, and her grandchildren
after them—as much as she could get away with.

She talked a great deal about the members of her family—and
they seemed countless—not because it was an old front porch
custom, as I once thought, but because she wanted her children
to know their every trait. If we knew their characteristics, she
said, we would know what talents and weaknesses to expect to
crop out in future generations. Every trait had its hereditary
origin; nothing could be attributed to individual originality or
environmental conditioning. I got my left-handedness from my
maternal grandfather and my peculiar way of putting my shoes
under the bed from the other. I used to stare at them and ponder
how I could rearrange them to break this genetic spell cast over
them and me. I wanted just a little credit for being what I was
and what I did. A congenital dent in my head was similar to one
in my mother's brother, Thomas Gordon McLeod, who had been
governor of South Carolina in the twenties. Didn't this mean
that I had his potential for success, perhaps even in the field of
politics? At times I felt imprisoned by my genes.

With all this stress on heredity, it was natural that aristocracy
should be the byword. In a South Carolina town of seventeen
families who owned most of the cotton land, it must have been
fairly easy to distinguish between the high and low castes. The
aristocrats owned the lands and the plain folk either worked for
them or struggled along on small, unproductive land of their
own. Some of these plain folk had a subclass called po'buckras or
po'white trash. There were occasional movements across the economic line when a commoner, by dint of industry and ambition,
acquired some wealth or perhaps a doomed-to-maidenhood aristocrat for a wife, or when one of the gentry fell into reduced
circumstances. But once the aristocracy of the community had a

couple of generations to crystallize, it could not grant that its
class could be broken into or fallen out of because of the fortunes
of finance. Memories were long in those days and though ac-
complishments were honored, origins counted for more.

The well-born passed off any attempted invasion of their ranks
by an unblooded person by saying, "The skin has riz," quoting
some hypothetical Negro sage. It was remarkable how convinced
they were that the Negroes had accepted this stratification of
society and how many pithy sayings about it were attributed to
them. The Negro's apparent approval of this caste system among
the whites seemed to be their sanction of the more pronounced
one which separated the blacks from the whites. Further Negro
affirmation of the system came from the fact that the Negroes
established their own hierarchy on the basis of which white folks
they worked for.

What amazed and frustrated me was that my mother, even in
her early married years and in a new and strange city, continued
to use this standard of human differentiation with complete confidence. She tagged the people we knew by the hereditary traits
that showed through them and revealed their origin. Birmingham didn't exist until seven years after the end of the Civil War,
and for the first several years it was a lusty coal-mining camp.
The aristocracy developed there on the guts, gall, or luck of
fortune hunters who came from everywhere, even the North. It
didn't have enough years behind it to become refined and genteel. She would never adapt herself to this materialistic method
of determining human worth and was somewhat nettled all her
life because our family, living in moderate circumstances, was
not recognized for what it was. It didn't occur to her that every
aristocracy has a material base after which the bloodlines begin
to show. Hers was based on land, the new one on fluid capital;
and capital we didn't have much of. She couldn't accept Birmingham's pig iron aristocracy.

She was particularly proud of our homogeneous ancestry. She
was a McLeod, her mother a McLean, and her grandmother a
McEachern (pronounced McCahan, as the initiated know). Her
father's people came over by way of Ireland when they took the
side of Bonnie Prince Charlie and exile for their choice, and got
hold of some rich low-country Carolina farm land. I was con-

vinced at an early age that I was an exceedingly lucky person to
be white, American, and Southern, but above all to be of Scotch
descent, and from the Isle of Skye at that. This Irish business was
never stressed because our migrating family didn't stay there
long enough to cross bloodlines. A brief respite there and they
were off to America to plant a new Scotland, free from the complex politico-religious alliances that had often pitted them
against the English and their own clans.

Beside the coat of arms there was a picture of Dunvegan castle
reverentially hung on our living-room wall. This castle on the
Isle of Skye was the ancestral home of our people, presently made
famous by the promotional wandering of the charming Dame
Flora McLeod, who keeps it in business through contributions of
McLeod clubs ingeniously organized by Flora in Canada, the
United States, and Australia. Mother prophesied that I would
someday visit that castle. And so I did. When I came back and
described this Scottish Zion to my mother, adding the deflating
note that all who came from that part of the island, laird and
crofter alike, were McLeods and that we had about one chance in
eight hundred and eighty-six of descending from royalty, she
looked at me with pitying tolerance as if to say, "Those are all
the odds we need."

What puzzled me as a child was that this fortuitous breeding
of mine which went back from South Carolina plantation to the
Isle of Skye, citadel of the world's choicest people, didn't cut
any ice with my contemporaries. It didn't make me automatically
excel either in the classroom or athletic field. Alternately, it
consoled me in the belief that excellence was not a matter of
personal achievement and drove me to attempt the impossible.

Thanks to my mother's persistent indoctrination I either developed or accepted an extremely romantic outlook. To me the
Southland was still paradise on earth and the Scots were the chief
contributors to its excellence. The South had been wronged,
spitefully hurt, by the rest of the nation. Appomattox had to be
reversed. The old order of gentle living, gracious manners, and
benevolence toward inferiors must be remembered and preserved. When a people had wrought an idyllic civilization, why
should they be either punished or forgotten? So with eyes glisten-

ing I vowed that I would do something for this city and this Southland of mine. My sector had done so much for me, why should I not give myself, even sacrificially, back to it? And why should not its beautifully distinctive qualities be cherished above all mongrel ideas of material progress? As early as I can remember I felt this way.

Yet there was another strain in me that produced ambivalence toward the Southern mystique. My father was not inferior to my mother—he was only of rougher finish. Long before I ever heard the epithet "redneck" I marveled at his two-toned skin. He had not plowed since he was seventeen but his neck remained a walnut brown color with a reddish underglow to it. The rest of his body, excepting his arms, was almost paper white. In no other way did he bear resemblance to the proverbial redneck or "wool hatter." I believe he came from what Southern historians are now calling "piney woods folk." His life began in the red clay hills of central Alabama. Apparently a little colony of Scotch-Irish, second-generation settlers from eastern North Carolina made the westward trek in the late 1700's and moved parallel to the Appalachians, which took them southwestward into Alabama. There they found land similar to what they had left—and very little civilization. The tombstones in the old Hatchet Creek churchyard record names like McDade, McKay, McElrath, McDiarmid, Patterson, Carmichael, McNeill, Brown. I could never figure out what brought Brown there, but he had eight daughters and through them all the Scots became related to each other.

The Hatchet Creek church had an arbor behind it, a kind of open-air pavilion. The congregation probably got its start under it when it was put together with poles, saplings, and branches. When the people built the church they promoted the arbor to permanent status. Firmer than the old makeshift one of pioneer days, it served as a reminder of the church's hardy origin.

Occasionally my father took me as a boy into these woods to visit the few relatives that were left there. Goodwater, the nearest town to my host-cousin's farm, was sixty-five miles from Birmingham—an all-day trip by the Central of Georgia Railroad. We spent the night in Goodwater and borrowed a horse and buggy to drive the four miles to the farm. We forded Hatchet Creek, the horse swimming and the water coming up over the floor board. The fields were rugged and eroded. The houses were typical pioneer, which can be best described as two boxes with a dogtrot between. (The house in which my father spent part of his early life was a corncrib the last time I saw it. I have never since regarded Lincoln as a man of humble origin.) The primitive conditions of these people belied their quality. They were living there and under these circumstances because this was the kind of life their fathers and grandfathers had deliberately chosen, and it was good for another generation or so.

On Sunday the members of Hatchet Creek gathered at the plain but well-kept little church for worship and for what was probably their only social occasion. The clear glass windows were wide open in the warm seasons. The benches were handmade and appeared to be constructed more for penance than for comfort. The birds and insects could be heard outside and occasionally flew in, to nobody's concern. There were spittoons under the benches for those who didn't get a window seat. As in most pioneer communities the men and women sat on opposite sides of the aisle. No one knows exactly how this custom got started, but even in recent years I have seen the division occur simply because each sex had clustered outside, swapping gossip or talking business, and each moved in together as a body. In the old Hatchet Creek church, however, the spittoons were an added reason. Segregation of the sexes meant only half as many spittoons—and in better range.

Before the worship service the men gathered under the arbor behind the church to hear my Uncle Joe Carmichael teach the Sunday school lesson in the awesome tones consonant with his Calvinistic proclivities. The circuit-riding preacher came there about once a month, so professional religious instruction and exhortation were infrequent. One Sunday in the mid-twenties when I was there, my father unwittingly threw a deacon into a mild predicament. The offering plate couldn't be found and he had to take the collection in his cupped hands. My father, who appeared and perhaps felt rather affluent compared to these backwoodsmen, folded up a bill and thrust it into the deacon's bulging palms as he passed before him. This stunned him for a moment because nobody in the Hatchet Creek community could afford to be so generous. He leaned down and whispered into my father's ear, "You want your change?" My father didn't but he was tempted to say he did, because the deacon couldn't have counted it out for him without first depositing the entire collection in his pocket or growing a third arm.

These ruddy-faced, gray-eyed sons of the hills were nothing like my animated, fun-loving kinsmen of the Carolina low country. By contrast they seemed austere, humorless, lacking in vitality. This was not the case, however. Their wrestling with the elements and their intimacy with nature made animated self-expression difficult and perhaps unnecessary. Hard physical labor develops a communication among people that doesn't have to be verbalized.

There was real ambition among these people despite their primitive conditions. Much of the time they didn't even have the proverbial red schoolhouse. Families would go in together and form a school of their own. The family with the most children furnished the place to meet and the oldest boy who got to the county seat for some formal training acted as teacher. Pupils came out of this rustic educational system with encyclopedic minds and the greatest asset of all, the desire to keep learning. Uncle Joe's brother built a little study room fifty feet from the house and required his children to spend an hour a day in there the year round. This family and this system produced eight boys who all eventually earned their doctorates.

One of the Carmichaels was Oliver Cromwell, who was president of the University of Alabama in 1956 at the time of the Autherine Lucy case. He did not take the stance of grimness that the South expected of one of its sons. Another Carmichael, Omer, a first cousin to the eight boys, was superintendent of the Louisville, Kentucky, school system and worked out the now famous plan of peaceful integration. These are my kinsmen, according to the flexible genealogies these people employ. And then, of course, there is Hugo Black, the most unequivocal spokesman on the Supreme Court for racial equality. He came from Ashland, the county seat, just a few miles away.

Since race has been the great social issue of the twentieth century, I can't help comparing my father's kin, near kin, and neighbors to the family on my mother's side as they have responded to the issue. Her double first cousin was Cotton Ed Smith, who stomped around the United States Senate for thirty-six years and led his state's walkout at the Democratic convention in Philadelphia in 1936 when a Negro offered the invocation. Another cousin in Sumter, South Carolina, brought suit against a local Negro minister for libel when they engaged in a dispute over civil rights. (The Negro had no chance before a white South Carolina jury so had to settle out of court for ten thousand dollars. This amount was paid by the United Presbyterian Church U.S.A., called Northern, because he was their minister and they stood firmly with him.) A brother was chairman of the membership committee for the White Citizens Council. He and his son in succession have served more than forty years as circuit solicitor over a district which includes Clarendon County, noted as one of the places which furnished a case which resulted in the 1954 Supreme Court decision on integration. A nephew, now attorney-general of the state, ordered all South Carolina state parks closed in 1963 when a federal court directed that they be integrated.

These men are typical of the state as it has been represented lately by the national press—when they fight they ask and offer no quarter, they fight fairly, and they lose like gentlemen.

The irony of it all is that the sons of my piney woods forebears, who should have feared the Negro as a potential economic rival, have emerged as the men of good will, while the sons of the planters who are long on *noblesse oblige* have become deterrents to racial equality.

So I began life with two different but not necessarily diverse strains in me. I was imbued with the Southern mystique, indoctrinated in its faith. I was also urged to rely more on my intelligence than my heritage and to get on with the business of maturing in a fast-growing city that never knew the old South. These influences were never thrown into open conflict with each other. But the conflict was in me, restless, irresolvable, and for a long time unidentified. I was half piney woodsman and half aristocrat. From my earliest years I didn't know which mien to assume, which strain to follow.

Chapter Three

I was reared in Birmingham
on the less expensive hill across from Red Mountain. Geologists
and topographers call it Enon Ridge; my mother gave it tone by
using the less familiar name, Graymont Heights. Today this
ridge is known nationally as Dynamite Hill. Our neighborhood
was on this ridge, with Birmingham-Southern College at one end
of it and an enveloping Negro population on the back slopes and
in a gorge that cut through the hill near the other end. Their
section was called East Thomas.

It was a good neighborhood, made up of middle-income people
and seasoned with enough faculty families to enable us to boast
of our cultural atmosphere. There was a fraternal spirit among
the adults that tended to develop a fierce loyalty among the
younger boys toward each other and a jealousy toward the borders of our neighborhood domain.

There always seemed to be two threats to us and they were
closely related. We feared the encroachment of inferior whites,
and even more, of Negroes. If inferior whites moved in there
would be less desire to preserve the integrity of the neighborhood; if Negroes moved across the zoning line and got away with
it, the value of the property would be reduced to the point where
the undesirable whites could move in. Very early I was taught
the fine points of this double-barreled alienation. We couldn't
understand why these Negroes in this pincers movement around
us were so restless. They had their own territory, why did they
want ours? Could it be that they wanted the heights and the

status among their own people that went with it? Were they no longer content with being black people and living in valleys?

The vague uneasiness of the parents over the occasional tampering with zoning ordinances was picked up by the boys and converted into belligerence toward any Negro children who even dared to walk through our community. Usually such an intrusion resulted in a rock battle, with nobody getting hurt but with the colored boys retreating before superior white forces which seemed to spring up out of nowhere, much like the men of Sherwood Forest. I can remember the cock-of-the-walk exhilaration we felt as we saw the enemy disappear over the hill in full flight. I believe we would have cried if we had hurt any of them, but our fierce loyalty to our kind dictated that we abase them. We missed them with our rocks not just from poor aim but from the schizoid temperament already growing in us that allowed us to degrade but not to injure. Occasionally, a lone Negro boy might have the audacity to stop off and offer to join a marble or football game. If we were in the proper mood we not only permitted him to play but made a pet of him, especially if he was discreet enough not to excel us. Inevitably, however, some watchful mother would see that the game was broken up, the brash colored boy sent on his way, and the usual lecture delivered about the impropriety of mixing with a diseased, immoral, and dirty race. "Now go wash your hands and wash them good; you can't tell what you might have picked up."

It was not pleasant for a white boy to go through Negro neighborhoods, either. What saved him from being roughed up was the Negro parents' fear of serious reprisal from the adult whites. But the Negro boys never forgot our indignities against them and they bristled openly with hostility. If they could just catch one of us out of sight of any witnessing adults . . .

During kite season a few run-ins with Negroes could be expected. Southerly winds carried our kites from our ridge over the valley of East Thomas. If our strings snapped, as they frequently did, our kites would drop right into the Negro ghetto. From a distance of several blocks we could see Negro boys collect under the falling kite, snatch it up, and run for cover. It was useless and unsafe to give chase. An ingenious scheme they had was, when the wind was right, to put up a kite in their valley that would become entangled with ours. Then they would wind their kite in and ours with it. Once my line broke and I decided to give chase. I arrived at my kite simultaneously with several Negro boys. I flexed my muscles and spoke some threatening words to them, quite sure that they knew my reputation on the hill for having things my own way. They didn't. They weren't impressed and, in fact, their leader came up close to me with right fist cocked and sparks of hate flashing in his eyes. I saw I was outnumbered and outbluffed, so I scooped up my kite and retreated, letting them win the showdown. This was something new to me. Negroes were supposed to cower before a white when he spoke with authority. They were supposed to because they always had, and they always had because groveling was their means of survival. But for some reason this tough little piece of ebony hadn't been taught to fear the white boy. It was a sobering experience. I hadn't been challenged in a long time and here was one beneath consideration who would have relished a fight. Why didn't he scare as he was supposed to?

I keep pushing back into my memory, trying to fix upon some event that first demonstrated to me what segregation was. I believe it was a streetcar incident that caused the light to break for me, if you can call it light. My mother used to go to a good many club meetings around town and the streetcar was the chief mode of travel. When our cook was sick or malingering, Mother would take me with her. The meetings she attended were interminable and boring, but I was compensated by refreshments and the big trolley ride both ways. Big yellow Seven, Owenton-Ensley; what a sight she was after waiting for what seemed like hours. There were all kinds of commercial cards along the walls, most of which advertised pleasant things to eat or drink or chew. A detailed study of these cards plus the images they evoked could consume the whole riding time. The conductor always had a little kidding routine with the children which included pretending to punch their ears with his clippers. And speed! There was a stretch of several blocks on Eighth Avenue where the motorman could really bear down on the throttle. He became Casey Jones at that moment, gulping down the distance and bringing her in on schedule. The rails sang, the big yellow coach rumbled and lurched and swayed as if it didn't intend to stay on its rails once it got its momentum, and an occasional Essex, Maxwell, or Ford driver would look up in dismay as the electric monster barreled by him. The jaunty ride was over all too soon.

One day I climbed aboard the trolley and went on ahead of my mother, who was paying the fare, to select a seat. I found one and quickly realized that somebody else was seated there next to the window. I looked up into the grinning face of the darkest man I ever saw. His smile was all ivory and gold, encased in blue gums. He was impeccably dressed in what must have been clergyman's clothes (none but preachers would be wearing their best at that time of day), and he had a big gold chain strung across his bosom. Come to think of it, from the size of the chain he must have been a Methodist bishop. I liked this man instinctively and immediately, and I took his disarming smile to be an invitation to sit with him and maybe to find out what was at the end of that chain.

I heard my mother call my name and the next thing I knew, my black companion, still grinning, had lifted me over a barrier and deposited me beside my mother. Dimly I sensed that some kind of division was made between people, that maybe skin color had something to do with it, although that didn't make sense to me. After I had learned to read I saw that the barrier said "white" on one side and "colored" on the other. This division for whatever reason seemed to be all right with everybody concerned, because my Negro friend was still grinning when he removed me from his territory to my mother's. And Mother was gracious about it, too. They seemed to treat the incident as a little joke between them that I was too young to appreciate.

"Gracious" is the right word to describe my family's attitude toward the Negro people. Graciousness was Southern tradition and anyone who acted or spoke ungraciously was not in the tradition, not a real Southerner. That's why old-line Southerners today can without hypocrisy or self-contradiction abhor the Oxford violence and the Bull Connor-type officials. Graciousness, of course, applied only to person-to-person relationships and not to laws. I was bred upon it. Like most middle-class Southern children I was raised by a Negro cook-nurse. Some of my most pleasant hours were spent around the coal stove in the kitchen watching Cook prepare dinner or listening enchantedly to the whoppers Cook's man could tell. I have often wondered why they didn't despise us for the carriers of bigotry that we were instead of practically adopting us as their own. Perhaps it was because they felt, at least subconsciously, that we small white people could really love them in return if left to our own impulses and weaned from the parental milk of racial arrogance.

My association with Negroes was closer and wider than that of most boys my age because of the responsibilities my parents delegated to me. If we had a cook who was afraid of the dark and didn't have a man to come for her, I had to walk her home. We had some wooded areas to go through and there were no lights, so the nights could be pretty dark and scary. I had nothing for comfort except a flashlight or kerosene lantern, and my dog, a beautiful Maltese-colored greyhound who looked formidable enough but would have been a completely disinterested spectator if we had been attacked. I think it began to dawn on me that this escorting the cook home was a real adult responsibility and that I must be a rather unusual boy to be trusted with it. I was just a runt of a person, maybe twelve, small even for my age, and I was the appointed protector of our household servant; I was expected to fend off any attacker, no matter how large or vicious. This is what I meditated upon on the lonely trek back, this is what I talked about to myself when I looked up at the starry sky. Was I destined, I wondered, to be a protector of people, even these people? Was I chosen to perpetuate the graciousness and all the other fine Southern traditions that I was learning? I looked often at those starry skies. God seemed so close and intimate. I felt so much a part of His planning because I felt so important to people.

There were times when I was directed to go into East Thomas on even more responsible missions. If our cook was sick or had quit, I was assigned the task of securing prospects for replacement. This meant going from door to door inquiring if anyone was interested—and that I either got into or looked into a good many shanties. I had to make a quick judgment from the appearance of the woman and her living room as to whether I should encourage her to come talk to my mother about employment. I never ceased to wonder at the makeshift way they lived—several beds in one room, the walls covered with newspapers to discourage the wind that whistled through the cracks, the oil lamps, the ever-present smell of collards or turnip greens seasoned with fatback and eaten with corn bread, the iron wash-pot in the stump of a yard, the sagging clothesline, the countless cats on the porch, dogs under the house, and little brown faces peeping out from everywhere. Seldom was a door opened to me until I had stated my business through it and had been looked over through a window. It took me some time to realize how much these people dreaded the sound of a knock on their door, especially that of a white person. There were so many policemen, process servers, and collectors who combed their neighborhood. Once that flimsy door was opened there was no escape from the white man's law or his tongue. So I had to get used to being looked over pretty carefully before I could even see the person I was talking to. These junkets into the Negro ghetto not only forced me to see how they lived, but required some judgments from me that I might never have made had I not been given the responsibility. I was early developing a social conscience without realizing it.

Every little boy has a domain, I think, an area over which he imagines he presides. It may be no more than a corner of his house or his yard, but in it he is the supreme authority. If he is the roving kind he may annex territory beyond the borders of his parents' property. How far he extends his reign often depends on how much the adult neighbors like him and how respectful the other boys are of his physical prowess. Thus in addition to my own yard and the wooded area in back of the house I took in the Beecher residence next door. It had many things to commend it. It covered half a block and was equipped with a spacious lawn, all kinds of hedges to hide behind, and a tall fir tree that I could climb. From its high limbs I could survey without being seen. This is where I went when it was too hot for games and I felt like an hour of reverie.

Everything else about the Beecher place was either mystifying or foreboding. The house was imposing, but its roof slanted down to the front porch in such a way as to resemble a beetle-browed scowl. There was a bas-relief on the wall of the porch which we couldn't understand at all, and knowing the Beechers were Roman Catholic we associated it with their faith.

They were very different from the rest of us. Mrs. Beecher had a voice lower than a man's and large deep-set brown eyes. She sounded awesome whether she was reciting poetry to the literary club or scolding us for getting into her flower beds. Mr. Beecher we hardly ever saw, but we knew that he was rich and that he drank bootleg whiskey because his bootlegger mistakenly left a burlap sack of the stuff in our garage one night. This was nothing short of astounding in a predominantly Methodist neighborhood during Prohibition. I would never have had the nerve to annex their spacious yard if I had had to confront either of them. They were too formidable and too little versed in profounder aspects of ownership. They actually thought the property was theirs because they had legal title to it.

But I had an ally on their place. He was the butler-chauffeur-yard man named Bob Perdue. He was truly a splendid person. If he were a young man today he would be a professional man in high standing. There wasn't anything he couldn't do. All the household problems assigned to me that I couldn't handle I took to him. He had nails, wires, scrap lumber, tools, everything. I was always borrowing. Once he painted a soap-box car I had built and christened Betsy Bell after one of Zane Grey's characters in *The Day of the Beast*. Bob had a way of whistling through his teeth, just two notes, that he used for a greeting, to indicate fatigue, and to tell Maggie, the cook, that he was ready for his mid-morning pitcher of ice water. He understood little boys. He, too, didn't want them trampling the flower beds, but he knew that I couldn't hurt anything up in the fir tree or when I lay on the lawn at night staring up at the stars. He respected my right of domain, knowing that by honoring it he was encouraging me to influence my playmates to be solicitous of the property. Bob Perdue was a superior person, a colored man I looked up to.

I learned in later years that he had a marked influence on someone else, the Beechers' only son, John. He was eleven years older than I so we didn't have much association with each other, except when he occasionally persuaded me to steal oatmeal cookies for him from my mother's inexhaustible jar. John was a prodigy, and was educated in private schools for the most part. His father was treasurer of the Tennessee Coal and Iron Railway Company, which is a subsidiary of United States Steel. This made him one of the top executives in the city in a most conservative industry. He was a direct descendant of Edward Beecher, a brother of Henry Ward Beecher and Harriet Beecher Stowe, all abolitionists. Apparently he carried only their name and none of their social concern.

John's mother, however, possessed the social conscience as well as the literary gifts of the two and was able to mold him in her image. When he reached manhood he embraced liberal causes and threw himself solidly behind the philosophy of the New Deal. He became a cause of consternation and a source of embarrassment to his father in the higher financial echelons. As an avowed liberal he lost his standing, his position, and finally through divorce his wife and children. He left the South, taught at some of the eastern universities, and finally landed on the west coast, where he became one of the seven professors there who refused to sign the loyalty oath imposed on educators during the McCarthy era. John is now poet-in-residence at Santa Clara University. He is as indignant as his abolitionist forebears and twice as much involved in the race issue.

Hardly would I have believed that this young John Beecher would refuse the legacy of affluence to cast his lot with his yard man, to hammer out his indignation at his own kind in a poetic cadence that pummels the conscience. I didn't know John very well then—I only stole cookies for him. But I believe I would steal for him again if we could only return to our place of origin, side by side, and he could be a part of my mystic domain and I could share the compassionate cries of his gentle heart while my own heart was still in its formative years.

The most beautiful nature I knew at that time was that of my brother, Walter. He was seven years older than I and was like a third parent to me. Though plagued by ill-health all his life, including diabetes at the age of fifteen, he never lost his masculine sweetness. He spoke to me often of the plight of the Negro people, their poor wages, long hours, and patient acceptance of abuse. He spoke of them in tones of sadness rather than of righteous anger. Young as he was, at least from adolescence, he knew the guilt was corporate, that he must share it along with the toughest bigots. His conduct toward any Negro he met was neither crass nor condescending. He seemed to go out of his way to make their condition not only durable but pleasant.

Late one afternoon as I was returning home from kite-flying, a Negro night watchman of some road machinery asked if I could bring him some supper from our table. He explained that he hadn't brought any food and couldn't leave his post to buy any. He said he had money to pay for it.

"That's all right," I said, "we always have plenty left over, so I won't charge you."

After supper I prepared him a plate, mostly string beans and biscuits, and started out with it. First, however, I had to clear with my father, and to my consternation he told me to charge the man fifteen cents. As usual, I took my problem to my brother. I had promised the watchman to give him food that we would have thrown out anyway; how could I charge him for it—and fifteen cents?

"Take him the supper and give Daddy this," my brother said, as he produced the money from one of those hidden places where boys keep their treasures. My charitable gesture nearly cost me embarrassment, but it had cost my brother something of value. There was no self-righteous indictment of our father or the system to which he adhered, only a touch of sadness that all of us of white skin were guilty of fostering such a system—all of us.

Chapter Four

Graymont Grammar School was a square red brick building three blocks down the hill from my home. In those nostalgic growing-up years of mine I would never have dreamed that this modest building would become the center of racial strife and the first public school in this volatile city to capitulate to integration.

There were seven grades—high and low—fourteen classrooms and the principal's office, no cafeteria, no auditorium when I entered. I went the first day when I was six and was so repelled that I stayed out another year, which was permissible in those days. I don't believe I have ever liked school since that first day, yet I have forced my way through ten years of college and graduate work. I didn't like the regimen, the austerity of the teachers, the intellectual competition and showmanship, the slack-jawed bullies who ruled at recess, the smells of unwashed bodies and overripe bananas in lunch boxes.

Like it or not, I couldn't stay out forever. I had to become a prim little member of the social order. No longer could I roam my domain or climb the giant fir or daydream at will. I didn't like to sit there in class as part of a human cluster, I didn't like to listen, I didn't like to recite. But I had reached the advanced age of seven and had to settle down.

Ironically, I was the first in the class that year to learn to write and the prize was a trip across the hall to the low-second grade to demonstrate my genius to my superiors. My instructions were to write "Merry Christmas" on the blackboard, after my purpose and I had been properly introduced by the second grade teacher. So in a trance of fear and grimness I scratched out my message on the board. When I finished the entire class burst into laughter. I was bug-eyed with dismay—what in heaven's name had I written? Well, it was "Santa Claus," which was not too far off, but these superior little second-graders disdainfully laughed me back across the hall to the lowly hutch where I belonged. What a lousy turn of events; I could write only two short sets of words, a fifty-fifty chance, and I had come up with the wrong one.

My diligence had earned me embarrassment—why be so eager to excel academically from now on? I had learned to write before the rest of the class, had tried to impress the class above me, and had proved to be anything but precocious. Besides that, my teacher had taught me to write with my right hand, not knowing that I was left-handed. Either because of a slow right hand or a slow head I gradually fell behind the class in writing speed and was seldom able to finish written assignments.

My grammar school days were more memorable for the extra-curricular activities. The scene I can't forget is the rows of pink or blue rectangular lunch boxes at each entrance to the building just before the opening bell sounded. We formed lines to go everywhere in the building and on the grounds, and importance was attached to being first in line. So while at play before school began the little girls would stake out a claim to position in line with their lunch boxes. The boys didn't have boxes; they packed their lunches in brown paper bags and they were a little less eager to get to class first anyway. Refusal to honor a claim to position was an unforgivable breach of the code and could lead to some unfeminine pushing and hair-pulling. Love would play its role occasionally. Since the girls formed one line and the boys another there was opportunity for pairing off. Unabashedly a boy and girl might intertwine fingers as they marched in, enduring for sweet affection's sake the merciless jibes of all the others. If a boy dared go as far as to match up with a particular girl, he would put his brown paper sack lunch alongside the box of his girl, and the fun began. Either he had to be thick-skinned or physically strong to stand off the treatment he got from his fellows. Conformists that we were, a boy might risk a public courtship, but he wouldn't be caught in daylight with a lunch box. It was brown paper sack or go hungry.

When we weren't playing organized sports, such as football or baseball, top-spinning and especially marbles were the big games. At recess every bare spot on the playground was used for a game called "Cincinnati." Peewees had gone out by my time, and the most beautiful glass spheroids we mistakenly called agates were the taws and the medium of exchange. Two to six were sold for a nickel, depending upon size. A real agate, which we called a stone, cost from fifty cents to a dollar each. Players matched off against each other according to their measure of skill. We had an infallible rating system which nobody had attempted to work out; it just evolved, and each boy knew where he ranked without ever seeing a form sheet. There was some dispute in the championship bracket among the top two or three as to who could break the others, and these contests were the most exciting, sometimes ending in a fist fight if the score was close and any cheating was detected.

The players kept up a steady stream of noises intelligible only to the initiated. After each shot one would grunt "Vance," an abbreviation of "advantage," which meant that if he were still shooting he had the right to dust off his line and tee up the marble in the ring. Sometimes his opponent would say, "Hard down, study knucks thu," which meant, keep your knuckles flat on the ground and don't lag in the circle. There were some expressions used, too, along with wagging the hand over the target to put the hex on the shooter, which I have purposely forgotten. The cheating that was done occurred when a player in one fast motion picked up his taw, brushed the dust from his hand with his little finger, and replaced his knuckles an inch ahead of where his taw had been. Watch duffers on the putting green and they will do the same thing. They learned it on the school ground playing Cincinnati. I was a pretty fair shooter, one of the best I would say from watching the others, but I had no rating. My parents wouldn't let me play for keeps on the ground that it was gambling and would condition me for gambling with money in the future. So I was strictly amateur.

I think teachers hated the marble season above all others, and it was then that they exercised their full powers of tyranny. Marbles made noises; they rattled in the pockets, they clattered like hail on a tin roof when they spilled out of one's pocket onto the floor. A good taw that fit the knuckles just right and was a fellow's lucky color was a rare and lovely thing. How could he resist fondling it at some time during the boring classroom hours? But how could fate invariably cause that sparkling glass to slip from the boy's knuckles, crash to the floor, and roll unfailingly up to the teacher's desk? With a glower of triumph the teacher confiscated every marble that hit the floor, unless some barefooted friend was able to catch it between his toes as it rolled by. Without dusting her knucks the teacher ended the season ahead of everybody, and all of us groaned inwardly as we heard our favorite taws rattle among scores of others every time she opened her desk drawer.

During the summer months we played sandlot baseball in the schoolyard, but without the organized adult supervision that Little League has today. At the age of twelve I was playing manager of the Graymont Hillbillies in their across-the-ridge rivalry with the Fountain Heights Wildcats. My counterpart on the opposing team was Bobby Bragan, presently the manager of the Milwaukee Braves. The image of a ball I hit up against the school house in the ninth inning to win the game and the series is as vivid as if it had just happened. We won the game 19–18, or was it 29–28? How can Bragan live the memory down? How can he step out on a diamond today with any degree of confidence with this managerial failure in his background? When I see him on television today I say, "Bobby, how in the name of Branch Rickey can you expect to succeed at managing when my Hillbillies beat your Wildcats when you were twelve years old?"

There is a somber scene connected with old Graymont school that I can't forget. My father was scoutmaster of Troop 22 and the meetings were held in the school building. I was too young for scouting, but went along one Friday night with my father and brother. As they were about to enter the basement door they noticed that the lock had been jimmied. As they opened the door somebody rushed out and ran into the mass of sturdy scouts. When the scouts pinned him down and shined a light in his face, they saw they had a young Negro burglar on their hands. He was about to get away with a wheelbarrow-load of produce, although I don't know what food was doing there since to my recollection we had no lunchroom at the time.

My father went for the police and left the prisoner in the stairwell with the assistant scoutmaster and about fifteen husky boys guarding him. The boys had whatever crude weapons they could find—sticks, an axe handle, a pitchfork, bricks. I had never been so excited—here was a real burglar and old Troop 22 had caught him. We had had our house burglarized several times at night when we were asleep, so this kind of criminal was out of the phantom world, something demonic, something to be crushed and chopped into pieces like a snake. And here was a real live one, sweaty black, nostrils dilating, eyes bulging, and casting wildly about from one would-be assailant to the other, lips trembling but speechless.

Oh, the fierce joy of witnessing this fear! Here was a half-man who was guilty of two crimes—of breaking the law and, worse, of sedition against white authority. Why take a chance on his escape? Clobber him senseless—he'll have plenty of time to heal in jail—and plenty of time to repent of his offense against the white man.

But he did escape; he suddenly bolted through that cordon of teen-age guards and lit out across the playground into the darkness. The assistant scoutmaster, who was lighting a cigarette when he saw him break loose, took out after him with sparks flying from his mouth, making a trail in the dark for his troop to follow. But it was no use. Once the prisoner was out in the open no one of his captors wanted to catch up with him and tangle with him. I couldn't hide my disappointment; I had been deprived of an opportunity of seeing guilt-blood drawn from the dirty, black body of one who by this larcenous act had spit in the eye of the white man.

It never occurred to me then how inconsistent I was in my judgment of the Negro. How could I so piously despise this poor hungry devil and blame his thieving nature on his Negro-ness? Cook and Bob Perdue were an integral part of my life—admirable people—and I either forgot they were colored or was glad that they were, for they in their dark skins had something unique to offer me. But why am I surprised at my inconsistency? Consistency is the first virtue to die at the moment one man consents to enslave another. I knew Cook and Bob Perdue and grew to love them. But I didn't know these thousands of other Negroes. I sensed somehow that my people had treated them in such a way as to merit their repressed hatred. So like all my kind I feared Negroes and hated them for making me fear them. If perfect love casts out fear, as the author of I John says, then the absence of love compounds fear. **1302092**

Graymont school—a terrified Negro streaks off into a night as dark as he, his liberty and possibly his life depending on his fear-charged speed, and forty years later two little children of his color with that same fear in their throats walk bravely into that same school, not to steal but to learn. My school—the place where I learned to write "Merry Christmas" and become a social being under protest, the place where hard-knuckled boys lived to clean each other down to the last taw, where brown paper bags made love to pink lunch boxes at recess, where Bobby Bragan along with his brothers suffered the most ignominious defeat of his managerial career, and where I tasted my first passion for the blood of a fellow human being. Thank God for those two brave little brown children for choosing this school to be the first in the history of this city to be opened to them, for they have redeemed my memory!

My high school days, 1928 to 1932, are a blur to me. Ironically, my school, Phillips High, was the first that Negroes attempted to integrate. In the late fifties I was startled to see on television a riot on the grounds of this school. My most vivid recollection of the riot is of a long-legged Negro sprinting across the grass to avoid the crunching blows of white men, who were flailing him with link-chains. The Negro was Fred Shuttleworth, one of the earliest and most effective leaders of the Birmingham movement and minister of one of the local churches. Once again I saw a man flee for his life, but as an adult I could see how debasing flight is, and I found myself hating the evil that reduced a man to a single, wild reflex that knew no purpose except to survive. Heretofore I had thought amusing the stereotyped flight of the Negro, whether in blackface comedy or in real life, but now I was

filled with shame at this indignity forced on any man, especially
a man of God.

I remember so little about my high school years possibly because I was so small. My post-puberty growth simply would not
come, so I wasn't a part of the life of the school. It was a period
of abysmal inferiority for me. The social leaders of the school
were from the exclusive south side and the athletes came mostly
from the parks in the tougher sections of the town. I didn't get on
socially or athletically, and since I had never learned to shake the
habit of daydreaming I was no pundit in the classroom either.
My development was at a standstill during these years. I was an
insignificant, knee-britches runt whom nature had forsaken, and
it was only in my dreams that I accomplished anything. What I
would do with my life I never asked myself, because I wasn't
entirely convinced that I would ever grow up.

Finally, however, by the time I enrolled as a freshman at Birmingham-Southern College in 1932, a local Methodist institution, I weighed in at a gawky 130 pounds, all bone and gristle. I
went out for all the athletic teams, to the consternation of the
coaches and the amusement of my classmates. The varsity football coach looked me over and observed, "Nothing but a string of
guts." I figured differently; if I could just get my adolescent arms
and legs to move as I wanted them to I would show them some
hidden talent. I got my chance in a freshman game at Tuscaloosa
against the University of Alabama, which during those years won
several Rose Bowl games. Those were the days of Dixie Howell,
Don Hutson, and Bear Bryant. A minute before the end of the
game in which we were getting systematically clobbered, Coach
Ben looked into my pleading eyes and said, "You really want to
play?"

I didn't answer him; I just catapulted onto the field, scooping
up a headgear as I went. He grabbed me just in time to instruct
me, "You play safety, not ours, yours."

In that minute I made our two longest gains of the game. The
first was on a fifteen-yard penalty—one of their big ends came
down field, missed his block on me, but caught me in the mouth
with his feet. It could have been Bear Bryant, but I wouldn't
swear to it. On the next play, Alabama punted to us for the first
time that day. Coach Ben hadn't counted on that and he was

horrified to see me standing there at safety waiting for the ball to come down. I caught the punt and set out for the distant goal, running from sheer terror. Those big red-shirted giants looked as though they wanted to eat me, not just tackle me. I tore out for the side lines, picked up some timid blocking, and amazingly got by all but the safety man. When I hesitated to figure how I would pass him, the other ten bruisers caught up and hit me in unison, piling me up under the player's bench. When I could see daylight again I heard applause from the stands for me for the first time in my life. The University of Alabama cheering section was actually applauding a play of the opposition. They could afford to be generous—they were ahead forty-five to nothing at the time.

This was heady stuff, and I wanted more of it. I was giving away an average of seventy pounds per man and I had them moving backwards for the first time that game. This Scotch-blooded boy was going to reduce the mighty Crimson Tide to a pink trickle. Fortunately for them the game ended on the next play. But I had my resolve; I was going to play the long odds from then on because my heritage made me just the fellow who could do it. I had hit the glory road.

The one moment of glory turned out to be a flash in the pan. I kept charging the insurmountable and challenging the impossible. I went out for varsity football and found myself on a team that became one of the six undefeated in America, even beating Auburn University in the opening game. The place I found on the team was not so imposing. On Monday afternoons the assistant coach and scout would take a squad of us aside and for half an hour would teach us the up-coming opponent's plays. Then we would be fed to the first and second teams in a very earnest scrimmage. A sweat shirt would be put on me bearing the name of the star ball carrier of the next Saturday's foe. As we trotted to the line of scrimmage the big lineman on the other side would chant, "Get Dombrosky! Get Vogle! Get Smith!" depending upon whom I was impersonating that week.

I got the worst beatings of my life in these scrimmages. Half the time I got up dizzy or out of breath, but I trotted back to the huddle feigning a look of wanting another crack at them. After all, I figured, I had to endure this beating while waiting for my weight and coordination to come to me. Not enough of either came. I was still cast in the role of the tailback villain on Mondays the next year, and the next.

I won a few things out of sheer persistence. I backed into the presidency of my fraternity because the depression stripped us of most of our upperclassmen. I made the varsity basketball team, which lost most of its games on the schedule, but I had the exhilarating experience of wearing that big black sweater with the yellow letter on it. I got into campus politics and was elected to the student senate. I was beaten for the student body presidency, however, and ended up as vice-president. As a climax I was tapped by Omicron Delta Kappa, the honorary leadership fraternity.

As a senior, I looked back over my college career and saw that I had fallen short of my expectations for myself. I had lost as often as I had won and the big prize always seemed to elude me. I picked up a few silver and bronze medals but never the gold. Those who did get the coveted awards seemed to do so with such effortless ease. I was never willing to concede that I was out of my class, that I was a welter among the heavyweights. But I relied on the belief that there was no obstacle so great that I could not overcome in time. I was nearly right, but not quite.

In the spring of my senior year I was like many others, wondering what I should do after college. One day in chapel a tremendous man was sprung on us by the college president. Henry Hitt Crane, a giant in Methodism, was introduced to us as our Religious Emphasis Week speaker. We didn't even know it was Religious Emphasis Week. Nothing had been said about it, so the president had obviously pulled a fast one on us. Customarily the North Alabama conference furnished for the occasion some leather-lunged cleric who would invariably put the rousements on us—the revivalistic term for arousing the people to penitential pitch. The students, except for the missionary band, the Y.M. and Y.W.C.A., and a few other conscientious ones saved their chapel cuts so that they could escape these religious services without academic penalty. But after Henry Crane had addressed us once and the word on him had gotten out, the students surged into the chapel early to keep the townsfolk from getting their seats. Ordinarily these adults occupying students' seats were a godsend, but this time they were almost resented.

Crane was a big, strong fellow with a leonine head and the grace of an athlete. He wore a blue shirt with white detachable collar and gold tie which made him the last word in stylishness. He was full of fun and mimicry with which he softened us up, and then he proceeded to punch us groggy with his convictions on social issues that caused the North Alabama Conference to blanch and made the student body ready to march on Congress.

I was fascinated by this man; he was the most impressive man I had ever encountered. I had to see what he was like close up, so I took my place in line to have a few minutes' private conference with him. His burning blue eyes boring into me, he asked, "Rob, what are you going to do with your life?"

"I don't know for sure," I answered honestly, "but I plan to go to law school and see where I go from there."

"Have you ever considered the ministry?" he inquired quietly.

"No, sir," I answered quickly. "I don't believe I would ever be called to do a thing like that."

Somehow I had wanted him to ask me that. I wanted to know if he saw anything in me that was of the same substance as himself. But then when he did ask it I felt uneasy. The presumptuousness of it, the incredibility of it! He gathered himself up for a quick offensive against my now vulnerable will and thrust this word into me: "Rob, let me tell you, it's a thousand-mile drop from the lowest pulpit to the highest pew—if you are called."

That's where we left it. I strode out feeling the new strength that one man can give another if their eyes and hearts lock for an instant and one covets the other for a high calling. With this kind of strength I could go out in search again for impossibilities, whatever they might be. The mystique was alive and valid again, I was equipped to confront the insurmountable. I kept repeating to myself, "A thousand-mile drop, a thousand-mile drop—if you are called."

So I graduated from college in the middle of the Great Depression at a time when the nation's economy had practically nothing to offer the new supply of potential employees, no matter how well trained. My brother had graduated seven years before in 1929 and had picked up whatever jobs he could, working for as little as ten dollars a week as assistant manager of a theatre, and finally getting on with the government as recreation director of a transient camp, a kind of hobo jungle under federal auspices. My father and mother continued to live normal lives. Though he was medium-salaried, he had what so many of his more affluent business associates lacked—security. They never knew when their businesses would fail entirely. His employer had consistently practiced such caution and frugality that even a major depression found him impregnable, and my father was his right arm. However, during the latter part of these depression years my father began to show symptoms of a heart condition that finally cut him down in the winter of 1937. In the meantime, I was getting ready for law school to prepare for a career—or was I just staying in school because the world beyond the campus didn't need me and my fellow graduates?

Chapter Five

The religious faith of my family was Christian, Protestant, and Presbyterian. My mother was reared a Methodist, but in defense of this fact she quickly explained that it was only because there was no Presbyterian church in her town when her people came here from Scotland by way of Ireland. When she married my Presbyterian father she eagerly reverted to type by joining his church.

Protestantism in the South in the early twentieth century was for the most part fundamentalist, which meant biblical literalism, puritan piety, and an other-worldly slant. The Presbyterians were more doctrinal, more orderly, and less emotional than Baptists, Methodists, and the numerous denominations and sects, but they were fundamentalist along with them. The great doctrines of grace, justification, santification, and predestination were preached with great earnestness but little clarity. Occasionally a revivalist was brought in to bear down on sin and repentance and to stir the people into an emotional experience, saving a few of the unredeemed and shaking the complacent ones out of their spiritual doldrums.

The approach was individualistic and I am afraid it still is. We were to repent, believe, be baptized, grow in grace, and hope for the return of the Lord. Above all we were to avoid works-righteousness, which was an attempt to save ourselves by the good acts we perform. We were harangued over the corruption of our souls and the evil of our deeds, but there was seldom a hint that there was anything amiss in the social order or that our wrongdoing could be collective. Apparently the scriptures inveighed against looking critically at corporate life. We were to accept the social order as we found it.

"Let every soul be subject unto the higher powers . . . the powers that be are ordained of God." So politics was out as the preacher's rhetoric.

"The poor always ye have with you," said Jesus, indicating that a reverential act toward him was more desirable than feeding the hungry. So public charity was a dubious ministry.

"Unto every one that hath shall be given," said Jesus to conclude his parable of the talents in which the one-talent man came in for heavy condemnation for burying what he had. So people of limited skills, manual laborers or field hands let us say, should be content with their limited wages and their periodic unemployment.

"Seek ye first the kingdom of God and His righteousness, and all these things shall be added unto you." So the man who gives his heart to the Lord has a right to assume that he was first righteous. And so on. When it came to the race question, segregation was perfectly valid because God "hath made of one blood all nations . . . and determined . . . the bounds of their habitation." Besides, segregation was an edict of ordained government, essential to an orderly life. If the Southern ecclesiastics were hard pressed on the issue they could become pretty raw and fling the Hamitic curse at their antagonists, which relegated the dark descendents of Noah to the menial tasks of "hewers of wood and drawers of water" forever.

In early childhood I never thought religion would be an important factor in my life because of both the awesomeness and the dreariness of it. Our family belonged to First Presbyterian, a stately church in the heart of the city and across the street from the famous Birmingham jail. There were times when I felt an affinity with the prisoners there—the difference was that my incarceration was only for three hours on the Sabbath.

As a child I always developed a headache on Sunday; why, I have no idea. The figures in the stained glass were foreboding, even frightening. The histrionics of the preacher and the grimaces of the paid soloists were incomprehensible. The substance and terminology of the sermons seemed completely removed from reality. Maybe I *do* know why I had my headaches—I was exposed once a week to a region somewhere between life and non-life, a purgatory where everything seemed either grotesque or

shadowy. I must have been torn between conformity and resistance, and my system became upset over the conflict. I took the
coward's way out; I fell asleep in my mother's lap or on her
shoulder as soon as the sermon began.

In adolescence I began to listen and my headaches ceased. The
church was beginning to mean something to me, I was responding to it for some unaccountable reason—the moving of God's
spirit in me, some theologians say. I do know that I was consciously responding to the attention I received from my elders. In
Sunday school, unlike public school, I was a model student. I
always studied my Bible lesson, did my memory work, and re-
cited flawlessly. The fact that even the brightest children neglected to do their homework made me the star, more by their
default than my virtue. This diligence of mine in matters spiritual was immensely pleasing to the teachers, and I was the object of their compliments, which they frequently made in my
presence. I counted for something around First Presbyterian and
I found myself developing a proprietary interest in the place.

This led to a romantic attachment to what was espoused there.
As I look back on this experience I will have to admit that what I
had committed myself to was as much folk religion as the Christian faith. Here was a tight little ideology, based on the mores of
the people, that promised comfort, prosperity, and perpetuity to
those who professed it. This is not to say that the Bible, the
creeds, and the spirit of God were nowhere present and acknowl-
edged; but it is to say that the folk religion was the native faith
and the Christian faith the intruder when any concrete application was made. This folk religion was the sacerdotal counterpart
of the Southern mystique which I had so thoroughly embraced.
So we had a rare blending of God-blessed and enthused sectional
patriotism going for us.

Through my high school and college days I went along with
this kind of religion, mainly because I heard little else except on
rare occasions from some malcontent or some beleaguered
prophet. The fellowship of the church was the warmest relationship that I knew. The church was a large family of kin and near
kin. These people seemed to appreciate me because of my obvious desire to serve, to please, and to commit myself to some
ideal.

I found the same spirit in youth conferences which I attended
in late high school and early college days. Here were clean-cut,

starry-eyed young people who, like me, were looking for something enduring to which they might commit themselves. At night just before taps they would gather in the arbor and sing the favorite hymns of that day. They sounded a lot like love songs, which encouraged some innocent and wholesome courtships. I can remember two songs in particular:

> *To knights in the days of old,*
> *Keeping watch on the mountain height,*
> *Came a vision of Holy Grail*
> *And a voice through the waiting night,*
>
> *Follow, follow the gleam*
> *Banners unfurled o'er all the world,*
> *Follow, follow the gleam*
> *Of the Chalice that is the Grail.*

Another one was:

> *"Are ye able," said the Master,*
> *"To be crucified with Me?"*
> *"Yea," the sturdy dreamers answered,*
> *"To the death we follow Thee."*

And the refrain came from those youthful voices, full throated and clear:

> *"Lord, we are able." Our spirits are Thine.*
> *Remold them, make us, like Thee divine.*
> *Thy guiding radiance above us shall be*
> *A beacon to God, to faith and loyalty.*

The deep emotion that this singing evoked was difficult to suppress. This was an outpouring of the soul, a lyrical, but none-theless vague commitment. Even today I marvel at the disparity between what we sing and what we profess, which is almost as great as that between what we profess and what we do. Apparently we have no sense of being under oath when we sing the hymns of the church.

In our classes at these camps and conferences I recall nothing that even alluded to the problem that plagued our corporate existence. We received creedal and biblical instruction that pointed inevitably to personal salvation and piety, but nothing was said about social unrest. Our religious inversion was enough to satisfy and occupy us. We received lasting inspiration from these religious retreats, and we saw how beautiful life could be if the society to which we returned could only learn and practice our consciousness of God and our code of self-giving and loving concern. We were challenged to go out into the world and re-make it in the image of a summer conference.

Many young men and women committed themselves to full-time service to the church and the mission field under the spell of the final candlelight service. Though deeply impressed, I felt no such urge to enter the ministry. There was a subconscious feeling in me that there was something not quite real about this utopian atmosphere, that the world was not looked at as it really was. I knew nothing of the so-called social gospel, but I must have sensed its absence from our thinking.

I didn't think ministers were real people either. Even Peter Marshall, who had been a member of our local congregation, with all his manly charm and winsomeness, didn't seem to me to be part of the authentic world. Had he known my feelings, I am sure he would have taken me in hand and attempted to convince me. Ministers seemed to be so patronizing and so obviously conscious of the spiritual image they must project. As a group they seemed earnest and good but irrelevant. If they wanted to spend their lives being spiritual and keeping the temple fires burning, I would respect, support, and even love them, but I couldn't see myself in their place. Besides, one had to have a compulsion—a call to preach, some kind of divine break-through to the heart which clearly indicated that one was a chosen servant of the Lord and His church. I just wasn't the type to receive such a call; I wasn't by nature clairvoyant. But the spiritual exhilaration had been there, and despite a hidden strain of skepticism I had partaken of it and could not forget it. These religious thoughts and experiences of mine occurred in a period that covered my last year in high school and the four years of college climaxed by my confrontation with Henry Crane at the time of my graduation.

In the fall of 1936 I enrolled in law school at the University of Alabama in Tuscaloosa. I was still hazy about a vocation. About all that I was sure of was that I belonged in the thick of things, and the profession that was most concerned with a proper regulation of society seemed to be the one that would fulfill my desire for human service. I didn't receive much advice from my parents or brother at this point. They seemed as unsure as I about what I was capable of doing. And Crane—I put him out of my mind entirely.

My initial experiences in law school were sobering. There were students and professors of character and intelligence there, but no spirit that I could detect of altruism or selfless devotion. The students seemed to feel that their profession required above all else that they be cunning, that law was to be respected, yes, but also manipulated. I shuddered to think what was going to happen when some of these legal schemers were turned loose on the state, especially if they entered politics. Others have shuddered since. Two of the products of that era were Si Garrett and Arch Farrell, both indicted for murder in the Phenix City, Alabama, scandal; and two more recent products are Alabama governors, John Patterson and George Wallace.

One professor, the avowed cynic of the faculty, propped his feet on the desk one day and said to the class, "It doesn't make a damn what's right, but what the law is." He was correct, of course, in the sense that a written statute is the community's collective opinion as to what is presently right. But his attitude seemed to say that it was none of our damn business as future attorneys even to think in ethical terms. Learn the laws and learn to use them for the benefit of yourself and your client. With this kind of indoctrination it is no wonder that our Southern gentlemen attorneys-at-law have nearly always stressed jurisdiction over justice on the question of slavery and discrimination. It's not what's right but who has the power to say what's right that counts.

This attitude plus endless hours of reading cases involving the quarreling and contentiousness of men made me begin to doubt that the study and practice of law would really help me to plumb the depths of human nature and take an effective part in the regulation of society. Law seemed so superficial, so conventional, the way the faculty and students handled it. The school seemed lacking in a dynamic jurisprudence.

My studies were fitted somehow into a forty-two-hour week as the night short-order cook in Dinty's Diner. The pace nearly burned me out physically. I couldn't find enough time to do collateral reading, I couldn't stay alert to hear the lectures, I couldn't think straight enough to write a coherent examination paper. At law school I was once again trying to do the impossible. In the early morning hours when my eyes were still burning from the grease smoke of the grill I began to think back over my impressionable high school and college days when I was looking for an object of supreme attachment, and I began to wonder if I could find fulfillment in what I was now doing. I was absolutely conscientious in my studies now. No longer did I daydream or malinger. I was intent on mastering the profession of law; but somehow my heart was not in it. Our law school dean exhorted us again and again, "Law is a jealous mistress." I was not lured by the flirtations of other mistresses—I saw none in sight. As for my mistress of law, I respected her but was not infatuated with her, and respect is not the feeling you commonly confer upon mistresses.

Inevitably my mind reverted to the spring day when the most vital man I had ever met, Henry Crane, looked straight at me and asked, "Have you ever considered the ministry?" I argued with myself that religion, aside from Henry Crane's, was not relevant, and the clergy, aside from him, wasn't real. But then the tormenting question arose, If they aren't relevant and real why don't you get in there and make them so? After all, you are the long-shot boy and you will have only most of the church against you at the outset. Sure, make the church over in Crane's image—or yours. If you don't like it as it is then get out of it and let it alone. But if you can't forsake it, then put some of your own muscle and guts into it so you can respect it again. This kind of thinking didn't occur often, and I gave myself credit for realizing I was in an abnormal state of mind when I entertained it. So I promptly forgot Crane and his thousand-mile drop—for a season.

At the end of the spring term after a year at the University I returned home to Birmingham, hoping I could find a summer job that would lessen my work load when I returned to law school in the fall. Through sheer luck I found one immediately with Linde Air Products, a subsidiary of Union Carbon and Carbide. This was 1937 and the depression was still hovering over us like a dirty fog. Jobs were extremely scarce and low paying. I went to work for sixty-five dollars per month as a mail and shipping clerk. I found out later that one of the applicants for the one opening was my old childhood baseball rival, Bobby Bragan, so I take credit for pushing him into professional baseball, where he is probably earning three times my salary. The corporation wanted me on a permanent and not a summer basis, so I had to do some quick thinking about my future. I reasoned that I should stay out of school for a while, save some money, and be close to my family because of the ill-health of my brother and the extra burden this placed upon my mother. I could go back to the University in a couple of years without having to receive financial help from my father or to work all my spare time on a hash-slinging job. In 1937 one could save considerable money on a salary of sixty-five dollars a month, and a raise or two was not out of the question. Then, too, I thought perhaps I should try my hand at this sort of business—I might possibly find fulfillment in it. I found some pleasant relationships and some exhilaration from playing on the company softball team, but the work itself was a bore even though in due time I was promoted to a correspondent with a raise to ninety dollars a month. My brother and I bought a chain of penny peanut-vending machines to operate in our spare time. This kind of work got me into garages, taverns, night clubs, pool halls—any place where people liked salted peanuts with what they were doing. I had seen a pretty good segment of human nature as the short-order cook at Dinty's Diner. I think I saw the rest of it on my peanut route.

I had worked at Linde only six months when my father died one night in bed of a heart attack. It was a hard blow—he had just begun to settle down to a pleasant middle age, his sons were educated, his debts were paid, and there were some satisfying experiences yet to be had. But one quick attack at midnight and he slipped away from us without a murmur while we held him in our arms. Mother showed her stoicism in these moments. She wept quietly, not out of self-pity or despair for her husband, but because life, as we limit it to our earthly existence, is essentially tragic. There is no other end than death; pain is our last sensation, failure our last effort, pathos our final emotion.

She wept quietly, not copiously, because she remembered the

promise recorded in Revelation that "God shall wipe away all tears from their eyes; and there shall be no more death, neither sorrow, nor crying, neither shall there be any more pain: for the former things are passed away." Her faith ran deeper than the folk religion we practiced.

My sweet, manly brother was a great comfort to everyone, more so than was I. He said when we returned from the funeral, "I feel closer to God than ever before." As a diabetic his very body bore the marks of tragedy, and he would go the same route as his father a decade hence. Very early in life, he had made his truce with pain and misfortune, so that death was not a total stranger to him, nor was it a sinister threat.

I was too stunned to act normally, so I tried to act as I thought one should under the circumstances. Mainly, I should play the man, keep a stiff upper lip, and carry on in the fine tradition of my Scotch forebears. Gradually the fact of my father's death became apparent to me and my facade of self-assurance was replaced by an open and sober awareness of my plight. I could no longer live in that hazy zone between youth and adulthood. Heretofore out of pride I had attempted to live on my own resources; now I had to do it as a matter of necessity. Now I had to mature; I could no longer postpone deciding which direction my life would take.

I could not wait; and yet I did. My mind idled a while longer, awaiting some break, some sign, some act of providence. I saw no future at Linde Air Products; I found myself not caring whether anybody wanted our oxygen, acetylene, or welding equipment. It was my job, after my promotion, to trace empty cylinders that gas users failed to turn in. I did it well enough, but mechanically. The job didn't tax my ingenuity or imagination, only my patience. I knew before long that my future didn't lie with this business or any other of its kind.

My thoughts returned to law school and I began to prepare myself mentally for the break away from this desk job at Linde. However, I couldn't be unequivocal about it with myself. I remembered my impressions of the cynicism of some of the faculty and students, the occasional bestiality of fraternity life, the undergraduate standards of value, all the rah-rah of collegiate existence, and the prospect of a return—well, it all looked jaded

to me. Where in such a milieu could I find my lodestar, my
reason to be?

As the time drew near for me to stride up to the desk of my
departmental manager and confess that I didn't believe my future lay with the company, that I had a stronger compulsion, I
began to feel the pains of skepticism. Was the study of law really
my compulsion? Was I really fitted for it and possibly the political arena? My decision now would be not just one more choice
in a series of choices—this was it, this was the big one. The old
small-hour-of-the-morning questions of previous years were coming back now like the pounding of a hammer, and they would
not accept postponement. Then for some reason the visage and
the words of Henry Crane crashed into my consciousness, and I
had to listen to the old refrain that now became an echoing
chant in a cavern—thousand-mile drop, thousand-mile drop, thousand-mile drop . . . if you are called, called, called.

Well, was I? It was possible, because there were nothing but
mortals to choose from. I had developed a deep affection for the
church, I was reasonably moral (a little puritanical, in fact), I
was of average intelligence, I enjoyed people, I was normal; but
more than anything else I had an insatiable curiosity about the
universe and an honest desire to discover the will of God for my
life. But I didn't want to be anybody's moral example, I didn't
want the awesome responsibility of interpreting God's mind to
people. I didn't want the aura of sacred essence imposed upon
me as though I were different in composition from other humans
around me. I didn't want to be set apart from the regular course
of life. I didn't want to take on the tone, mannerisms, and clichés
of the typical parish minister. I didn't want to carry a Bible
under my arm, I didn't even want to preach and pray. What in
heaven's name *did* I want? I didn't know how to put it, but I
think I wanted God to be such a reality in all of life outside the
church that people would be as conscious of Him and as desirous
of Him as of the sun on a dismally gray day. I wanted nothing
more than to be a reflector of that reality, always reflecting but
never self-conscious of it in word or manner. I wanted to be
servant to this task and none other. I wanted my mind and will
to be free from the pressures and dictates of all the little mortal
oligarchies around me that insisted that it was wiser to be realistic than to be absolutely free. I had come to despise "realism" as

being anything but real. Most of life as man had constructed it was spurious, I had concluded. Therefore, I wanted life as God, the originator, had made it. I knew now that I had to find this, devote my life to find it, and speak of it as I made discoveries along the way.

In a very real sense I was wrestling with God now, God as He penetrates a consciousness that divests itself of the whole clutter of ideas stored there as a result of perception that was both imperfect and unfree. This was one of the few times in my life I was willing to throw out the clutter to make room for the contest. God was at once adversary and friend. Divine and human wills were locked in combat. The human will dared test the divine only to discover its strength insuperable and yet more gracious to man than man is to himself. Therefore, man wins by losing, he receives his blessing by direct confrontation, even by conscious conflict, with God. The only losers are those who avoid the issue, who never come to grips with God as adversary. To take Him only as friend is to presume that this human stuff, untested and unpurged, is worthy of divine fellowship, and it is to miss the experience of the disparity between strengths.

In these agonizing hours of indecision I came to know God as adversary. Once I consented to suspend all human fealty and come to grips with Him on a winner-take-all basis I knew there was no turning back to a life which, though originated by God, was fraught with human modifications. If I entered the ministry of the church I had two choices before me, both of which I dreaded. They were neither clear cut nor rational, but nonetheless real. I could take the name, rank, title, and office of the church and with them a life encumbered by men's habitual fear and policed by human sovereignties. This choice might gain me station but would lose me my integrity. The other choice was the way of unqualified freedom and creativity, the serious acceptance of my uniqueness, being one's own man for God's use and no one else's. This meant nonconformity, dissatisfaction with sacrosanct tradition. It meant probable rejection by one's own people, who preferred the partial to the full life and modified to complete freedom.

This total concentration upon my calling practically entranced me. For days I lost track of time, ate irregularly, and tasted little of what I ate. I was distant and uncommunicative with friends and family. They knew that something had gotten into me, that I was not with them, not touching earth at many places. This was a perfectly normal abnormality, as nearly any clergyman will agree. No visions, no hallucinations, no voices, just a training of all one's faculties on an unseen God, a yielding of one's selfhood to a second making. In it there is as much agony as ecstasy, as much despair as joy. And when one comes out of it on the side of total commitment to God, a yawning gulf opens between him and the life that was his only days ago, a gulf that not many can recross except upon a bridge of cynicism and self-defeat.

All my life I had challenged the impossible on my own—now I was called to do it.

Chapter Six

My decision came so close to the deadline that it was almost a case of going to the ticket window and deciding after I got there to buy a fare to Richmond, Virginia, instead of Tuscaloosa, Alabama. The crisis was over; I had decided to go to Union Theological Seminary where I was to study for three years in order to enter the Presbyterian ministry.

The whole experience of making this decision lay so deeply within me that I could not speak to my mother and brother about it. I had to write it out and leave it on Mother's dresser for her to read while I escaped for the day. It shouldn't have been this way. I wasn't going into a monastery; I wasn't going to don a twelfth century cassock and take the oath of poverty and chastity. Protestantism doesn't set its clergy apart to live in a world entirely different from that of the laity. Yet there was an emotionalism, an other-worldliness, promoted among the young people of my generation, that made commitment to the ministry appear to be an escape from life. This made my decision exceedingly difficult to talk about. I think my mother and brother were a little dismayed by it all, but they took it in stride and even seemed proud that they had a "good" boy in the family who would now become professionally good.

In keeping with this unnatural feeling that everybody seemed to have about the ministry, I was immediately regarded as an untouchable by my friends, or so I felt. I was glad I was leaving immediately so that I could escape their quizzical looks and their new awkwardness in my presence. One day, a former basketball

teammate at Birmingham-Southern encountered me on the street
and asked what I was doing.

"I am about to leave for seminary," I told him.

"What's a seminary?" he asked suspiciously.

"A seminary is a school where you train for the ministry," I
explained.

"The hell you say," he exploded. "What's the matter, can't
you make a go of it in life?"

Another friend, a Jew, stopped me later and said, "Tell me
just one thing; did you see a vision?" I assured him that I had
not and he seemed partly satisfied.

I *had* had a religious experience, which I can't quite explain.
It was neither irrational nor suprarational. Yet I would have to
say that it was not confined to rational experience. I believe it was
a divine-human encounter to which my whole being responded,
and that my reason was heightened but not overcome by emotion
or volition. The experience certainly did not purify me. The
good and evil in me both responded to the occasion. About the
only thing in me that approximated purity was the singleness of
my desire to find freedom in God and freedom from the archaic
and artificial systems of men, from the humanly structured life
that made too-small allowance for the function of God.

I had a craving for freedom in God; this was a right motive—
but I also had a romantic attachment to the church and the folk
religion it espoused; this was a devious motive. Now my two
loves, the South and the church, could be wed and become one.
This merging was a near-perfect union, as I was to learn later,
ruefully.

When I entered the seminary campus in Richmond I memorized every step I took on the way to my room. This was a
pilgrimage I never wanted to forget. I met other young men as
starry-eyed as I who were still dazed that such as they should be
called to do the Lord's work on earth. The cordiality and cheer-
fulness of faculty and student body reminded me of the summer
camps of some years back. Here at last was a climate in which my
soul could breathe deeply and taste exhilaration with every
breath.

I had expected too much. We soon moved off the clouds and
got down to the business of living on hard and not too holy
ground. We learned that studying theology day in and day out

could be as tedious as studying any secular subject. We still had to conjugate verbs and the fact that they were Greek, the language of the New Testament, didn't make the discipline any less boring. We discovered that there were worthless courses in the curriculum and some trivia in all of them, just as in college. We caught on to the eccentricities of the professors, and mimicry became a popular pastime. We thought we could never get a snout-full of religion, but we could and did.

We discovered things about ourselves. We had submitted to a calling that would never pay us much in money and prestige. We were to be humble, to suppress personal ambition, to act as servants to the yearnings of our people. But within our own profession—although we refrained from using this secular term—we intended to be top dog. Privately we talked of the tall steeple churches and predicted which ones of our class would be tagged for future delivery to them. We compared looks, manners, resonance of voice, mentality, personality, everything. We speculated over who would win the fellowships and gain an added degree, perhaps from a Scottish seminary. We all seemed to want to be skillful preachers of the gospel, but to be so in positions of middle-class respectability and comfort. The idealism we brought with us tarnished gradually, and we conceded in our moments of candor that we were all too human after all.

There was a system in seminary that seemed out of place for men who were supposed to practice and preach humility. It was a table-seating arrangement in the refectory that actually organized us into clubs of eight. The new men were told to rotate among the tables for the first two weeks and get acquainted with the upperclass men, who in turn decided which two or three they preferred. The new men, called Juniors, wrote down their first, second, and third choice of tables and the upperclassmen did the same with the men. Tables and men were then matched. We joined a table as we had joined a fraternity in college. Most of the new men got their first or second choice, but a few of the pock-marked, timid, or socially ungraceful ones ended up at tables with the hand-me-downs of previous years. Table members would have parties together with their dates; they would troop around the campus together like a band of roving prophets. The whole thing reminded one of the old eating clubs at Princeton. So much nostalgia and tradition had developed around the system that returning alumni would make straight for ol' Table Five, nicknamed the Vatican, and punch up a few memories to remind the present members what noble forebears they were following. In our Virginia-gentleman atmosphere the whole thing seemed quite fitting. The arrangement was one of friendship, men of like mind and interests preferring to cluster together and enjoy what they reverentially called fellowship. But here was a case of snob appeal and we should have recognized it immediately. I think I did but I put aside that recognition quickly because I was a beneficiary of the system. I had good manners, could pass a football, and was not pimply-faced, so I was pledged to a table of bright boys. But there were some outstanding men who were passed over simply because they were not of "the image," and I know they felt their bruises from the system.

Near the end of the school year there was a movement on to abolish the system and I joined it. I realized that I had enjoyed the benefits of the system while at the same time being ashamed of it and of myself. A convocation was called to vote on the issue and we were soundly beaten. Feeling had run so high that one of our student leaders, in order to show the proper spirit, got up and said among some other gracious things that he was sure that the outcome was the will of God. I recall muttering to myself, "The will of God, the devil—we'll get them next year." I was getting my first lesson in the equation—the status quo equals the will of God. And I as getting it firsthand in a theological seminary!

We didn't get them the next year but the year after that we did, and by a much greater majority than the vote by which we had previously lost. We had broken a pattern that had lasted several decades. Today the seminarian is shocked to hear that there ever was such a system. The change was not without its bitterness, however. One of my classmates, whom I considered a good friend, looked me up the night before the convocation and proceeded to call me every uncomplimentary name this side of profanity and to accuse me of every dirty political trick in the manual. I had considered him to be of rather limited vocabulary until I heard that string of epithets, but I seemed to have brought out all his latent eloquence. The whole thing was so preposterous that I didn't get as mad as I should have. Here was a minister of the gospel livid with rage because an unfeeling

system in which he found so much security was about to go
under. He threatened to quit the seminary over his disillusionment in human nature. I suppose one of us had to suffer some
disenchantment; he just happened to be on the losing side this
time.

During my first year in seminary I was pretty much of a model
student. I tried very hard to impress, and I think I must have
studied harder than most of my classmates to make up for a
background deficiency in language, theology, and philosophy.
My college major in political science was valuable, but it wasn't
much help here. I recall studying all night until 5:30 A.M. for a
Greek examination which I must have written in my sleep. Because of all this special effort I became what is now known to
educators as an overachiever; that is, my results ran ahead of my
mentality. This was because I was trying to prove something;
something, incidentally, I was later to disapprove of.

At the end of my first year I was awarded the position of
student minister to a historic, picturesque little church in the
Virginia countryside. I say "awarded" because it was a prestige
appointment for a seminary student. The arrangement was that
from the fall of 1940 through the spring of 1942 I should drive
up every other Saturday afternoon and spend the night with a
family of the congregation, teach a class, conduct the Sunday
morning service, visit the members in the afternoon, stay for the
youth vespers, and drive home that night.

The church was neat and white, set upon a green hillside,
looking like the pictures on calendars that business offices display
to prove that they practice the golden rule. The Rapidan River,
in sight of the church, flowed through the valley bringing to
mind the brilliant exploits of Stonewall Jackson and of the
guerilla fighter, Major John Moseby. It was here that the glorious Confederates were at their best. The well-kept farms looked
fabulous in their richness, especially to me who had always associated farming with poverty. I could picture myself lying on
one of these lush Virginia hillsides on a sunny fall afternoon,
becoming quietly ecstatic from the insights the Lord God would
deliver to me, just as though I were some Hebrew shepherd boy
composing his psalms for the temple worship. The church bell
would toll on Sunday morning, the sleek cattle would look up

curiously from their grazing, the new lambs would leap joyously in the air at the sound, the insects would buzz their canticle to the sun's warmth; and the several families in the valley, looking clean and pleasant, would file in to their regular pews and gaze with serene expectancy toward the pulpit where an earnest young man would open his Bible and invite them: "Now hear the word of the Lord as it is written. . . ." This was the image; it was idyllic, and it was mine.

Not many of the families were equipped to take me on these week ends, so I was frequently scheduled to stay with a retired professor and his wife, who had one of the finest houses in this lovely rural community. This good doctor, eminent scholar and teacher, was counted as one of the grand old men of the church. I was prepared to have the rare experience of a disciple at the feet of his mentor. But something was wrong. I learned that he had an orthodoxy as inflexible as the Ten Commandments, and carved in harder stone. His orthodoxy seemingly heightened his sense of smell—he could sniff out a deviation from the way I cleared my throat. My very presence seemed to sour his countenance. His wife's orthodoxy was more social than theological, and more caustic. In their presence I felt as if my bones were showing and my mind was being monitored.

On Saturday night before retiring we had prayers together. The professor and the lady knelt at their chairs and I followed suit, although the whole scene was a little incongruous. I couldn't visualize these two people kneeling to anybody, and their doing so was like sprinkling a few pinches of humility into their pot of pride simply to keep it from boiling over. For Sunday dinner we usually had roast duck, a real delicacy to a student hardened on institutional food. With fine dignity the professor would carve the bird, and then he and the lady would proceed to carve up most of the nice people I knew, including members of the seminary faculty. I don't think the roast duck ever got to my stomach—it stuck somewhere in the middle of my chest. As far as giving me any sustenance was concerned, the poor bird could have gone south for the winter.

I tried to figure out what was wrong with me. These people were the gentry, theologically and socially. I tried to find the fault in myself, like the good little seminarian that I was. I knew I was a bright shade of green as far as experience was concerned.

I didn't have much to say from the pulpit, and I didn't relish saying *that*. I wasn't glib; I hadn't memorized the pulpit clichés which can be a beautiful cover-up for poverty of thought. So I did a lot of fumbling around, and this got worse under the hawkish glare of the professor and his wife.

Finally toward the end of the spring term I was notified that I was not expected to return there the next year, that the work could be done better by someone else. It was then that I learned that my entire salary (thirty-five dollars a month) had been paid by the professor and his wife, and they were the ones who decided who came and who went. I knew I hadn't done very well, but I also knew that by the prevailing standards I wasn't that bad.

This was my first rejection by the Christian church and it hurt, I admit. It's like being clouted by a parent: you can't fight back and you can't run. I could retch, but that was considered a weakness due to immaturity in grace. I have since learned better. There are some things about the church that should not be kept on the stomach; in fact, they should never have been swallowed in the first place. I salvaged something very important from that experience. One conviction set in very deeply—I hated snobbery. From then on I would not try to hide that fact, especially from the snob himself. What I didn't know then was the number of different forms of it I would encounter. But the line was drawn. I knew the face of the enemy I was engaging; I just didn't know the various uniforms he would wear.

Now I saw what I had done that I disapproved of in myself. I had tried manfully to be the conformist. I wanted to be the best by somebody else's standards. I didn't fit the pattern; I shouldn't have tried, for in doing so I had betrayed my integrity. I had seen and lived with a venerable man of the church. I had been diligent in my work at the seminary so that I might tread the path he trod. I had been ambitious—I had wanted the church for both throne and footstool and congregations for my cheering section—I was a phony. Thank heaven, the professor made a failure out of me! From then on I would apply myself only to what added lasting strength to the inner man.

These were the years just before we entered the Second World War. Ours was a rather pitapat existence. Faculty and students alike had little grasp of what was happening in the world and why. We didn't know specifically what we were for. I felt that we were being trained to take over the vacancies in a compact and solvent denomination, to run a tight ship, and to be artful dodgers when tough issues were thrust upon us. We were to preach on temperance but not prohibition, justice but not politics, greed but not economics, prejudice but not segregation, and so on. Our job was to be judicious and moderatorial so that neither side of an issue could ever take offense at us. The posture that was commended to us was similar to that of one of our 1964 presidential candidates who announced: "I am in between, not because that's where the most people are, but because in between is the best place to be."

We were not to concern ourselves overmuch with social ills because they were but symptomatic of the sickness of the individual sinner. The individual must get right with God and social matters would clear themselves up. In our preaching we could add some pith by Americanizing the biblical settings and characters, as Peter Marshall did so ably, but there was little encouragement to biblicize the cryptic American issues, that is, require our congregations to face our community and national problems, using biblical criteria and not their homemade ones as solutions to them. We were to be sent out as good little priests to keep the temple fires burning in the churches of our Southland.

There was an attitude around the seminary that this social action business was "works righteousness," as it was called. It was considered bad because it showed a lack of faith in and dependence upon the sovereignty of God. One of our projects was the Seventeenth Street Mission, down in the Negro section of Richmond. A group of us would go down every Monday afternoon and make house-to-house calls in order to keep up the interest of the people in the mission. It was not easy to get volunteers for this project. Some of our strait-laced students noted for their piety and inflexible orthodoxy would, when urged by the chairman, retreat to the one impregnable defense— "This is works righteousness. Salvation is not to be had by ringing doorbells of Negro people."

We learned about Amos, Jeremiah, and Isaiah and avidly read their writings, even in the Hebrew language, but these three wouldn't have lasted a year if they had been students with us.

They were too outspoken, too unequivocal, too often out there in the market places, the courthouses, and the legislative halls to ponder over our various theological niceties. The sentiment prevailed that our denomination was sound and solvent and that our religion pertained to God and His grace with only a speaking acquaintance with social ethics and corporate justice.

Where had I heard that before? My year in law school had etched on my mind that it wasn't "what's right but what's the law that counts." In effect, law is not primarily concerned with justice but with the way things are. Another way it was put to me was that law was primarily for the purpose of keeping order, and rendering justice was secondary. I had moved from law to theology and I was getting the same answers—justice is not our prime function. On the one hand find God, on the other find law. If you want to be a good lawyer or a good theologian find the subject of your profession and stick to it—don't go wandering into fields that are in some other professional province. I believe I could have moved through the schools of every profession and gotten the same answer, "a good shoemaker sticketh to his last."

This is no indictment of the theological faculty. I had great respect for these men, especially for some among them who were on the port side of conformity. Much of what I heard in criticism of the social gospel came from students who apparently had been indoctrinated by their old-fashioned ministers or college professors before they came to seminary. I suppose what I wanted was the faculty to devastate publicly this student smugness. However, the members of the faculty were like the students, products of a sectional church that was noted for playing its hand close to the vestments on matters of social concern.

My first formal experience in race relations occurred in my middle year in seminary. An interseminary conference was held at our school. I was selected as one of the delegates, through no desire of my own. To my surprise the conference was integrated. It had just never occurred to me that there were Negroes in these seminaries in our area, even though Virginia Union University, an all-Negro institution, was in the same city. I was also surprised that the seminary's attitude toward an integrated meeting was so bland, as though such was a usual occurrence. Among our students and faculty there seemed to be neither prejudice nor social concern. It was as though we could take it or leave it and the main thing for us to do was to get back to the business of exegeting the Pauline epistles. After all, it was an infrequent event with little likelihood that it could have any effect upon the social order. I have to admit that the seminary's neutralism on this particular issue was ethically superior to my negative views about it.

This was the first time I had encountered young intelligent Negroes whose education was comparable to mine. I was surprised, of course, as nearly any white person is at first contact, to see how easily they matched us in reasoning, judgment, vocabulary, wit. I came away a little embarrassed that I had planned to get down to their level, when the case was that I had to scramble to get up to theirs. The chairman of our delegation asked me to sit at a certain table so that all our visitors would have a local host.

"Will the Negro delegates be sitting with us?" I asked.

"Certainly," he answered. "Why?"

"Just curious," I muttered, "just curious."

So I sat and ate with them and tried to act normally, and I soon discovered that I was normal without acting. As I told some of my classmates later, "It wasn't bad at all, it didn't defile me." On this subject I had simply been a typical, unthinking Southerner. The issue had never been raised for me and the seminary did so only in an offhand way. I suppose this is why I have some sympathy for the trauma into which Southerners are thrown when the matter is thrust squarely before them. But my sympathy is also with the one who feels that he must thrust the matter.

My senior year included the terrible day when Pearl Harbor was bombed and we were suddenly at war. Soon after that the chief of Navy chaplains came to our campus to recruit members of the senior class for his branch of the service. Immediately I went to our president, Ben Lacy, whom we respectfully and affectionately called the Pope, to make application. I was outdoorsman enough to look forward to the rugged life of men who would be stretching their guts to the limit for a worthy cause. I wanted to be out there in their supreme trials with the men who would return and make over our civilization to come.

The president said kindly, "There have already been four applications and the chaplain only wants two from this class; you might be selected if you applied, but these other fellows need the experience and you are rough enough already."

As it turned out, our denomination sent two hundred per cent of its quota to the chaplaincy, which far exceeded that of most if not all of the other churches. I marveled at this aggressiveness from such a conservative institution. The president concluded that to stay out rather than to go in would actually be the harder way. That did it; I was always looking for the difficult part and here I was being faced with a challenge again. I would give up the opportunity of winning a silver star for bravery and stay home and fight the battle of ration points and U.S.O. doughnuts. I was the more heroic, I reasoned, for letting my colleagues be the heroes.

I had a desire for more education, at least a Master's degree, in a field related to theology. I was offered a position of minister to Presbyterian students on the University of Kentucky campus. It was only on half-time basis at a salary of eighty-three dollars per month. I wasn't ready for a conventional pastorate; I couldn't bring myself to accept the two or three churches in small towns that had been offered me. The half-time arrangement was to my liking because it gave me the opportunity to work on the advanced degree. I was glad when the day of graduation came at seminary. I felt overstuffed and undernourished. Theological school had not been the exhilarating experience I had expected. The blame was partly mine since I wasn't any paragon of inspiration there myself. But I had felt the cynicism, detected the veiled ambition, and sensed the cruelty of the church, and I wanted to go someplace where religious faith would be the seasoning of life but not the whole lump.

My move to Lexington proved to be a wise one. I picked up a Master's degree in philosophy and got my mind honed down to a cutting edge by faculty and students who gave me no quarter because I was of the cloth; in fact, they pressed me a little harder because of it. In this intellectually tough atmosphere I learned never to make assertions I could not support, for I had to reckon with the scientific point of view at every turn. This didn't mean that I had to support my views with scientific evidence, but rather that I refrained from either condemning or exploiting science in order to defend religion. I learned, too, to shake out the nonessentials in my creed and stress those points that made sense to intelligent people. I discovered that religion on a university campus came closer to being the pure article by reason of the buffeting it got from skepticism and even open hostility.

It was in Lexington that I met a precocious senior, Jeanne Lancaster, who was majoring in home economics and also serving as organist in the Maxwell Street Presbyterian Church, which was my headquarters. She was from the fine little town of Lebanon, Kentucky, and was of a family which had members on both sides in the Civil War. She graduated in 1943 and spent the next school year at Louisiana State University on a Danforth fellowship. We were married in August of 1944. By this time I had gotten my Master's degree in philosophy and had been put on full-time status as a director of student work.

The student population, I found, was restless for religion to be aggressive for human justice. However, student work was overseen and financially supported by the older generation and that meant conflict. One Sunday morning the Maxwell Street Presbyterian Church was thrown into turmoil over the presence (on invitation of the Session, which is the church's governing board) of a delegation of a Y.W.C.A. conference meeting on the campus that week end. The conference was interracial and the ushers had not been notified of their coming. This mixed delegation was seated but the minister was never forgiven by several officers for "mixing social life with religion." I took the position that occasional exposure to each other was good for both races; certainly it was educational. My lofty opinion satisfied neither the segregationists nor the Y.W.C.A. I was trying then what self-styled Southern moderates attempt today—finding some impossible middleground between the two extremes. The heat was on the local pastor, not me, so I came away from the issue unburned.

In 1945 we moved to Austin, Texas, where I was to be minister to Presbyterian students at the University of Texas. The problem of housing cut my work short there. About the only rental property available was on a month-to-month basis, made possible by the owner leaving town briefly and allowing us to keep the house for him. After a time I decided that, if we were forced to move again, I would take it as the call of the Lord to return across the Mississippi and settle down in a local parish which had, if nothing else, an empty manse to commend itself.

Even in that brief span of a year, 1945 to 1946, the race issue could not be escaped. My students wanted to invite a choir from a local Negro college for a Sunday night meeting. I offered them four alternatives: cancel the meal that night; invite them to come after the meal; eat together but segregated; or eat together integrated. The students would have no equivocation; they insisted on the last alternative. That's the way we had it and the word got out to the officers in a matter of minutes. We had a couple of grim Session meetings over it, during which time I came out pretty strongly for the right of the students to determine their own way of demonstrating their religious faith. I argued the secondary issue of student freedom; I don't recall saying anything about hoping the walls of segregation would come tumbling down. When an Elder cautioned against any further experiments in race relations on the ground that people were divided in their views of the matter, I responded rather heatedly, "I refuse to be a receptacle of diverse opinion." It was probably a good thing there was a housing shortage, for as we say in polite ecclesiastical language, "my effectiveness with the people was impaired."

I didn't leave these two university situations entirely unmarked. I was feeling some disenchantment with the church when I saw many of its astute members bare their fangs over the token gestures we had made toward better human relations. My conviction was being shaped not so much by my concern for the Negro as by the irrationality and nasty antipathy of those who opposed any kind of contact with him. I was also dissatisfied with my own indecisiveness. I didn't know what to think. I didn't like limping between two opinions. These brief encounters with the issue were beginning to nudge me off dead center, off the middleground of social expediency toward the side of unqualified justice. I recognized, perhaps belatedly, that racism was another one of those uniforms of snobbery that I detested.

Chapter Seven

We did come back across the Mississippi. Our next move, in the summer of 1946, was to a steel mill district called Fairfield Highlands, just outside my home city of Birmingham. I brought my young wife and nine-month-old daughter, Janet, into a compact little white frame manse to begin work in a place just twelve miles from where I had been born and reared, and yet a place totally unfamiliar to me. Nearly all the men of the community were members of the C.I.O. This was the real American working class, which I had not known too well before. My family could hardly be considered to be of the management class but most of the people we knew were. Among them organized labor was an object of suspicion and fear. So I was mildly surprised to find that these people that lived on the ridge above Tennessee Coal and Iron Company were entirely normal in their views and behavior. Most of them owned their own homes, most belonged to one of the three churches in the neighborhood, and almost to the last man they hated the idea of a strike at the plant. They were fine people, a little tempestuous, but thoroughly American.

This was my first work as the pastor of a church. I realized that a conventional ministry was expected of me, and I sincerely wanted to oblige as long as it didn't stunt my own mind and aspirations. Actually this would mean being an unconventional person in a conventional pattern. It wasn't long before the tyranny of routine began to oppress me; two sermons a week, Wednesday night prayer meetings, afternoon visits to the ailing, the backsliding, and the peeved.

All of this could have been pleasant if it had been productive, but the people had been indoctrinated with a fundamentalism that created suspicion of any teaching or demeanor that didn't toe the line of narrow conformity. Pastoral calling, for example, is a vital part of the ministry, but much of it is done defensively. The minister feels an obligation to call on a particular person, not because he feels that he can help that person but because he would anger him by not calling. This is a result of an inversion process that has been going on in the church in the last century, a process of turning in upon itself, of existing for itself. It leads the member to believe that for his faithfulness in attendance, his work, and his contributions he is due certain attentions from the paid executive, the pastor. Therefore the member watches the pastor to see whether he properly appreciates a diligent member and is alert enough to seek him out if he is ill or offended. There are beautiful exceptions to this—a person racked with pain or bent low by every adversity will glow with appreciation over the pastor's visit, but will protest that he should use his time for more constructive matters; and the pastor will go away feeling that he has been ministered unto when he went there to minister. Inwardly I had rejected this sterile kind of ministry, which was found in all the churches, not just the one I was serving; and yet I worked hard at it. I played the role. I didn't know what else to do that would be even partially acceptable to the people. So I went through all the motions, but internally I was knotting up.

I undertook a personal project of reading everything I could find on the race issue, not only to bring my mind to a definite conclusion about it, but to keep from drying up inside by doing nothing but the expected, the routine things. I started by reading Gunnar Myrdal's fourteen-hundred-page volume, *An American Dilemma*, the most comprehensive work in the field. Eight years later the Supreme Court made reference to it in its famous decision on segregation in public schools, which prompted the Court's enemies to accuse the Justices of socialism because of their agreement with the author, who was a Swede and a Socialist. Then I added several other classics to the list: Howard Odum's *Southern Regions of the United States*, Allan Nevin's *Ordeal of the Union*, Hodding Carter's *Southern Legacy*, W. J. Cash's *Mind of the South*, Lillian Smith's *Killers of the Dream*, Richard Wright's *Black Boy*, Claude Bowers' *Tragic Era*. Most of

these books came from the public library. One in particular was
on prominent display in the library because it had won some
literary award. What was so astounding was that the book was
unequivocally Marxist. The author had been a professor in a
Southern college at one time, and one of his pupils explained
that he got by with his political philosophy because he was so
abstruse that nobody understood him. Only a few years later, a
Montgomery librarian was put under extreme pressure over a
child's book whose illustrations had white bunnies and brown
bunnies playing together. And here on display in the literary
center of Birmingham was an American Negro's communist
manifesto, and nobody caught on.

It was about this time, 1946, that the political pot began to
seethe in Dixie. The Negro was showing restlessness after World
War II, a war in which he was a combat man and not a mule
tender as he had been in 1917. His blood had mingled with the
white man's on foreign soil, even if he was not completely integrated with him. Now his temper was being sensed in Washington, and in 1947 the first civil rights legislation since Reconstruction was passed.

The old ex-Confederacy was enraged. Rebellion was in the
air; secession from the Democratic party was inevitable. That
little haberdasher who backed into the White House, Harry S
(for nothing) Truman, was responsible for it and had to be punished. A party convention was planned, and as Alabama had
furnished the first Civil War capital, Montgomery, so it offered
its prize city, Birmingham, as a convention site for the schismatic
party in 1948. Harry Truman and his leftist hangers-on had to be
beaten and driven from the Democratic party, for they had betrayed the long-standing but tenuous compromise which had allowed a conservative South to mind its own affairs and yet stay in
an essentially liberal party. These grim Southerners were the
children who were going to spank the mother for making them
eat the unpalatable and for taking them for granted. They were
going to wreck the party in the 1948 elections and then wait to
be wooed back into the household with promises that never again
would their wishes be violated.

I made it a point to be at that Dixiecratic convention. I knew
that this would be one of a kind, one that history would not

relish to record. The unusual I was prepared for, but not this. At times I thought I was experiencing a nightmare, but it was a mawkish reality. Here hell did not yawn, it retched, and spewed every devilish thing imaginable. On the platform was a weird assortment of party hacks. The presiding officer was a local backstage manipulator who rejoiced in the new set of puppets this convention furnished. The welcoming address was given by none other than Bull Connor, who had won his place on the program by his leading Alabama's delegation in its walkout at the Philadelphia convention where, a few months before, Truman had been nominated.

A professional after-dinner speaker from Mississippi, a rather poor imitation of Will Rogers, accepted the welcome and the show was on. A former Alabama governor, Frank Dixon, added some dignity but little reason to the rabble with his keynote address against civil rights. The Kappa Alphas, his fraternity brothers from the local college, Birmingham-Southern, stampeded for him, holding high a portrait of Robert E. Lee, their "spiritual founder." How fortunate that this gallant Southerner was spared the sight of this disinterment of a dead Confederacy. A gum-chomping Texan delighted the crowd with sarcastic barbs directed at intellectual liberals. He used Arnold Toynbee as a target to prove that he himself was an intellectual. He could have put Toynbee in left field for the Dodgers and the audience wouldn't have known the difference.

During every salvo of cheers an old veteran whom they must have dug out of the ruins of Vicksburg stood up and waved a large Confederate flag, and hot-faced zealots crowded the microphones and spewed obscenities over the radio networks. It was a field day for second-rate and comeback politicians, for precinct patriots, and for hatemongers. If there was a clear-thinking, high-principled student of state's rights in the convention, he was not heard that day.

The man who caught my interest in all this was one who in later years was to become internationally prominent, or rather notorious—Bull Connor. He was the most unequivocal of the lot and about the only one in that 1948 Dixiecratic convention who was to be remembered and to enlarge his reputation. He possessed none of the refinements that the others had in some degree that would moderate his racial attitude. It is still hard to believe that a man of his caliber could cause such social anguish. However, it has almost become axiomatic that promotion to leadership in racist groups is in direct relationship to one's quantity of racial antipathy. Bull had a singleness of purpose, a dedication that could not help but move him to a command position.

I remembered him as a ham-bone radio announcer who broadcasted the baseball games of the Birmingham Barons. He was straight from the corn patch and made no effort to conceal it. He had a gimmick: he made two distinct syllables of the word "out" and ran into a falsetto on the last one. "Bancroft grounded to the shortstop and is ow-oot." When, as a teen-aged boy, I delivered papers in the afternoon, I had to hear that from nearly every radio on the route. There are fifty-four outs in a full nine-inning game, so one can imagine how grating his "ow-oots" could be—that is, unless the baseball fan thought he was clever and liked that sort of thing. The bald fact is that thousands of people did go for this bumpkin, and they gave him his start in politics because they had identified themselves with him on the radio.

"Bull" in a way is a misnomer. As police commissioner in the 1963 racial strife he was depicted as a bruiser, a bone crusher, a violent man. He isn't really, although he probably wouldn't mind people thinking so. He got the name of Bull very early in his career not because he was a ramrod, but because there was a humorous columnist in one of the Birmingham newspapers with a caricature face whose by-line was B. U. L. Connor. Almost any person whose name was Connor might be nicknamed Bull, just as a Dempsey might be called Jack.

Bull had another occasion to flex his muscles about the time of the Dixiecratic convention. Senator Glenn Taylor, the Progressive Party's vice-presidential candidate on the ticket with Henry Wallace, had come to an interracial meeting in Birmingham boasting that he would fracture the segregation laws of the city. Bull lusted after such a skirmish. The meeting that Taylor planned to attend was a convention of one of the many justice-seeking organizations of that day and was to be held in a little shack of a Negro church. Bull posted his policemen in front of the church to prevent Taylor or any other white person from entering unless he did so on a segregated basis. The local ordinance required clearly marked separate entrances and a barrier between seats occupied by the two races. Taylor headed directly for the Negro entrance, but a policeman stepped in front of him. In order to pass he had to make some bodily contact with this guardian of the law. A scuffle ensued, Taylor was jostled enough to get a bruised shin (which he displayed to the photographers to suggest brutality), and the senator from Idaho was unceremoniously taken to the Birmingham jail.

The trial was held in the Recorder's Court at City Hall. Here was another event in history I couldn't afford to miss. A friend of mine and I went early, and the courtroom was nearly full then. Later it became packed to capacity. While a few hearings preliminary to the main event were being disposed of, mostly concerned with the jail's regular patrons' bouts with the bottle, Senator Taylor came in quietly and stood at the back. He was nothing like what I had pictured a Midwesterner to be. He was foppish in appearance, smelling strongly of toilet water, and from time to time he smoothed his carefully trained hair with a manicured hand. He stood exactly between the white and colored sections, as though he were straddling an imaginary line. I had an aisle seat, which I offered. He replied, with no show of gratitude, "No, I prefer to stand." Then he seemed to straddle more firmly the imaginary line between the races.

The trial was ludicrous. A judge of the lowest court was to pass sentence upon a member of the highest lawmaking body in the land. In fact, the judge made that point as he began to lecture Taylor. The senator wanted to be convicted on the charge of violating the local segregation laws so he could appeal to the federal courts. The prosecution wanted to prove him innocent of this. So it was proved to the satisfaction of the judge that the policeman stationed at the door had prevented Taylor from breaking the segregation ordinance. Therefore, he was convicted of disturbing the peace and resisting arrest, and his sentence was suspended with the hope that he would leave town forever.

In the courtroom that night there was yet a greater piece of irony, a more woeful inconsistency, than had occurred heretofore. I hadn't noticed it until I was caught in the press of both races as I moved out of that room of insufferable heat—*there was but one entrance!* A man was arrested for entering a church that was required to have two distinctly marked entrances, "white" and "colored," but in the courtroom where that man was tried there was only one entrance. In our exit white and colored were not integrated; we were enmeshed.

Connor added another ribbon to his chest in the racial conflict. When the Freedom Train, displaying historical documents, was scheduled to stop in Birmingham, it occurred to someone at the last moment that the issue of race-mixing might arise. So it did, and Bull snorted that the viewing would have to be on a segregated pattern. He wouldn't even permit stand-up integration. Whites and Negroes could line up with each to buy groceries and stand together in elevators, but they couldn't stand side by side to read the Constitution and the Declaration of Independence.

These events plus my extensive reading were getting to me. I had already moved into that nebulous region called the middleground, and here I had hoped to be able to stay because I thought it was the ingenious position. I was now beginning to realize that it was more ambiguity than ingenuity, more expediency than conviction. It was now beginning to sound hollow when I proclaimed that I was against extremism on both sides or when I decreed a plague on both their houses. In this position I could not lead from strength. I had nothing to say except "on the one hand . . . but on the other." This discontentment with myself was building up to another conversion.

Occasionally I would drive by my old home and take a long, nostalgic look at it and the Beecher house next door, which had been the extension of my domain. Mother was a housemother at Alabama College now, and my brother was married and living in Atlanta. Neither of the houses looked the same. The memory was better than the present view. Each time I turned away, saddened and depressed, resolving not to disappoint myself again by looking upon them. The Negro encroachment was apparent now. House after house became vulnerable to them with each passing year. Those white families who were directly in the path of the movement did not give up without a fight. From the time we had sold our house in 1939 until now, 1948, there had been nine bombings on this ridge. I recognized some of the ruins as having been the former homes of white boys I had gone to school with. Even a white man accustomed to the sadism of racial animosity could sense the terrorism that hovers over these grave marks of hate.

One of the dynamited houses was that of a Negro dentist, who repaired the damaged part and continued to live there. I was determined to meet this man because, for one thing, he was showing uncommon bravery and, for another, I was beginning to experience a genuine identification with his people. In order to see him I had to get my barber to call and assure him that I was all right. My barber wasn't too sure of me at first. He had known me most of my life, but not in the role of sympathizer with his people. I will never forget how his eyes widened when I mentioned the dentist's name. It was nothing I said that convinced him of my sincerity—it must have been something in my manner.

When I found the house and rang the bell I was greeted by a wizened, white-haired old man, under five feet tall; infirm and yet gracious in bearing. Was this the brave man who had refused to be intimidated by those who would mingle his blood in the rubble? Despite the barber's recommendation the little man didn't warm up to me immediately. This intimacy invited by a white man, and one who had lived on the same ridge with him, was as new an experience to him as it was to me. Soon, however, he began to tell me his story, without rancor or bitterness. He had bought a lot from the city, not knowing or being told that it was within the white residential area. Before he built his home he appealed to the zoning commission, and had obtained a reclassification of the property so that his building would be legal. Ironically, the lawyer who helped him was a Dixiecrat who couldn't turn down old Jim when he needed help, because as a boy Jim had worked for his father.

After the awful day when the house was bombed the dentist was undecided as to whether he should rebuild. His son, away at college, convinced him that he should. He wrote that he had fought in Saipan alongside men who were perhaps like the ones who had dynamited his home, but they had fought on the same side for the same things. Rebuilding that house was a kind of fight, too, to stand firm on a principle until its enemies saw that it was too deeply rooted to be shaken. So he stayed on and rebuilt. Eventually one white neighbor offered the dentist's wife some climbing roses, and another got him to pull a tooth for his child. As I left him the tiny little man cautioned me with his eyes that the trouble might not be over, and that nothing should be spoken or written that would arouse his assailants again.

"I still don't see how you go through with it, how you keep your faith and your sanity," I marveled.

In reply he stood as erect as his hunched back would allow him and repeated:

> *The Lord is my light and my salvation;*
>   *whom shall I fear?*
> *The Lord is the strength of my life;*
>   *of whom shall I be afraid?*

The old man with the humpback got strength from some source that his tormentors didn't have. He dug in his own ruins and stuck it out for the sake of a freedom he himself would not live to enjoy. He was too old and his antagonists were too relentless for him to see the promised land. Once I had thrown stones at his people. Then when tension mounted someone threw dynamite. Finally, others may take up arms against them. What is the difference? It's the same contempt. Who is less guilty?

I went away that day both misty eyed and angry. What were we doing to these people? What were we doing to ourselves in process? After all these years, these blind years, it finally occurred to me what it was—we were making saints of them and beasts of ourselves. Suddenly my mind went back through all those years to my childhood. I saw my father strap on his gun belt at night, and the next day word got around that a Negro family had moved out of a house on the white side of the zoning line which they had occupied. This happened more than once, but I could never get either of my parents to explain it to me. It all seemed so heroic and yet I was denied the thrilling details of these exploits. This was soon after the end of the First World War, and the Klan had revived because Negroes seemed to think that wars changed our social patterns. I never knew whether my father and the neighbors were Klansmen, but they used the Klan tactics of that era to administer justice as they understood it. Their homes were threatened (the dollar value, that is); they were defending them from an invader—it was as simple as that. To me as a boy they were heroes. They were vindicating the stand of the old South and rectifying the wrongs of the Reconstruction. Had I been of age I would have strapped on my gun belt and joined them.

My mind replayed another event. I couldn't have been more

than five at the time. I was taken to a Klan parade one night. Scores of cars drove by filled with white-robed and masked men. Those sitting on the fenders of the cars bore torches. The procession was designed to strike terror in the hearts of the dark population, which needed a stark reminder every now and then. It probably worked, for it certainly terrified me. The whites were quite sure that all the Negroes crowded into their churches that night for a vigil of prayer and for safety. They probably did.

This had been my orientation, and here I was paying a call of penitence on a little old man who refused to yield under the white man's storm of torment. My people couldn't break him, but when he thrust his whitened head above his bowed back and fixed his tired, gentle eyes upon me and repeated, "The Lord is my light and my salvation," it was I who was broken.

These episodes in Birmingham in 1948 sobered me considerably. I was embarrassed over the irrationality, the cheapness, the buffoonery, the gut-boiling hate of my people. I marveled at the patience, the courage, and the faith of an oppressed black people. They were the admirable ones! I was ashamed of the ugly image the South was shaping of itself. Wasn't there some step short of total integration that would bring relief and restore sanity? Was I ready for integration if there was no other just way? I wasn't sure—I hated to think that integration was the final and necessary resort, not because of my personal feelings but the social convulsion I was sure it would cause.

Chapter Eight

After two years with the steel mill people in Fairfield Highlands I realized I wasn't doing them much good, that I ought to move on as soon as an opportunity came. It did come in the form of a call to a little college-town church in Jacksonville, Alabama. The church was a one-door, hundred-and-twenty-member congregation, with no great promise of becoming anything other than what it was. But there was something that intrigued me about the place. Just from being there a day to look it over I got the same feeling I had when I was perched atop my fir tree on the Beecher lawn. The place also seemed to speak to me of the Southern mystique, which had come alive for me again, at least subjectively, because my reading was immersing me in the old South. The people were fewer and the salary was smaller than in the Fairfield Highlands church, but it was beginning to initiate a mood in me, a mood of creative peace. I felt attached to the place as though it had once been my home.

Jacksonville was a sun-baked little hamlet of thirty-five hundred people nestled in the foothills of the Appalachian range. It was not prim and starch-collared, but careless and faded from too much heat and too little civic pride.

Ironically, the first house to catch the eye upon entering the city limits from the south was inhabited by a New Englander by the name of Ivan Greenleaf. He was *one* of the inhabitants; no one ever quite knew who or how many more were staying there. The house was ante bellum and from its tumbledown appearance it was hard to tell which war it preceded. There was a slave block in the yard where sales used to take place. Greenleaf had come from New Hampshire with orders to close the cotton mill. He decided it could be profitable with good management, so instead of closing it he prospered from it. But he never forgot his initial treatment by the townspeople. When they learned of his Yankee origin and his intentions they refused even to give him lodging for the night. Almost out of spite he got control of the water and light systems and much of the strategic property. This meant that industry couldn't locate there without having to reckon with him. As a result Jacksonville didn't get its share of modern industry and lost out to Anniston, twelve miles away, as the principal town in the county.

Local legend has it that Greenleaf vowed in 1936 that he would never improve his properties until a Republican president was elected. His own house, standing like a dead sentinel at the south entrance of the town, was falling down on his head. In 1951, however, he began to patch his roof, which provoked a great deal of speculation as to whether he had run out of drip pans or had been given an omen of Republican victory. Sure enough, Eisenhower was elected months later.

It was said that the chief industries of the town were a college, a cotton mill, a post office, and Alcoholics Anonymous. A poet would not be driven to ecstasy over its romance and beauty. A hundred yards from the town square was a field with a pretty good stand of corn, a tired mule, and a broken-down barn. There were few heirlooms of Confederate splendor. The Old South was here, but it was a modest South, tranquil and a little sad. One cannot imagine the gaiety and gallantry of a Montgomery ever having been part of the town. Rather one visualizes tired, red-necked pioneers tilting back their porch chairs in the cool of the evening, grateful that they could bring the wilds to order and hopeful that the land would sustain them another year.

It was deathly still at night. Every katydid and tree frog got a full audition. There was no distant rumbling of highway traffic, no puffing engines. One train a day came in on a spur line, with a mail car, an ancient passenger car, and a few freight cars. There were no hotels or tourist courts, so you either lived here or you didn't. Someone asked a native what would happen to this town in case of emergency. "Nothin'," he said. "We don't believe in 'em."

Sometimes late at night I would sit on the shoeshine chair in front of the drugstore which overlooked the square with its one undersized Confederate monument. There were no sounds except the click of pool balls at the Pastime Billiard Emporium and an occasional roar of the perennial war picture at the Princess Theater. I wondered how long this placid life would last. When would progress catch up with Jacksonville? When would industry crowd in and accelerate our living to the point where these gentle hearts could not stand the pace? Or worse still, if a third world war should come would the survivors crawl out of the rubble and recover the existence we call the Southern way? The pattern of gracious, kindly living—could it be traced in the ruins of homes and stores and personalities and be revived? I was beginning to love this town more than the natives did. They saw it as it was. I saw it as it had been a century ago—all the good aspects of it, that is.

Jacksonville had a special claim to fame. It was the home of the Gallant Pelham, a twenty-five-year-old major who had been Lee's chief artillery officer and had been killed in the battle of Kelly's Ford in Virginia. They brought him home and buried him, named the main street for him, and have never ceased to boast of him, especially when the most conservative citizens wanted to block a progressive measure. Then they would cry, "This was where the Gallant Pelham sat; how could you think of changing it?"

The Presbyterian church was built in 1857, by slave labor, of brick made by hand within a block of the site. The church has always been financially solvent because the contractor was a Yankee who was run off before he could collect his fee. This gave the congregation a good start and even a good name in those hostile days. The church is a perfect example of Georgian Colonial architecture, and a national architectural association has agreed to preserve the building if the congregation should ever give it up. There is a plaque in front stating that the building had been used as a Confederate hospital during the war. There was the usual slave gallery, which they say was never used as such. I don't think these people had that many slaves. One day a lady from the North asked if I would show her the church; she wanted to see the chains. I explained that there never had been any chains because Negroes didn't need to be chained to church, only whites. But I said that I would use the contribution she had put in the box to buy some chains to jangle for the Yankee tourist trade. She looked at me as if to say, "Appomattox hasn't convinced you, has it, boy?"

And so I was pastor of a dilapidated but stately church of the Old South that seemed to have mingled in its mortar both the folk religion and the mystique of a former century. It didn't seem incongruous to the nineteenth century forebears that a house of God, of all edifices, should be erected for them by slaves, who in turn could worship therein only if they distinguished their menial status by climbing the steep stairs and separating themselves from the official worshipers. Folk religion doesn't exclude the worship of God in all due reverence, but it selects requirements of the Christian faith that can be kept and rejects those that might upset the basic social structure, a structure more like that of a large family than of a heterogeneous society. And when has this selectivity not been the subtle heresy of Christendom, no matter what the issue?

The section having been predominantly rural, the churchgoers consisted of a few large families who were either kin or intimate with each other. Some of the plantation owners built chapels on their own land for exclusive use of the family. The clergy, often the circuit-riding variety, was not inclined to buck the system. What with sickness and death being ever-present factors and the cemetery adjoining the church, salvation, longsuffering, and heaven furnished the preacher with inexhaustible rhetoric. Somehow it was assumed that people were free to perform all kinds of deeds individually but God alone was responsible for social arrangements. So the churches, chapels, and even the brush arbors blessed the worshiping families and as heaven's halfway houses gave assurance that they would be reunited in eternity.

This refusal of churchmen to apply Christian criteria to systems as they did to individuals was labeled "spirituality." The reason religion was not allowed to sit in judgment on social systems is obvious: the systems couldn't bear the scrutiny. Slavery was militantly defended, of course, even by the churches. But the best defense, then as now, was to skip the justice aspects of it and fall back on jurisdiction. It is much easier to say that something is none of the church's business than to say it is right or wrong. If it isn't the church's business then one can fight without churchly considerations, and this usually means he can fight dirty. So the crucial issues of life are tossed into the zone of moral neutrality and the church minces on its spiritual way.

Slavery didn't have to endure the critical stare of the church because the church's eyes were averted or seeing nothing. So it has been with segregation, slavery's refined successor. We should not marvel at the church's attitude; it has had three hundred years or so to develop. This attitude is softening from sledge-hammer blows from without, but it hasn't changed radically. I could imagine James Henry Thornwell, the venerable ante-bellum South Carolina clergyman, thundering even from this modest pulpit in Jacksonville:

The argument of the philanthropists would condemn every arrangement of society which did not secure to all its members an absolute equality of position—it is the very spirit of socialism and communism. . . . The parties in the conflict are not merely abolitionists and slave holders—they are atheists, socialists, communists, red republicans, jacobins on one side, and friends of order and regulated freedom on the other. In one word, the world is the battleground—Christianity and atheism the combatants; and progress and humanity at stake.[1]

This Thornwell was no oddity—his was the grits-and-gravy thinking of the Southern people. This was their orientation. Exceptions were rare and brash.

My friend John Beecher's great-grandfather, Edward Beecher, and great great-uncle, Henry Ward Beecher, were two of the most eloquent voices against slavery a decade before the Civil War. The worst working over Henry Ward got was not from the Thornwell type but from a Northern rabbi by the name of M. J. Raphall. He thundered:

I would therefore ask the gentleman from Brooklyn and his compeers—how dare you, in the face of the sanction and protection afforded slave property in the Ten Commandments—how dare you denounce slavery as sin? When you remember that Abraham, Isaac, Jacob, Job—the men with whom the Almighty conversed, with whose name He emphatically connects His own

1 J. H. Thornwell, *The Rights and Duties of Masters* (Charleston: Steam Power Press of Walker and James, 1850), p. 14.

most holy name . . . that all these men were slaveholders, does it not strike you that you are guilty of something very little short of blasphemy?[2]

So the men who constructed the fine little church in Jacksonville with the labor of slaves, who would not share fully in the worship within it, had their rationale for their system, all the way from a South Carolina Presbyterian to a Northern Jew. It is no wonder slavery and segregation didn't seem contradictory to Christianity.

The stately old church looked pretty shabby when my wife and small daughter, Janet, arrived to begin a ministry there. The roof leaked and water stains were all over the cracked, unpainted walls. The distinctive long green shutters were rotten and sagging on their hinges. The carpet was shot. The straight-backed unpadded pews had been painted a chocolate brown by someone who had the paint left over from some other building project. The old pedal-pump organ with its gilt-painted, dummy wooden pipes had wheezed its last. The people were embarrassed over its appearance, but the little money they had saved was tagged for a small educational wing for the children.

One rainy evening at a wedding their chagrin reached the ultimate when the roof aimed its drips at the hat of the Episcopal rector's wife. She was not only to the manor born but wore the broadest brimmed fruit-and-flower-crested hats in town. The people could hear the spatter and while the Methodists and Baptists present chuckled the Presbyterians cringed at this broadcast of their poverty. Episcopalians and Presbyterians are in social competition with each other nearly everywhere, and it just wouldn't do for this rector's wife to be turned loose on the community with this kind of evidence of our reduced circumstances. So what God could not inspire, Lady Jane provoked. That leaky roof was going to be patched and those shutters repaired and the church was going to get dressed up.

It did deserve it. No one was more impressed than I with the quality of its construction. It had some interesting features that were worth showing—the oversized, handmade brick, the grapevines used to secure the crossbeams, the square-headed nails, the wooden pegs, and the wide-planked floors. So something had to

[2] M. J. Raphall, *Bible View of Slavery, a Discourse* (New York: Rudd and Carlton), p. 54.

be done to restore the beauty and dignity of this fine old Southern church.

What happened in the process of restoration made me a favorite of all the antiquarians and Old South lovers in the state. I
hadn't been there three months, and it is not discreet for a new
minister to present any sort of radical program to the congregation until he has become thoroughly and securely settled among
his people. But that leaky roof wouldn't wait; and if the roof was
patched then why not paint the stained, dirtied walls; and new
paint would make the carpet look even shabbier; and a new
carpet would probably clash with the chocolate-coated pews. So
there was no use to think in terms of mere human effort and
sacrifice—I had to come up with a miracle, and fast. I had to
start groping around in my bag of impossibilities again. In my
seminary days I remembered reading of a church in the Midwest
that enacted the biblical parable of the talents by giving the
collection out one morning instead of taking it, charging each
person to take a specified sum, invest it in some talent of his, and
bring back the proceeds on the Day of Reckoning. The idea got
hold of me and wouldn't let go. At first the officers weren't overly
enthusiastic about it as I revealed the plan, but they saw I was
enthusiastic enough for all of them. We kept the plan, called
Talents, Inc., a secret from the women, just telling them something momentous was going to happen on the next Sunday. This
turned out to be our best promotional technique. Their insatiable curiosity drove them to prod every living person in town for
clues to the secret, and as a result our little church was filled to
capacity on the big day. We tipped off the newspapers and even
the *Birmingham News,* seventy-seven miles away, sent a reporter
and photographer. The story was picked up on the wire services.
In both the Anniston and Birmingham papers it received front-
page coverage with pictures. There was an appealing little story
about faith and good will which crowded the V-2 bomb out of
the headlines for the moment. Hartzell Spence of *One Foot in
Heaven* fame came down and wrote the story for *Good House-
keeping.*

The Day of Reckoning was overwhelming. The congregation
had earned enough to beautify the old building, and people
around the state were so impressed with the effort to honor
antiquity that with a little prompting they contributed most of

the fifty thousand dollars that built and equipped a new educational building. Spence said that his publishers would not have sent him to do the story in any other section of the country, but for the South this outlay of energy was phenomenal. Our editor of the county weekly, a pretty ardent Southerner, was not very happy with Spence's reference to the "lackadaisical Southern somnolence," but he refrained from rebuttal because this was supposed to be happiness week for everybody.

I was not exempt from the talent project; in fact I was expected to set a fast pace for the congregation. A college professor told me that the University extension center in Gadsden needed a night teacher in philosophy and religion. So I invested my ten dollars in two textbooks and drove twenty-two miles once a week to teach five straight hours. My students were mostly war veterans who held down jobs in the daytime and were too tired by nightfall to learn much. After the third hour it was nip and tuck as to which would happen first, whether the whole class would pass out on me or I would talk myself into a state of complete exhaustion. All of us made it through the quarter somehow, but not without calluses on their seats and my lungs.

Another job I undertook was the hot-dog concession at the college football stadium. Several convalescing members of Alcoholics Anonymous joined me in this enterprise and turned out to be expert salesmen. There were no facilities at the stadium so we had to mustard them up at home and rush them over to the stands. Our second child, Frank, born a few months before, would stretch out his little hand from his crib and pull the buns into his bailiwick while we were not looking. Everybody got into the act; those who didn't help hindered.

Jeanne became local representative for a brush company which sold its products by having demonstration parties. She did well with it but the prissy sales manager insisted she attend sales meetings. She couldn't, so he fired her. The minister's wife had the distinction of being the only servant in the parable who had her talent cashed in before she could either fully invest it or bury it. She still feels in limbo over it, but she cleared a hundred dollars for the cause.

The funniest story to come out of Talents, Inc., concerned a traveling salesman who was so intrigued by the plan that he asked us for ten dollars to invest. We gave it to him but he didn't show up for the Day of Reckoning, nor for several months thereafter. One day he came into Johnson's Furniture Store and handed one of our elders twenty dollars.

"Where have you been?" the elder asked. "We've been through with this for three months."

The salesman grinned sheepishly. "Well, you see, I got my parables mixed up. I thought we were doing the Prodigal Son."

After this success, I was considered an aggressive, imaginative young man who loved the Old South and its traditions and had energy to burn to preserve them. I didn't covet this sort of reputation but I must admit I didn't mind it. It put me in the good graces of both the antiquarians who longed for the tranquility of the past and the successful capitalists who liked my free enterprise. At a time when young clergymen were being sniffed at for any kind of socialistic traits I was considered the safest, sweetest-smelling one of them all. This fellow loves our traditions and he knows how to run them right on through the twentieth century, they observed.

After this mild but heady excitement my family settled down to the tranquil, unhurried existence for which the town was noted. People in Jacksonville became a little eccentric as they grew older. So far as personal characteristics were concerned there was no premium on conformity, and being a little peculiar was a kind of pastime. A lady said to me one day, "This town is filled with characters and as soon as you know me better you will discover that I am one of them."

Even our living conditions were a little bizarre. Our next door neighbor's cow grazed in our back lot and we received rich milk in exchange for grazing rights. There was a Negro family living just at the end of the lot and their pig frequently came up around our house to forage. I can't recall their name except that they had a boy, Tyrone. This name sticks in my mind because Tyrone was never where he ought to be and his mother had to rely on her lungs alone to get him back in.

A tire swing hung from a pine limb near the garage, and it was here that Janet, then four, had her first real experience in integration. One of Tyrone's little sisters would come to our house to play. She and Janet would take turns swinging. One would curl up in the tire and be pushed by the other. These two kept up a constant stream of chatter, and one day I was startled to hear them arguing the racial question. The little Negro girl said, "I

ain't black. You see this here tire? It's black and I ain't its color."
Then she warmed to her subject: "You ain't white, neither. That
garage there is white and you ain't white like it." Her logic was a
little faulty but it was nevertheless convincing: "So you and me
is the same color."

Janet came inside whimpering a little at that. How did she
know at the age of four that blackness was stigmatic and one's
whiteness was not to be confused with it? Did she pick that up
from me; had I unconsciously conveyed this impression?

One day shortly after Tyrone's thirteen-year-old brother had
been stabbed by one of the town bullies, a sociology professor at
the Jacksonville State College phoned me and asked what I
proposed to do about the recent stabbing. With some embarrassment I confessed I hadn't planned to do anything, that I had
no idea what I *could* do. He asked me to join him in rounding
up witnesses and to give moral support to the prosecutor so that
he would know that the town wanted justice done. This was no
transplanted Yankee, but a South Carolinian with an accent as
thick as a cotton bale. I knew I had to help. It was a case of
elemental justice toward which no one could be neutral. I would
have taken the neutral stand if there had been one.

The case was not an easy one. There were several witnesses but
most of them had been scared off by the threat of a slashing by
this white bully. The professor and I persisted, however, assuring
protection of witnesses (though we never figured out how we
could back this up) and confidence in the prosecutor. A conviction was obtained and we felt that Negroes would be safer from
then on.

I was a poor second to this South Carolinian in pressing for
justice. I had begun to preach and write about it, in more or less
abstract terms, but I had not been really active. I had never gone
to the courts of law to see that justice was done. It was the kind
of justice, however, that almost any white Southerner would have
insisted upon. Physical mistreatment of Negroes was never con-
doned, even during slavery. So what I did was no cause for alarm.
After all, this was in keeping with our traditions, wasn't it, this
bringing to justice a white man (especially if he was white trash)
who had willfully injured a little colored boy? Nevertheless, the
experience was another step toward a commitment to unqualified
justice.

In fairness to the people of Jacksonville I should say that they took more from me than most Southerners would have. On Race Relations Sunday, when all loyal, well-meaning clergymen were supposed to champion tolerance, charity, and good will, I delivered a sermon entitled "The Dark Blot on Democracy," in which I said some provocative things for those times. At the end of the service an elder's wife spoke what I considered to be the general reaction of the congregation. She shook hands and said, "I enjoyed that sermon—no, I didn't—I needed to hear it."

Several months later, in 1950, I made my first appeal before the higher courts of the church. The synod, the state organization, had made me chairman of its Christian Relations Committee. This was one of the least important committees because it had little to do with policy, program, or money. At that time it had only to do with conscience, as if that were not important. This was one of those sad realities which I recognized very early; conscience was not paramount. Our report was supposed to deplore drunkenness, divorce, delinquency, pornography, and the like—subjects that would upset neither the church nor society. If it ever touched on the race issue, it was expected to rejoice that public lynchings had diminished in number from the previous year.

By happy chance our committee was made up of men who, although not anxious to do so, were willing to bear down hard on the conscience, even of eminent elders and clergymen. When I submitted a draft of the report to them they were a little stunned at first, but then they settled down to the task of editing and reworking the report, which kept us at work until two o'clock in the morning. I had already used some of the material in the "Dark Blot" sermon and I knew that there would be no ringing cheers for it. The best I was hoping for was what the elder's wife had said: "I didn't enjoy it but I needed to hear it."

The meeting was in Anniston, the city which, in 1963, had the distinction of being the first place where a Freedom Bus was attacked and burned. When the time came to read the report I felt more than the usual nervousness that attends a public address and more than the normal presumptuousness of a freshman facing veterans. A sense of dread came over me that the words typed on that paper could throw the church into turmoil, perhaps move it several degrees off its middle course. My dread was such that I was actually as much afraid of winning as losing. The report read in part:

Since a Dutch trader in 1619 unloaded twenty slaves in James-
town, Virginia, neither the Southland nor the Southern conscience has been normal. From the presence of the Negro has
evolved the insurmountable problems of our region: war, the
single-crop system, soil depletion, degradation of the poor white,
political demagoguery, congressional filibusters, poor schools,
high percentage in crime and disease, race and sectional hatred.
Yet the church approaches the problem on tiptoe, hoping the
sleeping giant will not be disturbed. In the words of John Ran-
dolph, "Our policy has been one of wise and masterly inactiv-
ity."

There has been a marked improvement in the condition of the
Negro in the last decade, but the Presbyterian church has not
been nearly so important an instrument as have been the secular
agencies organized for the purpose of breaking Southern tradition by appeal to Federal courts.

The Negro of the South is thrown into a galling dilemma. We
encourage him to be clean but rent him houses with no bath
facilities; to be healthy in moldy shacks on unpaved streets, in
bottom lands; to dress properly on a pauper's income, to pay
taxes when there is little property to own, to finish his schooling
when he has to work to eat, to vote when registrars ask impossible
questions, to love his country which shows little affection for
him.

The Negro is not the person we used to know. We can no
longer lay claim to an intimate knowledge of the workings of his
mind. The stereotyped minstrel-like character is a rarity. He is
replaced by a new generation that we do not understand. The
new Negro may seem like the old one but he is putting on an act
because we expect it of him, and to gain favor; but secretly he is
laughing at the white man and cursing him, too, for making a
clown of him. The young Negro is ambitious, smart in the tricks
of the world, less religious and far less superstitious, determined
to move out of his sordidness, bitter toward the white man who
suppresses him.

The new Negro will not accept our paternalism. What love we
say we express toward him, if devoid of justice, is sentimentality.
Genuine love cannot bypass justice in its show of affection. The
old system of every white man "looking out for his niggers"
cannot be relied upon as a present-day solution. The Negro
wants the opportunity of looking out for himself.

Church courts have been reluctant to declare our ultimate goal
in race relations. We are faced with two inevitables, the Federal
Constitution and the Christian conscience. Both dictate that

legal segregation shall not last forever, therefore we may as well admit the removal of legal segregation to be the end toward which we work. Segregation is living on borrowed time. With the Constitution being considerably more active than the conscience of late, the church might have to adjust its morality to measure up to the mores of the state. Legal segregation is stigmatic, oppressive. It can, and as a matter of prophecy, will be replaced by segregation by covenant. There will be no more danger of amalgamation or miscegenation than there has been. Natural preferences and antipathies will preserve the identity of the two races.

These things we can do today, tomorrow, and the day after. Work out by sheer logic and good conscience what our ultimate goal shall be and declare it. Work toward all possible accomplishment under the separate-but-equal doctrine now in effect. Evangelize the Negro people as we have never done before, improve the quality of their churches, increase the financial support of their ministers, commend the acceptance of their theological students in our seminaries. They are ready to accept the high qualifications of faith and practice we require.

When I had finished reading the report, the storm broke loose. The clerk of the synod, a Scotsman, moved that the report be thrown out because it had not been mimeographed and distributed a prescribed number of hours before the reading. When it was pointed out that very few other reports met that requirement and he was asked why he singled out this particular one for disqualification, he replied, "I dinna like this r-r-report." Another venerable clergyman, considered the dean and chief conciliator of the synod, moved that a fifty-word telegram from a committeeman voicing objection be considered a minority report and passed by the synod as a substitute for the majority one. Still another man was so enraged that his doctor later prescribed that he absent himself from all future meetings.

All negative motions failed and the report passed forty-five to twenty-two. Then an unprecedented thing happened. The opponents trooped up to the table and registered their names in disapproval so that posterity and the constituents back home could read the minutes and see for themselves that they were safe and sane Southerners. I was relieved that we had won but I could not miss the look on the faces of those who pressed forward to record their resistance. They were angry, of course, and resentful toward me and my colleagues for deliberately wrenching the church into the path of an onrushing crisis. They seemed a little ashamed, too, that they felt it necessary to demonstrate in this extreme manner their opposition to something that they honestly felt was not all bad. But there was also fear, fear that unless they broadcast their dissent in this way their laymen would grind them to pieces when they returned home; fear that if the gospel required that they turn against the laws and traditions of their own state they could not survive. I felt sorry for them at that moment.

If I had been more perceptive I might have reserved some of that pity for myself. These men and their kind would eventually corner and catch me and strip me of my place in the church. I would not lose out to the Klan or the White Citizens Council or any other extremist group. I would lose to these eminent elders and clergymen, respected and moderate in all things. I didn't think so then because I was a romanticist; I was part of a dream that could have only a happy ending. I was too confident of my strength and of their eventual capitulation to the only possible course.

The report, if presented today, would hardly cause a ripple of dissent. It was unusual only in the light of the temper and the political realities of that time. It was prophetic in one sense, but in another it wasn't. Legal segregation was "living on borrowed time"—the time was to be shorter than we thought possible. But "segregation by covenant"—what an impossibility that was. It was my feeling that the responsible leadership of both races could form themselves into a council and work out a biracial pattern that would remove the causes of grievance and yet keep the two people from getting in each other's way. Then the statutes could be removed from the books. You might call this gracious segregation. It was an impossible plan. The whites would never have consented to it because negotiation itself was a form of integration. And it would not have removed the grievances because segregation per se, whether enforced or voluntary, whether restrictive or conferring every possible privilege, was *the* grievance. At that time, I think, the Negroes would have accepted the plan because it was a step nearer their goal.

None of us envisioned that the Supreme Court would strike down segregation within four years after our prediction. We didn't think the courts would dissolve segregation by law until it was obviously disintegrating in fact. That's why we proposed the unlikely covenant idea. We didn't think it possible that conditions could be changed without changing attitudes first, and certainly attitudes could not be changed by fiat. This was axiomatic. Even the courts were under the influence of this viewpoint. But the Supreme Court of 1954 exploded this theory. It was not going to wait for attitudes to change before justice could be offered. In fact, it might have become convinced that changing the law would rapidly change attitudes. Many sociologists maintain this. I think the Court was right. It is remarkable how fast some people swung toward an enlightened position once they were convinced that the law was going to remain firm and require compliance.

My own position was still unclear. If the race problem were simply a matter of whether I would accept the Negro, not only outwardly but inwardly, on a basis of complete equality, it would not be the near irresolvable problem that it is. It becomes complex because of the political realities involved. It cuts across every social arrangement we have, and this, of course, includes the church. The responsible citizen, no matter what his color, wants to conserve certain fundamental institutions. Therefore, he becomes acutely conscious not only of his principles and his attitudes but his tactics. He wants to preserve order, preserve worthy institutions, yes, even preserve himself. There is something to be said for this self-preservation, if the underlying motive is to maintain a strategic position through which the cause of justice can be served on a long-term basis. However, it is here that we often make compromises in the name of strategy by keeping our positions at the expense of our integrity. Where is the brink? At what point do our compromises destroy us? This is the tormenting question.

So I would work toward desegregation; but how openly, and how fast? Maybe it wouldn't come in my lifetime, and maybe desegregation was just this side of integration. I was painfully aware now that there was a vast difference between treating Negroes on the basis of equality in person-to-person relationships and working for a change in the social order that would grant them equality at the outset, an equality not subject to the whim or the arbitrariness of individual white men.

Chapter Nine

Soon after the meeting of the Alabama synod in Anniston I dropped by to see Ivan Greenleaf. The slave block in his yard was covered with vines and surrounded by weeds. He harangued me for a while about excessive federalism, as was his custom, and since I was a clergyman he spiced up his tirade by accusing the biblical Joseph of being the first socialist. Joseph, he reminded me, taxed the Egyptian people out of their wheat during prosperity and then traded it back to them for their land during the depression. I half listened while pondering over the symbol of serfdom in his yard. Had this trading block and all that it represented made possible the Old South that was so revered? Could the Southern mystique have been possible without black bondage? Did slavery make our section radically different from, say, the New England of Greenleaf's forebears? Will the difference be dissolved when the Negro has finally moved from slavery through segregation to full citizenship?

The Southerner has never really asked where he got his blood-and-soil complex; he just assumes it. In its intensity it is strong enough to be reverence; in its quality it is something less. When other people like us it is sheer romance; when they don't it becomes snarling belligerence. When our way is challenged we become sectional hellcats. When segregation, the successor to slavery, is attacked, our people, from the claghorn politician to the prim small-town librarian, shift the issue to "the Southern way of life" versus the social heresies of other sections. Other ways of life, if there be any worthy of the term, have no character or value.

It was hard to concentrate on Greenleaf's conversation, or rather monologue, because his opinions had been so widely broadcast that the listener could anticipate where his diatribe would come out. So instead I tried to imagine what would be the feelings of the typical Southerner as he stood around that slave block with a few planters and farmers a hundred years before, sizing up the human flesh put on display. He would, of course, have felt superior to the black man, for he would have reasoned that the very fact that his kind had submitted to servitude was proof of his low caste. But why would he have felt superior to the whites to the north of him, Greenleaf's New England forebears for example, who at that moment were passing judgment on the Southern system? And, he would reason, they were condemning it not because it was wrong, but because it produced an enviable civilization of which they were not a part. The presence of these abject people in the South was evidence that Providence considered the Southerner not only worthy of their ownership but a benefactor to them by virtue of the arrangement. Conscience would have intruded in this chain of thought. Either the South should cry for pardon and release these people or become convinced that Southern culture and religion were so nearly perfect that anyone, even in bondage, should feel fortunate to live and serve here. Crying for pardon, however, was out. The mystique had to be reverenced, an idyllic civilization had to be protected, especially from the boorish and envious one to the north.

Some time before in my self-arranged reading course I had run across a quotation taken from the *Southern Literary Messenger* which perfectly illustrates this superiority complex. It appeared in an 1860 issue and was written by a "distinguished gentleman from Alabama."

The People of the Northern states are more immediately descended of the English Puritans . . . The Puritans at home constituted as a class the common people of England, at least a portion of it, and were descended of the ancient Britons and Saxons. They have severe traits of religious fanaticism. On the other hand the Southern states were settled and governed in great measure, under the supervision of the crown, immediately by and under the direction of persons belonging to the blood and race of the reigning family, and belonged to the stock recognized as Cavaliers, who were the royalists . . . and directly descended from the Norman barons of William the Conqueror, a race distinguished in its earliest history for its warlike and fearless character, a race in all times since renowned for its gallantry, chivalry, honor, gentleness and intellect. . . . The southern people come of that race.[1]

Sheer pomposity, but how convincing it must have sounded then.

The slave block was now covered over with vines and the ground around it, once kept bare by the feet of buyers, was grown up in weeds; but was slavery a forgotten institution, was the relationship between the two races radically changed? I couldn't say that it was. Individual planters owned individual slaves in a previous century, and in the present one a white society subjugated a black society.

One night a few weeks later, as I reclined on the lawn of our manse, breathing the distinctive honeysuckle air and watching a yellow moon trim the cedars in the pasture across the road, I heard from over the hill the ecstatic shouting of Negroes in a summer tent meeting. Ironically, this section of Jacksonville is called Needmore. There is little these people do not need, yet they survive, are generally docile, and give the whites very little trouble. You don't know these people until you hear them sing. They sing as though weary for another land. Their minor shadings and improvisations are not renditions but cries of a piteous heart, majestically sad and sweet. In my reverie I could see the Lord of Green Pastures stretching out his great arms and drawing them to his bosom, gently chiding, "Don't you fret now, it won't be long."

The Negro population in Jacksonville was typical of a semi-rural community. Those who write of the South must explain quickly what they mean by "typical," because the type is vanishing fast. The Negroes were docile, respectful, extremely poor, and sometimes given to petty theft in order to sustain themselves. One day I watched Old Tom, a rheumatic and palsied Negro, ease up to a soft-drink truck in the alley and with amazing alacrity snatch a bottle and drop it into his shapeless coat. He had done this scores of times, I know. His movements were strictly professional. As I approached him I started to say, "Better put

[1] Rollin G. Osterweis, *Romanticism and Nationalism in the Old South* (New Haven: Yale University Press, 1949), p. 79.

that back, Tom; I'd hate to turn you in." To my own surprise I walked by and said, "Good morning, Tom. Nice day, isn't it?"

This old Negro was a model of the post-Reconstruction South. We hadn't known what to do with him. We knew that he was filching enough to keep himself fed and warmed, but we preferred to let him steal moderately and be restrained by his own fear of punishment rather than change a system that made stealing a near necessity.

Occasionally my mother, who was still a housemother at Alabama College, wanted to travel, so I arranged to drive her. One of our junkets, in 1950, took us to lower South Carolina, to the place of her childhood. She and I visited various members of her prolific family and went to a couple of cemeteries where her ancestors were buried. She led me from grave to grave, explaining what kin these sleeping ones were to each other and to me. In one churchyard there were two headstones that appeared in Ripley's "Believe It or Not" column. Two graves, side by side, bore identical inscriptions. It seemed that John McLean died and his family procured a small headstone for him. Years later a pauper died. By now McLean's descendants felt they could afford a larger stone, so they placed the smaller one on the grave of the pauper. Since the poor man had made no name for himself they didn't bother to change the inscription, reasoning perhaps that he should be proud to bear the name of John McLean in eternity.

I don't think I fully appreciated what my mother was doing in those old cemeteries. She was taking her cup of nostalgia, running her wrinkled fingers over the blackened stones and tenderly reading the past in Braille, recapturing the mystique of her time, and subtly teaching it to me so that it might not die with her generation. She was also doing what most of us do when we reach a certain period in our lives; she was getting acquainted with death, seemingly selecting a place where she might lie down and rest until her burdens were no more, rising unencumbered to an eternal morning.

She wanted me to meet Cousin Ellie, she called him, her double first cousin and a United States Senator. He was Ellison D. Smith, known nationally as Cotton Ed. Two brothers had married two sisters in this proud little province in lower South Carolina. Senator Smith had a sizable farm of two thousand acres outside of the little town of Lynchburg, where my mother had lived as a girl. I couldn't help but grieve for her a little as we drove slowly through the town and down the road that had once been familiar to her. She pointed out some of the landmarks of her generation. They had not only changed; most of them were gone, including her home which had once sheltered not just a family but a social institution. Here my grandfather, a twice-wounded Confederate captain who never quit until Appomattox, cheerfully nurtured his boisterous family of nine children through the trying and humiliating days of Reconstruction. But there was nothing there now, not so much as a foundation stone that could testify that once this place had seen proud people rise from honorable defeat to reclaim their place in a great federation of states.

But Cotton Ed Smith was still in evidence, very much so. His property had been a grant to his family by George III two hundred years before. The house itself looked nearly that old. It had about it an air of amiable dilapidation, indicating that its owner would prefer to be classed as a good dirt farmer than a sometime successful planter. As we drove into the yard I noticed on one side of the house several old cars that were rusting on their wheels. I thought at first that my distinguished kinsman had a junk business as a side line, but as it turned out he was just a sentimentalist who never discarded anything that he had once become attached to. I could believe it when I saw him saunter down the steps to meet us. He was wearing clothes that cried for burial, or at least one last trip through the washer.

"That's not Cousin Ellie," I whispered to Mother, "it just couldn't be."

But it was, and as soon as we got acquainted, I realized there was quite an imposing character beneath this dirt farmer's attire.

History has classified Smith with Gene Talmadge of Georgia, Bilbo of Mississippi, and Heflin of Alabama. They were the claghorns of their time, caricatures of senatorial dignity and Southern gentility, but also unbelievably crafty. They knew what they were doing and what their public image was, and it made them unbeatable as politicians. Smith not only beat all his South Carolina opponents for six consecutive elections but humiliated Franklin D. Roosevelt as well when in 1938 Roosevelt tried and failed to purge Smith in a senatorial election by throwing his tremendous weight to Smith's opponent. He didn't wear the red galluses of Gene Talmadge, who himself was highborn, but he had his own ways of identifying himself with the wool hatters. Mother often remarked that the family complained of the many tactics Cousin Ellie employed that were "beneath him." They would rather see him lose an election than turn uncouth to win.

He and Mother cleared the agenda of family talk in a few minutes, and then he began to expostulate. At the outset I marveled at the eloquence of his profanity. It was so rich that I unconsciously dropped my head reverentially before I realized that he was swearing and not praying. As he explained it to me, and at another time to Beverly Smith who wrote him up in the now defunct *American Magazine*: "If I seem to cuss a good deal there is a reason for it. My father was a Methodist minister. My two brothers were ministers, one of them a bishop. My two sisters married ministers. Mathematically, I was almost a minister, but God knows how much I missed it otherwise. As the only black sheep I've got the cussin' for the whole family to do. I'll never catch up in my lifetime."[2] Apparently he had soaked up all the churchly language of his prayerful father and brothers and converted it to practical usage, especially when he needed a choice expletive. Occasionally he would demonstrate his remarkable talent by shouting for his houseboy, David, who would appear at his leisure and grin appreciatively through the entire string of affectionate epithets, even when they ended with "nigger." David properly reasoned that when the old man quit cussing he quit caring.

With great relish he reviewed his exploits at the Democratic convention at Philadelphia in 1936. He led a walkout there when a Negro minister was called on to offer the invocation. His motives were misjudged on this occasion, but he didn't go to any great lengths to correct the false impression. As he entered the convention hall he saw photographers surrounding a Negro who was posing in an attitude of prayer. Later, when the same Negro stood before the delegates to pray, this was too much; Ed's sense of reverence had been profaned, and not by his own vocabulary this time. "That Negro minister was not put up there to invoke divine blessing," he snorted, "but to invoke Negro votes. He was not asking divine blessing but primary blessing."[3]

2 Beverly Smith, "F.D.R. Here I Come," *The American Magazine* (Jan., 1939), p. 145.
3 *Ibid.*, p. 146.

Of course, the voters back home in South Carolina were not interested in such a fine distinction. They only knew their tobacco-chomping hero had spurned the prayers of a nigger preacher, had flaunted the Devil and the whole Democratic party with the only proper racial view there is, which is to keep niggers out of white men's affairs. This was totally consistent with his stand on the double-barrelled issue of state's rights and white supremacy. A less-than-positive stand on these meant political oblivion. To the more literate he had asserted: "History from Othello down is agreed that he is an inferior breed. The history of Africa proves that this race is mentally and morally in a category remote from the white race."[4]

He must have repeated that convention episode a hundred times over. It probably won him the next election. He told us that in one of his campaign speeches he made the mistake of preparing too sophisticated an address. In the midst of his prefacing remarks on Runnymede and the Magna Charta an impatient wool hatter with tobacco running down the side of his mouth shifted his quid and grumbled, "Aw, hell, Ed, tell us about Philadelphyi." With that the Senator slapped his leg and roared triumphantly, "—and by God in heaven, I did just that."

We took leave of the old warrior, the unyielding opponent of anti-lynching bills and woman's suffrage ("the women run things anyway"), and advocate of more sensible immigration laws (to shut out the scum and offscourings of Europe). We took leave of my proud family's contribution to the United States Senate for thirty-six years, a term longer than John C. Calhoun served. He wasn't a mean fellow and he wasn't a redneck. He was an aristocrat who was bilingual, he could quote Shakespeare out of one side of his mouth and spout po'buckra dialect out of the other. He was devoted to the Negroes on his farm but he feared and despised them as an ethnic group, especially if they challenged the prevailing system of social stratification. I left him, feeling that I had been in the presence not so much of an unusual personality but of an institution that had spanned two centuries but could not endure a third. He was at once laughable and lovable, flexible and implacable, provincial and extremely perceptive, bellicose and gentle, transiently astute and ultimately

4 *Ibid*, p. 145.

blind, loyal to his own and subversive to the larger human family. I liked him and I pitied him, but more, I pitied those to whom he was the symbol of what our civilization should be like. My family's gift to the nation, but to their undying credit they preferred his brother, Bishop Coke Smith of South Carolina, resigning themselves to the fact that Cousin Ellie Smith would go on cussing enough for them all, and for the Devil himself if he ever ran out of hot breath.

My next excursion with Mother, in 1951, was to New England. She wanted to go there, she said, because New Englanders seemed so much like Southern people. She thought of them as soft-spoken—speaking a dialect much like ours—genteel, proud, individualistic, and having pronounceable names. Of course, the historical explanation is that the two groups are of the same origin; both came from the British Isles and remained similar until fairly recent immigrations from the European continent changed the Yankee ethnic pattern. A political similarity is in the secessionist tendencies of both. New England threatened withdrawal from the Union as early as 1812 at the Hartford Convention.

To get to New England Mother, Jeanne, and I had to travel through some states that Mother wasn't especially interested in. First we had to drive to Kentucky to deposit the children with their grandparents. She wasn't prepared to like the scenery or the people in Ohio, Pennsylvania, and New York. What few people from these states she had known she did not particularly admire. To her they were crude, bumptious, lacking in manners and sensitivity. They were a hybrid people, not pure Anglo-Saxon like the New Englander.

We stopped at Salem, Ohio, where there was a shrine to a noted agent of the underground railway. As I read the inscription aloud I noticed Mother pursing her lips and looking straight ahead. This was one of those indignities she felt she must endure if we were to get our money's worth from the AAA guidebook. Several miles later when she spoke again it was to say that the South had laid plans to free the slaves long before the North decided to jump in and get nasty about it.

Of all the historic places, Concord, Massachusetts, interested us most. We joined a tour conducted by the Antiquarian Society which took us to the places now hallowed because of Emerson,

Thoreau, Whittier, and Louisa May Alcott. We were surprised that the Civil War was so important to these people several states away from where the battle lines were. We thought that only the South remembered. In the Alcott house we saw a secret closet where runaway slaves had been hidden. We had just seen the war trophies in the museum at Bennington, Vermont. It seemed normal that they would display captured regimental flags, but when we saw in a frame a tiny fragment of a banner allegedly shot from the staff over the Richmond capitol—well, that was rubbing it in a little too hard. In the Manse, I think it was, I witnessed a real sectional skirmish. The proud guide, dressed in her eighteenth-century costume, was giving her well-rehearsed lecture on the furnishings of the place. In the middle of it Mother interrupted and asked innocently, "Are these things antique?" Aghast at such impertinence, the imperious lady cocked her head and took aim at Mother over the tip of her Victorian nose, intending to devastate her with a glare. Mother responded with an arched eyebrow and a half smile of forced tolerance. A confrontation between two ironclads and it was obvious that the *Merrimac* had scored a direct hit on the *Monitor!* Appomattox had temporarily been reversed. I staggered out biting my wrist to keep from being convulsed.

Later that afternoon we went to an old cemetery on the Concord hillside. Among the angular gray slate tombs is the grave of an unrenowned Yankee slave by the name of John Jack. The grave, well tended and covered with lilies, is in the far corner of the burying ground. George Tolman remarked in a paper prepared for the Concord Antiquarian Society and distributed to tourists that he had

always found the graves of Negroes carefully relegated to the obscure corners of the grounds, along with the paupers and the criminals, as our pious ancestors had taken care that when should take place that opening of graves and literal bodily resurrection of the dead . . . these lower ranks should come up in their proper place—in the rear of the great procession.

John Jack was not famous in life but he was in death, for his marker bore this unusual, oft-quoted epitaph:

> *God wills us free; man wills us slave.*
> *I will as God wills; God's will be done.*

The irony appears when we are told that the author of these lines was Daniel Bliss, a prominent Massachusetts Tory and later a colonel in the British Army during the Revolutionary War. Evidently he heard no divine fiat that the colonists be free of British dominion, though his line, "God wills us free" became popular currency in the colonists' cause of liberty. He did see the startling contradiction in the patriotic clamor for freedom and the patriots' willingness to enslave John Jack and his kind. Bliss just couldn't be convinced that America was beautiful "for patriot dream that sees beyond the years" nor "for heroes proved in liberating strife." The cause of the impending revolt, as he saw it, was those "amber waves of grain" for which the people wanted to escape taxation. It was a matter of pounds and pence, not oppression—or why John Jack?

My mother saw this inconsistency even before she read the Concord Antiquarian Society's pamphlet on the subject of this noted tomb. Pious, abolitionist New England had its slavery, too, and its second-class citizenship even in the kingdom of heaven. And these colonists who had started this fracas against its government wanted not freedom in the abstract but freedom to run their own affairs. So here was pretty good precedent for the South's position, she reasoned.

Mother was right in that there was a time when leaders of the South thought seriously of emancipation without duress from anyone. The remarkable Virginia Resolutions read in part:

> Resolved that the African trade is injurious to this colony, obstructs the population of it by freemen, prevents manufacturers and other useful immigrants from Europe from settling among us, and occasions an annual increase of the balance of trade against this colony. . . . For the most trifling reasons and sometimes for no conceivable reason at all his majesty has rejected laws of the most salutary tendency. The abolition of domestic slavery is the greatest object of desire in those colonies where it was unhappily introduced in their infant state.[5]

Similar resolutions were passed by both Georgia and North Carolina conventions. Thomas Jefferson's original draft of the Declaration of Independence included a tirade against the King

---

[5] Daniel R. Goodloe, *The Southern Platform* (Boston: John P. Jewett Co., 1858), p. 3. (From the American Archives, 4th Series, Vol. 1, Prince George County Resolutions, Virginia, p. 494.)

for permitting slavery when the colonies had petitioned him to outlaw it. George Washington freed his slaves, effective on the death of his wife. So did Robert E. Lee half a century later. Perhaps the most eloquent and introspective note was struck by Patrick Henry in his letter to Robert Pleasants:

It is not a little surprising that the professors of Christianity whose chief excellence consists in softening the human heart, in cherishing and improving finer feelings, should encourage a practice so totally repugnant to the first impressions of right and wrong. . . . Would anyone believe I am the master of slaves of my own purchase? I am drawn along by the general inconvenience of living here without them. I will not, I cannot justify it. . . . Let us transmit to our descendents, together with our slaves, a pity for their unhappy lot and our abhorrence of slavery.[6]

So the Southern people in the early stages were not oblivious to their moral inconsistency and the consequences of slavery. John C. Calhoun himself confessed that though the Constitution had intended slave trade to be tolerated until 1808, "I feel ashamed of such a tolerance, and take a large part of the disgrace, as I represent a part of the Union, by whose influence it might be supposed to have been introduced."[7]

These eighteenth and nineteenth century Americans had inherited their pattern from at least two generations of forebears. They did well to confess the evil in those days of militant imperialism when codes of ethics often pertained only to one's own kind. The correction of the evil seemed beyond their capacity. But these confessions by good Southerners indicated that there was a strong feeling that slavery was not good Americanism.

The question that was posed for me that day was, How would New England have differed from the South if its climate and terrain had been compatible with African slavery, if there had been thousands of John Jacks there instead of an occasional one? Did New England have a mystique like that of the South? Regional pride, yes, but not the mystique. And if not, could it be because they had no substratum of human servitude to produce a society of self-styled masters and inordinate reverence for this immoral arrangement?

6 *Ibid.* (letter to Robert Pleasants, 1779), p. 79.
7 Margaret L. Coit, *John C. Calhoun* (Boston: Houghton Mifflin Company, 1950), p. 110.

Chapter Ten

We had spent four happy and profitable years in Jacksonville, a town that had not moved completely into the twentieth century. The afterglow of the Old South could still be seen. Echoes of gentle voices could be heard in the cool, high-ceilinged parlors of old houses if you listened. The town was no ante-bellum reproduction; there was nothing artificial about it. No phony colonels sat around in the public square ruminating over Chancellorsville or Signal Mountain. No zealous president of the United Daughters of the Confederacy proposed that the town be recreated in its prewar image. The Old South that I came to know there was genuine. It was not there because the citizens consciously retained it, but because "progress" had not moved in entirely to replace it. I had loved its languidness, its unrehearsed enjoyment of modest things, its willingness to be just what it was and nothing else, its bemused tolerance of both the peculiar and the pretentious. I will long remember its fresh pine smell, the shadow cast by the tag end of the Appalachian range, and its musty old houses looking forlorn amid ranch-type companions, or self-conscious in new coats of paint.

The time for me to move, though, had to come. A young minister can do only so much in a particular place and then he becomes restless for what is called "a new challenge." Since there are always more churches than clergy there is a constant rotation. Scarcity of ministers is the bishop of our church.

One Sunday morning in early fall some strangers appeared in our congregation. They divided up at the door and sat in different pews. About the only time we ever had that many visitors at once was at Christmas, when all the Currier family returned for a reunion. All of them were known to us, even to the most reluctant in-law. Obviously, then, this was a pastor-seeking committee from some other church. As the late Halford Luccock of Yale Divinity School once said, such a committee is about as inconspicuous as an elephant on a lettuce leaf. To make matters even more interesting, there were two committees present from different churches, and each recognized the other as a scouting party even though they had never seen each other before.

I was overwhelmed by this sudden burst of attention and was unequal to the occasion. During the prelude somebody tripped and unplugged the cable to the electric organ. I had to come down unceremoniously and plug it in, which caused the organist, Jeanne, to cast a grateful glance in my direction; which in turn caused one of the committeemen to observe that, from the size of the look, the organist was either my wife or should be. I had been out of town all week and had what is known in the trade as a "quick mix" sermon. It is something grabbed hastily from the top of the mind that requires a little more heat and stirring than usual to make up for the lack of fresh ingredients. The one thing that didn't go wrong was that my greyhound didn't make his usual appearance inside or howl an anthem outside. "That's the last I'll see of those fellows," I thought. But pastor-seeking committees are a strange breed. They are completely unpredictable, hopelessly abnormal.

One of the committees or, I should say, one of the units of one of the committees showed up at the manse after church and began to talk as if they were interested in having me accept a call to the First Presbyterian Church of Columbus, Georgia. I was overwhelmed, because this was a fine old church of twelve hundred members and I was then serving a church of a hundred and twenty. It seemed that they had enjoyed my discomfort, my manful efforts to pull some meaning out of mediocrity, and all the little folksy miscues that transpire in a small-town church. What they wanted, it seemed, was not a pulpiteer but the un-starched, friendly sort with a good background who could make everybody like him and everybody like everybody else. I learned later what they themselves were probably not conscious of at the time: they didn't want a big man in the pulpit because he might become unmanageable. They wanted an amicable fel-

low because they had an element in the church consistently hostile to their ministers.

After some low-pressure wooing on their part they informed
me that they felt led of the Lord to call me, and after being
properly coy with them for a discreet time I told them I felt led
to accept their call. My world was brightening considerably. I
was vaulting into ecclesiastical prominence, serving a church that
outstripped even the Atlanta churches in per capita giving. We
would be living in a house big enough for my growing family
and receive an income adequate to all our needs. I couldn't help
thinking of these little fringe benefits as I asked the Lord for his
judgment. I didn't quite forgive myself then for these worldly
thoughts that influenced my decision. I can't quite forgive myself
now for not being honest enough to admit these were for the
most part legitimate considerations, all part of the call.

I really had no idea what I was called to except a greater
opportunity to work harder among more people. My worldly
thoughts were that I was called to a position of prominence;
what I couldn't know was that I was called to tragedy. I would
never have willingly accepted this.

Columbus, Georgia, is situated at a bend of the Chattahoochee
River. It was formerly a village of the Creek Indians. Immedi-
ately across the river, which is the boundary between Georgia
and Alabama, is the once infamous but now exemplary Phenix
City. In the forties and early fifties it was called by Secretary of
War Stimson "the wickedest city in the United States."

I stood on the breastworks of Wilson's Raiders on a hill in
Phenix City overlooking the river and Columbus across from it,
which had been within range of the Union forces. I marveled
that these Georgia people should flaunt the meek surrender of
their town to the hated Yankee by frequent reference to it at
Confederate Memorial Day exercises and on other occasions
when the past was disinterred. But if the Confederacy was to
glory in the Lost Cause, this little hotbed of secession was going
to muscle in for its share of it.

Columbus is still a cotton aristocracy, reigning now through
the textile mills rather than the old plantations. Some of these
mills originated in New England, having moved South since after the war. Some of the old family names in Columbus are

traceable to Yankee capitalists and technicians who came to Georgia when the state was prostrate at the war's end. Cotton is not the despot it once was, but it is still venerated. The town is one of the largest textile centers in the South.

Columbus began to burgeon in the 1940's from a population of 40,000 to three times that in the mid-sixties. Fort Benning, the world's largest infantry post, just outside the city limits, has been primarily responsible for this growth. The fort brought in many substantial citizens from other sections of the country and almost made Columbus a cosmopolitan city—but not quite. It surrendered to Wilson's few-score Raiders, but has been able to secure a truce of coexistence with these Federals of the twentieth century. I found the fort and its people to be refreshing in that their orbit of thinking was so much wider than that of the townspeople. It was especially refreshing to see so many young soldiers in the Sunday congregations representing most of the colleges and universities of the nation. I found myself slanting sermons toward them, which caused me to tip my hand a little more than I had planned.

The city is a comely place, well laid out and well tended. Its streets are wide and its stores fairly new. Its residential districts are filled with compactly built ranch-type houses shaded by the short-leaf pine trees that monopolize the Georgia soil. The more affluent homes are ablaze with color during azalea and camellia season. Camellia culture is a fine art. The object is not only to produce perfect specimens of the standard types, but by grafting to create new ones. The rare achievement of a new plant is cause for celebration and for having a flower named for oneself. Kentucky horse breeders couldn't be more zealous or ingenious.

Except for the torrid summer months the climate is ideal. Frosty winter mornings become shirt-sleeve weather by midday. Columbus children have never seen a heavy snowstorm and if a few lost flurries fall school is let out for the day. The people think they lead hectic lives, but compared to other sections of the country life is both casual and pleasant. There is so much grilling of steaks on outdoor barbecues that a stranger from another generation might think that the natives were engaging in some kind of religious rite of burnt sacrifice. The countryside is dotted with small artificial lakes where large-mouth bass and blue gills

abound. There are larger lakes for boating and skiing. Life is
good there.

The historic First Presbyterian, Baptist, Methodist, and Episcopal churches, all stand near the center of town, on choice plots
given to each by the city. There are some 7,000 members in these
four churches alone. In jocular moments the four ministers
would remark that we knew that our churches were within a
stone's throw of each other because we threw stones at each other.
The townspeople loved our show of tolerance, solidarity, and
even of genuine friendship. We had a weekly television panel
that included three of the four of us and an astute suburban
Methodist.

"Isn't it just wonderful how they get along with each other?"
the people exclaimed. "Look at them—you'd never know that
they were in competition with each other."

Our love affair was brief, however. The winsome Baptist died
of a heart attack. The brilliant and attractive Methodist became
mentally ill and had to leave the ministry. He started his life
over, loading crates for the Royal Crown Cola Company, and is
working his way up. When I left only the affable Episcopalian
remained and year after year he has held his position.

Long before we were forced apart, however, we had begun to
drift apart. The Big Issue, integration, was intruding and we
were beginning to feel a little self-conscious around each other. If
the racial viewpoint of one of us was not liked, some members of
his congregation would shift to one of the rival churches. Naturally there was some resentment on the part of one minister
toward another for undercutting him on the price of Christian
ethics. So we were friends only so long as the Christian faith was
an altogether lovely thing to preach.

Thirty-seven was the perfect age for taking an important pastorate. I was old enough to have made my serious mistakes and
young enough to be worked to death, as somebody put it. The
comment was made to one of our members that the Presbyterians
had certainly gotten themselves a young minister. The reply was,
"Yeah, but we age 'em fast."

I approached my work with real exuberance. I didn't have the
slightest doubt that I could live up to expectations and handle
any difficult situation. I had a good education, was used to long
hours of hard work, had good study habits and some degree of

imagination. Furthermore, since I had not spent all my life in fasting and meditation I was not easily shocked and had no illusions about human nature. I was as quick with the quip as the next man, which went far in convincing the luncheon club people that I was a fairly human sort. In fact, it got me up to the podium more often than I like to remember when there was some levity to be dispensed.

I was not depressed by poverty or overawed by wealth. I had good table manners and could keep a conversation going. For the modern ecclesiastical corporation all these were desirable if not essential traits. This was the new image of the clergy that had replaced the austere type whose very countenance was a reproof to all those within range. A minister could be normal; he wasn't expected to be a prophet Elijah, and sticky piety and phony tones were out. However, there was something just as false about this new image as the older authoritarian one. The prosperity of the church now was more important than the quality of its preaching. So first of all a minister should be a good organization man, and this required an affable personality and a cleverness in handling people. Members often comment on the salesmanship or political skill the pastor has or doesn't have. He need not be a good preacher; he need only seem to be. If he can punch together something pithy and short and give it the right tonal treatment, he is ace high with the people who come to church mostly for that feel-better feeling. And if they seem to depart each Sabbath looking as if they had a warm glow around the spleen, that makes the officers who arranged the last mortgage on the church happy.

A slick preacher could and still can get away with murder, and murder it is when human souls are kept on a starvation diet. Many a resourceful, dedicated young fellow has felt himself being jockeyed by a superficial civilization into the position of a religious pitch man. I know the feeling, and not just from hearsay. Study hours are shortened, books are secured not for their depth of content but for their fast digestibility; contemplation is nonexistent; imagination, which is so vital to preaching, is exhausted on canvasses for more and more money. The church plant expands, the steeple heightens, the gospel sounds pleasanter; but the spirit of the people famishes. No controversial issues have any place in such a context. The moral fibre of the people is nowhere near tough enough to grapple with them. The minister who has achieved his position by being a fancy Dan blanches at the idea of even climbing into the ring with a real issue. All his training has been toward reconciliation, unifying, and proclaiming an abstract love.

I came to Columbus with no standard to unfurl, no windmills to joust. I soon learned that all my predecessors had some deficiencies that had made their going hard. I was advised that my immediate predecessor had been too autocratic; the one before him had been a man of high esteem but had gone astray on the race issue. He was all right, one of the officers said, after they had straightened him out on the Negro question. He had seen a helpless Negro woman cuffed around at the police station and had said too much about it from the pulpit. He wouldn't get off the subject until the elders called an extraordinary meeting and confronted him with the defective side of his ministry, which meant regurgitating some of the real or imagined grievances that rested heavily upon their stomachs. The pastor before him was a grand old man but had gone dry in the pulpit, they said, and had outlived his usefulness there. And so on, back as far as 1895.

What kind of superman or angel did I think I was to believe I could avoid the same kind of psychological mugging they had gotten? But I was young and confident and believed I was wise enough to steer a careful course among these shoals. I was going to be all things to all men, always facing down any difficulty with prudence and humor.

I was never one to confine my ministry to my own people. Community life appealed to me, so I soon found myself on more boards and agencies than time permitted. But I liked the role of "everybody's minister"; it was both refreshing and flattering. I took my coffee breaks and ate my lunches at the biggest hotel, where most of the successful businessmen gathered. Before long I was doing more preaching and theological debating at lunch than I was in the pulpit. Here any inquirer, honest or not, could engage me in a lengthy discussion of subjects he wouldn't have the nerve or inclination to bring up in his church, that is, if he belonged to a church. Before long I was invited to sit at lunch with a group called the Knights of the Round Table. The Knights were business and professional men who liked nothing better than to argue as they ate, and the hotter the argument the

better they liked it. There's one like it in every town. The men
were not necessarily compatible with each other before or after
lunch. They ran the gamut of political persuasion and religious
affiliation. The one thing they had in common was a thick skin.
They had to be able to take every quip, prank, and insult in high
humor, and to drop every formality and restraint. This was no
place for holding back anything. One could say anything he
wanted to on any subject without fear of angering or shocking
anyone, or of being quoted to the wrong people. This was the
only free forum in town.

I was welcomed there not only for my thick skin and acid
tongue but because the men could unleash on me some of the
hidden hostility they felt toward the church. Although most of
them were churchmen of good standing, they had some repressed
resentment toward the clergy and the operational procedures of
their respective churches. They dared not offend their own ministers with their complaints, so they unloaded them on me. Naturally, the race question entered our discussions, and I found
myself to be the lone exponent of a better way than segregation.
I liked nothing better than to joust with them on this subject, for
it gave me a chance to express my views in bolder terms than I
dared use from the pulpit. They ganged up on me, of course, but
they always left knowing that it was not a foregone conclusion
that good conscience and sound judgment were on their side.

Another group I had more than casual contact with was made
up of several young couples who frequently gathered at one of
their homes for drinks and grilled steaks. They, too, were purposely argumentative and there was no limit to the subject matter. Some were churchmen but several were doctors who at best
were agnostic. None made any pious pretensions, none was
iconoclastic, and none had a mature grasp of the Christian faith,
or of any religion for that matter. They were very intelligent;
they sought the truth, and they were not afraid of finding it.
Jeanne and I were frequently invited to their homes because
with us they never felt apologetic for their behavior and because
theology was one of their favorite subjects. They gave me full
permission to convert them if I could, with the proviso that I lay
myself open to conversion by them. So during our evenings together I learned far more about the workings of the human mind

and the yearnings of the spirit than in our prim little Bible study groups in the atmosphere of well-guarded orthodoxy.

I often felt penitent about these people. They were either out of the church altogether or on the fringes of it because we, the churchmen, had put faith on a moralistic basis. Our preachments had said to them that it was a sin to doubt, and the reason for doubt was some other sin one cherished that veiled his eyes from God. That sin was usually of the flesh, such as drinking or sexual desire. And what was it they doubted in the first place? It was our theology, cast in the mental categories of past generations, outmoded and irrelevant, and our competence to know enough of the truth to be dogmatic about it. So in my presence they drank, indicated by their conversation that they had healthy sexual urges, and doubted. I didn't have to be highly perceptive to realize that these people by being honest were free, and their freedom was a better ground of beginning than the cautious belief-by-rote of the more religious. I didn't commend them, of course, for their thirst, passions, and skepticism, but neither did I declare these as disqualifications in their theological quest.

This intellectual freedom of theirs certainly made them more perceptive in social issues. Regarding the race problem, for example, they were much more reasonable than the official boards of the local churches. This led me to believe that there was more faith in them than in "the faithful." For those who are not honest with themselves are not free and where there is no freedom there can be no faith. Was there a church for these people? I didn't fool myself into believing that they would come to mine. I was trying to establish a place of freedom for their type but I knew the mold of convention was too hard for me to break. So on occasion we had church right there where they were. It would have repelled them to call it that but they were a fellowship seeking God, earnestly and honestly.

I had not been in Columbus long before I was warned about two people. The first was Hugh Bentley, the leader in the reform movement across the bridge in Phenix City, then at the height of its moral decadence. He lived over there but had a sporting goods store in Columbus.

The squalor of Phenix City defies description. During the depression of the early thirties it was about to go into receivership.

Since all the taxable industry was on the Columbus side, the city fathers decided to yield to the persistent pressure of the gambling element to "open up the town" to the soldiers at Fort Benning. The gamblers agreed that in exchange for this tolerance they would sweeten the coffers of the city treasury when they got low.

It was only a matter of time before politically controlled gambling became gambling controlled politics. The racketeers became the leading citizens. The dice table and the roulette wheel were soon followed by open drinking, prostitution, abortion, baby-selling, narcotics, hired murder, safe-cracking, manufacture of crooked cards and dice. At first the out-of-town soldiers were the main patrons, but eventually kicks-seekers from all over slipped into this dirty little place. Big-time gamblers from the North would stop off in Phenix City for a little practice with the dice on their way to Miami.

The city fell completely under the rule of the gangster element. Even the churches were controlled after a few of the racketeers' men were elected to their boards and a few large contributions were made to their building funds. Influence, however, could not remain local; it had to move into the state capital to insure freedom from molestation from some crime-fighting governor or attorney-general. Those at the capital were approachable because here in this little town was enough surplus cash to win almost any state election, not to mention the personal gratuities that made life interesting. So "satchel men" made regular trips to Montgomery to keep state officials happy about the little recreational center on the Chattahoochee.

In the late forties Hugh Bentley came into being as a reformer one night when he was converted by a tent meeting revivalist. As he left the meeting he looked about him at the red and green lights blinking their lurid bids to pleasure-starved citizens, heard the raucous drunken laughter of soldiers on holiday, and said, "God don't like what He sees here."

Soon after that he headed up a vigilante group that eventually turned the city inside out. He and his spunky little band scouted every illegal operation in the city, drawing floor plans of each one of them, marking the location of gambling machines and following them as they were moved to hidden storage houses whenever a raid was on. They recorded the malfeasance of officers of the law. They tried to clean up voting lists, awaken grand juries, encourage honest citizens to run for office, protect the elections from corruption. Regularly, they appealed and protested to city, county, and state officials, pleading that they do nothing but guarantee a fair election and enforce their own laws. They took their message to the people by radio, pamphlet, newspaper, and door-to-door canvass.

Pressure was building up against the hoodlums. Bentley had to be reckoned with, so he became the prime target of their brutality. Mobsters ran him off the highway in their big cars; they beat him into a bloody mess on the main street on election day; and finally they dynamited his home. His house was completely demolished, but his wife and children escaped serious injury, and he was not at home at the time.

The most significant move this reform group made was to stump the state for Albert Patterson, who was running for the office of attorney-general. Patterson had once defended one of the gambling lords in a murder case, but had in recent years turned toward the reform camp. The office of attorney-general was more strategic for reform purposes in Alabama than that of governor. He was elected, and his victory threw the vice barons into a panic. This was the first serious threat to their dynasty. One night before he had even taken office, as he was about to drive homeward from his law office, two assailants shot him in the mouth. He staggered out of his car and died in a pool of blood on the street, trying in vain to tell a passer-by the names of his assassins.

This brutal murder electrified the nation and aroused the stupified consciences of the people in and around Phenix City who had thought it was just a "fun place." Qualified martial law was declared and the wrecking crews of the National Guard showed everybody who dared look just how hideous this town was. After this physical clean-up the moderate element of the town, that is, those who took a position somewhere between the gangsters and the reformers, pulled down the "business section" of the city and rebuilt from the ground up. The next year, 1954, "the wickedest city in the United States" was given the national award of "All-American City." But Bentley and his friends were not on the bandstand that day—the moderates had taken over. I was advised to avoid Bentley because he was a trouble-maker and a glory-seeker. He was exaggerating the evils of Phenix City because he was a do-gooder who would never be happy unless he was reforming something. If I were seen often with him I would become identified as his type.

Such advice only spurred my curiosity. When I met him I saw not the proverbial fire-eater but a tranquil, sweet-natured person whom I would have nominated for the most likely person to hide under a bed at the first clap of thunder. During our conversation, though, I touched his shoulder, and realized that he was all steel under his shirt. During the next two years of being seen with him I learned he was all barbed wire under his belt. The man was pure guts. Through the whole long, nightmarish episode he had never lost his composure or his humor; and he had never lost his purpose. I not only didn't avoid him; I took pride in keeping his company in public. When the Phenix City Story became a movie his role in the clean-up was minimized and that of John Patterson, son of the assassinated attorney-general, was built up. Patterson afterward became governor, defeating the present governor George Wallace because, as Wallace put it, "He out-segged me." On racial justice Patterson was as hostile as Wallace will ever be. And Hugh Bentley, the alleged headline hunter, never batted a twinkling eye over being ignored when the accolades were handed out.

The other person I was advised to ignore was a renegade Southern Baptist minister by the name of Johnson, who referred to himself affectionately as Parson Jack. He was a scurrilous little fellow whom I never saw in all the years I was there, but whom I felt like poison ivy. He published a weekly newspaper, the *Georgia Tribune*, in which he preached his doctrine of hatred toward Negroes, Jews, Catholics, main line Baptists, and anyone who ever spoke a kind word about any of them. "Harmless old crackpot," people said of him. "Nobody pays any attention to him. Don't let him get under your skin and by all means don't tangle with him."

I saw people read his paper and chuckle over its absurdities. But I was not convinced that he was harmless or that nobody paid any attention to him. I learned that he had come to Columbus about thirty years before, and though he had only a handful of members he was able to put up a combination church, school, and news office. Most people didn't know how all this was fi-

nanced. It was hard to believe that his congregation could pay
him an adequate salary or that his newspaper was self-support-
ing. Those who should know and were willing to talk confided
that the textile industries subsidized him. It was explained that
he was influential among the "lintheads," the common laborers
in the mills, either through his preaching powers or his ability to
convince them he was their kind of man and would look out for
them on matters of employment. Apparently he was able to convince the mill operators that he could manipulate these restless
people and it would pay them to strengthen his hand in the
community.

The big factor is that even today the textile mills do not have
organized labor. This was Parson Jack's high card. He could talk
the unions in or talk them out. But even this shrewd little
conniver needed more than verbal persuasion to keep the lintheads hitched. The operators had a fear—the unions. The employees had a fear, too—the Negro. Why not play one fear
against the other? This is what the little parson did. He got hold
of pamphlets—or printed them himself—showing pictures of
labor leaders standing beside or shaking hands with fellow
unionists who were Negroes. These he would distribute whenever some organizer was attempting to get into the mills. This
would turn the trick every time.

Politically, textile mill employees are the descendants of the
Populist movement that swept the South in the late nineteenth
century and brought on the Jim Crow laws and lynchings. As a
class there is not a more degraded group of whites to be found in
the South than these common laborers in the mills. They had
reason to fear the Negro, for the Negro was economic competition. In all likelihood the Parson was able to convince the operators that a newspaper would be his best instrument in the control
of his people. So he got his newspaper. It could never have paid
for itself with subscriptions and advertising. Jack was the fellow
who kept alive the dying organism of the Klan, and he made no
bones about it.

The little man as a person was not worth my worry because
nobody respected him. He was despised by those who dealt with
him, especially when the dealing was under the table. It was
what he represented that was so galling. He was the dirty linen of
Columbus. The mill owners were the pillars of the big downtown

churches. Each one of those tall steeples depended heavily upon the leadership and money of the textile industry. Yet on one hand these respectable men were supporting an earnest preacher and on the other they secretly backed his diabolic opposite, who heaped smut on their minister whenever he could. It was another way of keeping their men of God "honest." These mill managers despised this man, and they would never repeat aloud that they approved of him, the Klan, or even the White Citizens Council; but in undertones they would admit they thought the presence of these extremists acted as a deterrent to the extremists on the other side, who in their opinion were the Negroes, the labor unionists, and the starry-eyed humanitarians. They played the age-old game of pitting extremes against each other, thereby strengthening their own position in the middle.

This undercover alliance between the textile operators and Parson Jack Johnson was almost unbelievable, considering the disparity of social and economic rank between them. But the Negroes and labor unions were both feared, and Jack was an instrument for keeping them down. That's the sordid side of the way a power structure operates. Actually, among the upper classes organized labor was feared more than the Negro. The Negro could be given social equality and still be avoided. But organized labor was a threat to their economic existence, and they were thrown in violent contact with the unions time and again. If I had spoken in favor of unions rather than racial justice, I wouldn't have lasted half as long as I did.

To the credit of the textile industry, it belatedly discovered that the best way to fight the unions was to offer higher wages and better working conditions. This took some of the wind out of Parson Jack's sails, but apparently the operators never quite considered him expendable. In their minds there was no question of morality here: it was a matter of economic competition and survival. If the clergy of the city took a going over in the *Georgia Tribune* each week and on a local radio station every Sunday morning, they were advised either to laugh it off or quit saying things of a controversial nature that piqued the little man's ire.

The real temperament of the town was beginning to stand out. The people didn't like reformers like Hugh Bentley. In fact, to take a friend or client across the bridge into Phenix City for some night life was quite a sporting experience. Why should anybody dedicate his life to the destruction of this business?

However, Columbus feared the equalitarian movements within the ranks of the poor whites and the Negroes and was ready to suppress anyone foolish enough to espouse their cause. So they played these two groups against the other and used a jackleg preacher to do their dirty work. Add to this the fifty-year record of the church I served for resisting its ministers if they got out of line or grew old on the job. The gentility of these Southern folk should never be taken for softness. They could cut you to the heart without raising their voices; they could curse you and end the curse with "sir." Their stately pines whispered a sinister warning, and their blood-red camellias held a wasp at their center. I was beginning to hear the warning and feel the sting.

Chapter Eleven

A pastoral honeymoon lasts a few months up to a year, depending upon how willing one is to ride the momentum of his predecessor and refrain from starting anything radically different. Things were going well with me. We were in an era of good feeling. The sanctuary filled up on Sunday, the people were paying their pledges, there were no factions, and nobody seemed to have any serious objections to what I did or said. The fact that I projected no program over which they could take exception helped keep the atmosphere cordial. So until the winter of 1954 life in the church was tranquil.

One day I received a telephone call, and I knew the honeymoon was over. The caller, Mr. Sam, had been one of the first in the congregation to cultivate me. We had belonged to the same college fraternity. He was an admirer of people with artistic skills and considered public speaking a special art. He even wrote a poem about one of my sermons in Edgar Guestian rhyme, which he could do with no great effort, unfortunately. We had lunch together, and he often called or stopped by the study to discuss something of concern to him.

Mr. Sam was the town's "aginer." He served on many of the boards and committees of the city and could always be counted on to uphold the negative. To him America's fortunes took a nose dive with the Roosevelt Administration and is still in a tail spin. Centralism, big spending, bureaucracy, high taxes, were plunging us into socialism, and he was going to fight them all wherever he found them. And he found them everywhere, even in church. He and I never really conversed when we were together; I was his audience, his foil. He didn't so much befriend me as appropriate me.

On the telephone he was noticeably agitated. He had been in a Florida church recently and that fine church was about to be split over the matter of reuniting with the Northern church, meaning the United Presbyterian in the U.S.A. What could we do to prevent this from happening to us, he wanted to know. I advised him to say nothing about it because it was to be decided by the General Assembly, our highest representative body, with three fourths of the presbyteries concurring. It was not a local church matter, so there was no reason to make a controversial issue of it in the congregation. This was Presbyterian polity, I explained, strongly similar to the sytem of our federal government. This didn't satisfy him. He wanted an opportunity to vote on it.

Here was a Civil War issue all over again. Our branch of Presbyterianism, called Presbyterian in the United States or Southern, had broken off from the national church in 1861 and had chosen to remain separate after our nation's political breach had closed. So now the word "union" was bandied about, and the very word itself reawakened hostile feelings. Some thought our church was going to vote on whether to favor unions in the textile mills. Others could think of nothing but the humiliation we had once suffered by the invasion and occupation of Union forces. Those who knew the issue a little more intimately saw this big superchurch from the North engulfing us and forcing its racial attitudes upon us. To return to the Northern church would be to forgive former indignities. The Southern states had had to return to the Union against their will, but the Southern churches didn't have to be reunited with their Northern counterparts. In symbol this was a way of declaring that Appomattox wasn't so and a kind of spiritual independence was achieved. With a sense of dread I heard the call to arms in Mr. Sam's voice.

His next move was to call our "venerable elder" and inform him that a group of men was in his office discussing the matter, and since our pledging season was upon us they wanted to know what the church was going to do before they committed themselves financially. "You've got to give a little and take a little," the elder advised me, even though he recognized this as a bare-faced economic threat. I explained that the vote was to be taken in presbytery where an elected elder and I would represent the local church. They would be satisfied, he said, with a kind of town meeting arrangement where the issue would be thoroughly discussed. If given this they would not press for a congregational vote. Reluctantly, I consented to this and the "town meeting" was held. No sooner was this over than a clamor arose to let the congregation decide how it felt. Again the "give a little, take a little" philosophy was invoked, despite the fact that the anti-union group had indicated that it would not push for a vote. What would be wrong with a plebiscite to give these people a chance to express their opinions? So again I yielded, but it was firmly understood that our representatives to presbytery would not be bound by the outcome. We held the plebiscite, which we agreed was nothing but a straw vote. Some 63 percent of the congregation present voted against the idea of reunion. Now they have had their sop, I thought, and will let me alone.

Mr. Sam and one of the elders called me the day before I went to presbytery and informed me I was morally obligated to vote the congregation's opposition to union. The camel had finally taken over the tent! I protested that this was a violation of the Presbyterian system, that I was not going as an instructed delegate but as a representative to vote my convictions, not theirs. They couldn't care less about Presbyterian system and the General Assembly to them was in the same class with the federal government, and I knew what they thought of that. I was morally obligated!

These men knew how I felt, how I intended to vote, and how I did vote. I even made a speech on the floor of presbytery in favor of reunion, and of course the word got back that I had deliberately defied a directive of the congregation. Not all the antiunion people held this against me, but to the regret of all the well-meaning people they saw an opposition party forming against their new pastor. They had seen this happen to every minister within their memory, and they resigned themselves to an interminable season of bickering and harassment.

The wonder of it all was what made Mr. Sam and his kind run. What possible difference could this make to them, who though routinely religious, were spiritually insensitive? I couldn't answer this except to guess that for some reason certain things about the church gave them a sense of security, rational or not, and tampering with those things actually threatened their psychological balance. Union, to them, would take their church out of the South and put it in the despised North.

Mr. Sam broke with me soon after that. After I had shown my hand on the union issue he found all kinds of faults in me and made it a point of telling me about them. He dropped out of church, and when I went by to try to effect a reconciliation he climaxed his rebuke by calling me the leader of the pinkos in Columbus.

The issue of union with the Northern church was defeated by the failure of three fourths of the presbyteries to ratify the favorable action of the General Assembly. In fact, more than half the presbyteries voted against union. This plus the negative vote in our local congregational meeting put me in a bad light. It made my opinion a minority one not only locally but nationally, "nationally" meaning the eleven Confederate and five border states. So I was put in my place; the place in which most clergymen find themselves sooner or later, especially in the South. It is the position of defensiveness. When they are maneuvered here they begin to feel all kinds of restraints and intimidations. The threat now is, either you move carefully, speak softly, and act meekly or you will alienate a few choice members who already regard you with suspicion, and the unity of the church will be lost. If this happens you have had it.

To come out of this corner I decided to work hard at something that I thought we could all agree upon—local stewardship. In my eagerness to increase the generosity of an already affluent church I encouraged the officers in 1955 to employ a professional money-raising organization to conduct our canvass. This was a mistake for two reasons. One, it raised our giving by fifty thousand dollars or so, and this couldn't hold from year to year unless the officers really worked at it. Two, the professionals used some high-pressure tactics that nettled the congregation, especially those who were practicing what the pros called "pocketbook protection."

For six weeks I was nothing but mediator between the money-raising agent and surly officers. The results catapulted us into fifth place in the General Assembly in per capita giving but the hostility of the people pulled us back to normalcy within the next four years, and this retrogression represented the failure of the minister rather than officers or people. This allowed the disgruntled ones to push the panic button. In today's church the financial report is one of the main indicators of success or failure of the minister. If the figures dip noticeably, he is in trouble. Ours did, and the reason given was that the congregation was no longer in accord with the minister.

In February of 1956, one Saturday night around closing time for merchants, a Negro doctor by the name of Brewer went back to the office of the white proprietor of a small department store, as he had often done, for the two ostensibly were friends of long standing. Apparently there was a brief argument, and when the doctor reached for his satchel the merchant grabbed a gun and pumped seven bullets into him. It never came to light what they argued about or whether the Negro was really going for a gun which he carried in his bag or not.

Brewer had been the titular head of NAACP locally, and had been considered belligerent by the whites in pushing for equality. By present standards he would be considered timid, but a decade ago he was despised by the whites as being too pushy. He wasn't the best of doctors, either, and this was advertised by the medical profession. He wasn't greatly admired by his own people, but he was a relentless champion of their cause and they had to respect him for that. But now he was dead, and rendered so in the worst possible way—killed by a white man who in fear or hatred or both seemed to want to decimate his body as well as end his life.

The next day being Sunday, the clergy was expected to comment on the homicide, at least during the period we call "announcements." A newspaper reporter canvassed the ministers of the city to find out what they had said to their congregations about the homicide. The minister of the Central Christian Church chastened his people for saying privately when they heard the news of the killing, "good," "amen," and "thank God." One Negro minister urged his people to "go quiet and go slow." Several other Negro clergymen didn't even mention the incident to their people. The rector of the Episcopal church recommended the reading of three prayers from the Book of

Common Prayer. I had forgotten what I said on that occasion, but I found that the reporter's newspaper quoted the text in full.

At this time I feel as did John C. Calhoun as he uttered his dying words, "The South, my poor South; what will become of her?" Last night a life was taken. I am not primarily concerned with him who committed the act. We do not indict on hearsay evidence nor convict by rumor. He shall have his day in court and justice will be done.

I am primarily concerned with thousands of us who created the spiritual climate that made this act possible and with those who approve it.

The issue now is beyond segregation. It is even beyond the contest between anarchy and law. It is deeper, more fundamental, and theological.

This is the issue: when we pray, "Our Father, Who art in heaven," do we consider the other men of the earth, diverse in color and in origin as brothers, creatures of God, justly deserving our reverence for their personality?

No human emotion is ever hidden. It will find its kind in someone else and just as the sun draws moisture from the earth and forms thunderclouds, so there is a force that draws our feelings from us and forms a cloud of wrath. The cloud breaks and we wonder where it came from. If you would know, then look within yourself.

"You have heard it said of old, 'You shall not kill' but I say to you, every one who is angry with his brother shall be liable to judgment."

In my brief ministry I have prayed much over this dilemma. In recent weeks I have prayed much more. Now I think it's time that you pray for yourself. I shall not put words in your mouth. Let us, then, so pray.

It was at this time I was supposed to offer what is known as the pastoral prayer. That day I asked them to pray silently, of course. I have often wondered what they prayed on that occasion and what they thought about my practically forcing them into an attitude of prayer.

I had said that justice would be done to the killer. I'm not sure that it was. He was not even indicted by the grand jury. A year later he was found dead in his car, apparently having taken his own life. The community seemed relieved; killer and his victim were both dead. The books were closed; some sort of impersonal, abstract justice had asserted itself and secured its own atonement.

Television was beginning to be recognized as a valuable medium for the spread of religion. Four of us, Baptist, Methodist, Presbyterian, and Episcopalian, became a part of a regular Sunday night panel based on questions telephoned in by the listeners. We had to answer directly: there was no opportunity to screen out undesirable questions or think about difficult ones. Every now and then a racial question would be received, and it was not just the luck of the draw that caused this type of question to land in front of me. I was a little bolder than my colleagues in attempting to give forthright answers, and maybe for this reason they gave me the quick pass, thinking I really wanted them. The television audience may have respected me for not being the artful dodger, but they didn't think much of my chances of staying around very long if I persisted in making my views plain on the race issue.

One of the most progressive things our church did was to televise its morning services, signing a five-year contract with a local station. Through this service we made real friends with the Negro population, since so many of them were unable to be in their own churches at that time. Every now and then I would receive a letter of gratitude from one of them, indicating that they were getting the message, even that unspoken message that all of us were equal in the sight of God and should see each other through His eyes. The television of the service became more important to me as time passed, for the very reason that the Negro community was hearing and responding. In fact, our organization of a church for Negroes in a community called Carver Heights was made easier for us because the Negro people had known what we were like through television. My antagonists sensed that we had a large Negro audience and so set about to break the contract with the station. They would have succeeded except for some outside money, raised by anonymous friends, that came in at the last minute, which our officers reluctantly accepted.

Concurrent with the union issue was the Supreme Court's deliberation and decision on school integration. To favor union was to favor this decision, for naturally the Northern church was for integration. This didn't help my position any, but at the moment it didn't hurt much because our people were sure the decision would not be implemented. Deliberate speed meant whenever convenient, and that meant never.

The county superintendent of education was almost jaunty about it. Not only would it not come in the foreseeable future, but when it did he would be ready with his own plan, which he had carefully worked on for years. He had so placed the new schools he had built that assignments to schools by residence would automatically separate the races. Even gerrymandering wouldn't be necessary. He was not only a rigid segregationist but a clever one. I went to his office one day to propose that our church rent an unused frame house which was on a new elementary school campus for Negroes. We were organizing the church that would be called Carver Heights, for the Negro residents in that area. It is not uncommon for school boards to do this on a temporary basis until the church can organize and construct its own building.

I got a complete rebuff. He could not allow integrated meetings on school property. I was amazed. We had arranged for a retired white minister, William Bourne Clemmons, and his wife Marian to organize the church while we sought a Negro minister. So if one or both of them conducted a service for Negro people, this was integration. Furthermore, he continued, if the minister's wife should apply for a position in the public school she might be turned down because she had taught an integrated class and some child's mother might call up and complain.

"What about Schweitzer, what about Livingstone, what about your maiden aunt Sally who taught the plantation Negroes on the verandah on Sunday afternoons?" I challenged. "Are they integrationists?"

I could see I wasn't getting anywhere, and as a parting shot he advised, "Don't stick your neck out—don't you get in trouble over this."

Several of his board were members of our congregation, and I could just hear him quoting himself to their conscientious but slightly stubborn clergyman, steering him clear of a sticky situation. Sure enough a member of the board who was one of our chief elders came by to dissuade me from taking the matter to their board, and to his credit, offered his own money to finance some other method of housing the church. This was to spare me from any further humiliation and tarnishing of my reputation.

Bill and Marian Clemmons were truly beautiful people. He was born on a poor farm in Georgia and had received his formal education in a one-room school, where strangely enough he studied Latin and Greek. He was so bred upon Confederacy and slavery talk from his parents and kinsmen that at times he felt he had lived in that era. When he left the farm he clerked and kept books for a merchant and eventually owned his own store. But he "felt God tugging at him," so he gave up his store and studied theology privately for three years with one of my predecessors at the Columbus church. At the outbreak of World War I he was turned down by the Army because of defective vision, so he entered Y.M.C.A. service overseas. He was cited for bravery by General Pershing for removing the wounded from the battlefield. When he returned home at the end of the war he accepted small pastorates and went through high school while well in his twenties. Later whenever his work was near a college he attended it, always adding a little more to his formal education.

Bill never became a big-time preacher. Reverently, I say thank God for that. I don't believe he ever intended to be. His motive in the ministry was as nearly pure as I ever found anywhere. He spent most of his life in the home mission fields in the countryside, which is the real scout work of the church. He had always been poor and he looked it. He drove a car of ancient vintage, his suit was slick and shapeless, his shoes were cracked and looked as if they were held together by the shoestrings alone. He had a rasping voice which would crack at times and jump an octave. This didn't make him the most mellifluous preacher, but it did make him the best reader of *Uncle Remus* in the state. He was an expert in bird lore and was the early morning companion of many a young scout trying for his merit badge. He was also an expert in Civil War history and could describe its battles down to regimental action. His last purchase before he died was Sandburg's six volumes on Lincoln, which his widow gave to me in the unopened carton. Immersed though he had been in the pride and despair of the Confederacy by his forebears in south Georgia, he got a sense of justice from somewhere, probably from the same forebears, that would not let him condone any kind of racial servitude or discrimination. He wanted to give his last year or two to the serving of those who had always been his servants

Bill had lost his first wife. Marian, his second, was much younger than he, and she continued to call him "Preacher" as she had done when she had worked for him in church extension. She had come from Virginia but had nothing of the hauteur sometimes associated with Virginians, only the accent. She had served as a school teacher, mountain missionary, director of Christian education, and social worker—a perfect complement to him. I asked her how she had come to be "liberated" toward the colored race, and she couldn't quite say. She did remember, however, that her mother was the first person she ever knew to use "Mr." or "Mrs." in addressing Negroes when everybody else was calling them "Uncle" or "Aunty."

Bill and his wife wanted so much to see this Carver Heights church established. It was to be his last ministry on earth, and he knew it. It was not easy for whites to go into an all-Negro community and organize a church. But the Clemmonses were so earthy and lovable; there was not an ounce of condescension in their manner, no saccharine piety oozed from their natures. They were the pure article, so color was forgotten. None of their Negro successors has inspired more confidence than these two. By coincidence, Marian had organized the first church I ever served, as pastor in the steel mill district of Fairfield Highlands outside of Birmingham, converting a dance pavilion into a place of worship. The grateful people there had named their first frame building for her.

It was ironic that my bitterest antagonists were the ones most zealous for the organization of Carver Heights. This was Southern ambivalence all over again. They wanted this church because the Catholics were threatening to take the neighborhood and because it would represent a Presbyterian outstation to forestall integration and because—well, there was the matter of conscience again. The white man had a compulsion to do something for the Negro, to atone for keeping him in a subordinate position.

It was my idea that the Clemmonses go out there and not wait until we secured a Negro minister. We would have been still waiting if we had hesitated, because there are hardly any to be had. Negro Presbyterians in the South are scarce, and a Negro Presbyterian minister even scarcer.

For a white clergyman to preach to the Negroes on occasion was all right, for this was lofty pulpit down to menial pew, but for a white couple to put themselves in the service of the colored folk was too demeaning. This took away the enthusiasm for the project, and I had committed another tactical blunder.

The Clemmonses were beginning to feel the isolation accorded those who live and work with Negroes. Marian's future as a wage-earner in the educational system was in jeopardy. Their high-school-aged son was being taunted because his father was a "nigger preacher." They were tolerated by our white congregation, but not acclaimed for the significant work they were doing. First Church continued to beat the tom-toms for foreign missions, but was cautious in expressing praise and gratitude for these ministers within their city limits.

The Klan was beginning to make piping little noises, especially through Parson Jack's *Georgia Tribune*. The Klansmen established headquarters on the Macon road a few miles outside the entrance to the city. They had posted a sign with the letters KKK for everybody to see, especially visitors from outside the South who would be both shocked and afraid at what so bold a display indicated.

One morning Bill Clemmons came into my study, his craggy face white with anger and his eyes ablaze. He handed me a note which read, "White man, get yourself a white church. This is your last warning." The note was written on the back of a Christmas card that carried a message of peace on earth and good will to men, and was singed around the edges. This, of course, was a threat of arson to the church.

The old man was so incensed that he could hardly speak. He would have set upon any Klansman of any size if he could have found one at that moment. "I have thought about giving up the work out there but not now I won't, not after this," he rasped between set teeth.

The night before, the Klan had paraded downtown, stopping off on the street where the white store proprietor had killed the Negro doctor, and climaxed the ride with a march around the Carver Heights church, slipping the charred note under the door.

I went immediately to the city manager and had a conference

with him, the city and county police chiefs, and the chief of detectives. I was pretty incensed myself and told them so. Only one of them had a suggestion to offer. The chief of detectives said he would talk to the Klan leader and call him off these activities.

I asked incredulously, "You mean you know the man?"

"Sure," he answered. "I know all of them."

I asked him to set up a meeting for me and the Klan leader alone, but he begged off this and pleaded that he be allowed to handle it quietly his own way. Then I asked each chief point-blank if he had Klansmen on his force. They all vowed that they knew of none and would fire anyone who was.

Despite their disclaimer the Carver church was watched by an off-duty policeman in a patrol car and headquarters either had or would admit to no knowledge of his activities. On another occasion, an alliance meeting attended by white and Negro ministers and chaplains from Fort Benning, a couple of plain-clothes men parked in front of the Carver Heights church and watched every move we made. I went out and asked why they were there, and they stated they were there to prevent any kind of violence. I told them they would see more violence at sleepy-time in a day nursery, and invited them in to have a glass of pallid church punch and look around all they wanted to. Since they wouldn't accept, I took a couple of glasses out to them. I was determined to kill these legalized Peeping Toms with kindness. But neither Bill Clemmons nor I ever got the chance to accost our adversaries face to face.

He didn't get himself a white congregation, either. He and Marian kept on developing their Negro members into a spiritual unit, formulating programs that would assist them in their daily affairs, teaching them a set of doctrines that would shore up their vague, inarticulate beliefs, and calling in their homes and endearing themselves to Negroes by being two white people who graciously accepted their hospitality, not just their menial service. He and Marian came to be recognized as genuine integrationists because they were neither professional nor quixotic in their approach. Neither recruiting zeal nor abstract principles showed in their relationships. Though Southern to the core, their graciousness had no social limits. I would like to think—in fact, I do think—that this is what the Christian faith did for them.

They stayed on, and the glad day was finally announced when

the church would be officially organized by the presbytery, and a Negro minister whom we pilfered from the Methodists would be installed as pastor. Installation was to be on Easter Sunday and it was to be a big day for the community, especially for those admirers who wanted to honor the man and woman who had practiced daily sainthood among them. They were going to welcome their new minister of their own color, but they weren't going to forget the man and his wife who regardless of color were of their own spirit. During the week before Easter, however, Bill was taken to the hospital—he had had a heart attack. I couldn't believe it was serious or that the old trooper could be taken out of the ranks at the very moment fulfillment was in sight.

That Easter afternoon I dropped by the hospital to see him before going to the church dedication. He was sitting up in bed, but was in an oxygen tent. I reached through it and squeezed his wrist, and assured him that though he wouldn't be there for the christening of the church, I would get him out there pretty soon to gloat over it. I left him smiling as I always remembered him. We were about to begin the service when the message came—Bill Clemmons was dead, another attack had taken him, and he was with us no more. So celebration turned to requiem, a day of pride had become a time of stunned mourning. He was gone, but was he? This church was blood and sinew of Bill Clemmons.

How my soul wept at the loss of this staunch friend! In his plain and disheveled way he had epitomized all that was good and decent and gracious and kind in the Southerner; he was the best representative of the South I had known. He was one of the few, even among the clergy, in whom the Christian faith took full and firm control. Poor friend, he was not there to receive his just plaudits. In fact, never in his life did he show up when awards were given. The final trophy was his, though, the one that's given to the man who steadfastly refuses to compromise his integrity. My only worry is that when he strolls through that "land that is fairer than day" he might catch and beat hell out of some robed angel, mistaking him for a Klansman.

We had been in Columbus five years now. Our family had increased to five with the birth of another boy, Walter, who was now aged two. Mother had moved to Troy State Teacher's College in southern Alabama, serving as director of one of the dormitories. My brother, for whom our second son was named, had died of a heart attack in Atlanta six years earlier. Jeanne and I had been given a wonderful trip to Europe, as the result of my being invited to address the Protestant Men of the Chapel at its retreat in Berchtesgarten, Germany. This is an organization of military personnel connected with the overseas armies. The friendships made with the personnel at Fort Benning have resulted in invitations I would never have gotten otherwise. I believe I can say that I was happy in those five years—in a harassed sort of way.

In 1957, after being in Columbus five years, I sensed that the race issue was now paramount in the thinking of the people. No one knew for sure where I stood, except that I was left of center, and I didn't know myself. It was apparent now that the Supreme Court meant business, that "deliberate speed" didn't mean never but soon. The well-meaning Court, had however, allowed time enough for the opposition to solidify. Out of extreme fairness it had granted reprieve to school districts that had a tradition of segregation, in order that they might adjust to the decision. But school districts had no intention of complying as long as they were sheltered by local and state laws. In Georgia the laws were made even more stringent, being directed now toward whites, especially teachers, who attempted to carry out the directive of the Supreme Court. Governor Ernest Vandiver promised in his campaign that he would "fight integration with every weapon in the state's arsenal, that no school would be integrated" during his administration. This was the political pattern from the highest to the lowest office. If you were not a segregationist you need not run—except for cover.

The newspapers merely echoed this sentiment. The one notable exception was the *Atlanta Constitution,* with the beleaguered Ralph McGill hoisting his standard every day in behalf of sanity, law, order, and justice. I could hardly have survived without his reassuring daily column, which became a little bolder the tougher things got. His Scotch-Irish Appalachian stubbornness was beginning to stand out like Stone Mountain.

Our local papers went along with the chants of the crowd. However, the Columbus evening paper, the *Ledger,* was showing signs of conscience. Its city editor, when he was still a reporter, had spied on a meeting of the Klan outside of town one night and was caught. He was forced to drink a fifth of whiskey and when he had passed out he was dumped at a place where the police would be certain to pick him up and jail him.

Three of the younger *Ledger* reporters often ate together and invited me to sit with them if I happened to be at the same restaurant. We argued good-naturedly over many things, including the Big Issue, with all three taking the gentle segregationist's view. But something happened to all three. One received a Nieman fellowship to Harvard and came back thoroughly unprovincialized. Another was given a Nieman travelship to Africa, and he saw the ugly side of apartheid there. The third, a conservative Jew, was shaken by a sermon from his rabbi. When we reassembled after these experiences we found we had much to discuss but nothing to argue about. At a Christmas Eve luncheon of the Knights of the Round Table, the publisher of the *Ledger* confided to me that he and many others shared my point of view; they just didn't see any advantage in coming right out and saying it. I was grateful for that confession, even if it did come after a couple of glasses of Madeira. *In vino veritas!*

With the politicians, newspapermen, and school boards meekly acquiescing to the tyranny of the majority, it was a precarious business to express any contrary opinion. I had said as little as possible but racial incidents, occurring more frequently than ever, thrust themselves upon us and required a definite response. Evasion had become an impossibility—at least for me. One night at a meeting of the Session it was mentioned that some emboldened Negro students were invading church services and were likely to hit us next. Stop them at the door and keep them out, was one rough suggestion. A smoother one was to smile and usher them to the balcony. I was getting a little overheated by now.

"Look," I said, "if they come sincerely to worship we can't by our own church laws prevent them nor make any distinction by seating arrangement. If they come to make a test case of us we play into their hands by keeping them out or segregating them. Isn't it the better part of wisdom to admit them and let them sit wherever they want?"

One of the elders blurted out, "The people they sit by will walk out of the church."

"Anybody who would do that," I said coldly, "is ill-bred."

I lost that elder that night. He went out repeating that I had
called him ill-bred. How did I know he was talking about himself? I admit I used the wrong word when I said "ill-bred." If I
had said unchristian I don't believe it would have sounded half
as offensive. But to make an appeal to Christian ethics or graciousness at that moment would have been considered by many
of them as beside the point.

About this time, the summer of 1957, the school crisis hit Little
Rock. Our local First Baptist preacher did a disservice to the rest
of us harried ministers by preaching a defiant sermon against federal troops attempting to impose with fixed bayonets an alien
morality upon a law-abiding people. That is the way the issue
was twisted. The troops were not there to protect nine little
children and to prevent rioting; they were there to ram an unpalatable edict down the throats of American citizens who had
the right to determine their own social patterns. The sermon was
printed and distributed by the thousands over the city. Several
were poked at me with a smirk which said, "Why don't you
preach like this?" After that, we not only had to take sides on
Little Rock but on what the Baptist minister said about Little
Rock.

On Thanksgiving of that year it fell my time to speak at the
union service for the downtown churches, to be held in the First
Baptist Church. I had to answer this man who had made recent
days so difficult for the rest of us, and what better place than in
his own pulpit! The irony of it appealed to me. I had to rebut
him, yet without giving the appearance of doing so. The Southerner is adept at this kind of subtlety, especially if he is something less than a sectional chauvinist. The conflict of interest
between conscience and survival requires it. As I look on that
speech it seems a little rococo, but the foibles have to remain as
part of the chronicle. Here is the text of it.

I shall never forget a fifteen-year-old page boy in a hotel in
Glasgow by the name of Archibald McAusland. What a neat,
winsome little gentleman he was with his black-and-red uniform
and rows of silver buttons. I couldn't resist engaging him in
conversation to find out what Scottish boys of that age did and
thought. As we left for the airport he followed me out and asked
my name, explaining, "When I come to America—and that's my
dream—I want to look you up." Just the other day I received a

letter from Glasgow—it was from Archie McAusland—and in a postscript he asked, "Tell me, Sir; what is America like?"

That's one of those questions you think you can answer immediately and then realize you might not be able to answer at all. How would you answer it? I thought of the passengers next to us on the plane—a boy from Finland and a family from Scotland immigrating to America—maybe their expectations would form a definition. I thought of those faces of all nations I saw at the Federal Court as one hundred and fifty foreigners were sworn in as new citizens of the United States. Maybe their impressions of this new land would be my answer. But why couldn't I say from my own experience what America is like? I have lived here since birth. My people came here in 1750. I have studied its history, I have heard scores of speeches on the glories of this land. Yet I suppose you don't analyze something you live with all the time. You have a subconscious impression that you like what you see but you miss most of the details somehow. But the young Scot deserves an answer so I wrote this letter:

Dear Archie:

So you want to know what America is like? I admit you have challenged my patriotism. Every good American ought to have a ready answer but it has taken me some time to prepare this one.

First, the easiest part of the answer is that America is a place. A beautiful place, it is, but so is yours, and so are those nations around you. We sing:

> O beautiful, for spacious skies,
> For amber waves of grain,
> For purple mountain majesties
> Above the fruited plain!

But what people with any sense of awareness do not find something in their own surroundings to inspire praise? I suppose you might say our land has a versatile beauty about it. You have your Loch Lomond and your Loch Tay but we have Minnesota, the state of ten thousand lakes. You have the wild, unspoiled splendor of the Highlands, covered with fern and heather and tumbling burns. We have our Black Hills of South Dakota. The lush green grass of Germany grows in Kentucky and Vermont. The snow-crested Alps of Switzerland have their little brothers in Washington and West Virginia. The sunny peninsula of Italy swings onto our own land—we call it Florida. There are Black

Forests in Bavaria but there are redwoods in California. Oxford and Cambridge and Edinburgh have offspring in Yale, Harvard, and Princeton. The ships that dock at London are the same that sailed from New York. The skies reddened by the mills of Mannerheim and Glasgow are the hue of Birmingham and Pittsburgh. The dainty rose of Denmark has spilled its color upon the camellias of Georgia. Beauty you find everywhere, Archie, and you shall not want for it here.

Perhaps the difference in this place called America is that we have room to move, to expand, stretch out. We have land uninhabited, trees uncounted, rivers unused, minerals undiscovered. In fact, we are an extravagant, wasteful people for this reason.

Something we have that we ought to pay taxes on—we have sunshine, glorious, constant sunshine that warms the back and thaws the face so that we greet each other with, "Nice day, isn't it?" We expect the sun to be with us each day, the sun is no surprise to us, and it seldom disappoints us.

We don't know this about our country, Archie, I had to leave it for a while to discover it.

What is America like? Well, in the second place, America is a belief. Strange how a land can get inside a person and become a kind of creed within him. I have an idea, Archie, that the American creed began to take shape in your country and the other parts of the Old World. Men of stature came to some noble conclusions over there. So they came to a new land where their conclusions might become the premise of a new life, where their afterthoughts might become forethoughts, where no heaviness of tradition existed to suppress a new creation. What is this belief of ours? You might say that basically it is in the inherent dignity and worth of every man, based on the fact that he is a creature of God and none other. Anything we do to debase or diminish that dignity and that worth is to create an artificial standard and to violate the standard of God. Only after the recognition of this does freedom come, and about this are our laws formed. America then cannot subscribe to any law or absence of law that does not safeguard the dignity and the worth of every man. Here are several byproducts of this larger belief:

It is self-evident (meaning requiring no proof) that all men are created equal, that they have the right of life, liberty, and the pursuit of happiness.

No man shall be penalized because of his birth so as to limit his progress, fix his status, or limit his natural rights.

Every man is presumed capable of managing his own family
and affairs.

No man is considered worthy of owning the life of another.

Government is the servant of the people and not the master.

Every man must formulate his own faith through whatever
means he chooses.

Democracy can become an exalted word if love and reason
prevail.

Judaic-Christian faith is essential to any experiment in freedom.

There is another outcropping of that larger belief, Archie. It is
our confidence in youth. We are never satisfied with a program
or product unless it catches the fancy of the young. They are not
required to fit into our ancient molds nor accept our rigid
patterns. They create their own forms of expression and bring
them along with them into adulthood. Each generation of them
has its own songs, dances, modes of dress, customs of courting.
We think some of them are wild and crazy and wish Europe had
better sense than to import them. But we can at least take hope
in this—our youth are creative. Maybe a young land can only
think in terms of youth, because there is so much progress yet to
be made and it takes the supple sinews and the off-beat imagination of the young to do it.

Finally, Archie, America is a dream. It is a place where a belief
is not yet accomplished. We set our goal high and have not made
it. But the striving for a high goal is better than the achievement
of a low one. We have a way of life that is not static but ever
refining. We have a Constitution that is dynamic and we are ever
moving toward a more sensitive realization of its intentions. We
have a faith that will not let us rest short of the Kingdom of
God.

America is still a dream to us, who have been here always. Yes,
and it is a dream to those who have recently come. The Irish
came and we put them in our factories. Now their sons are our
priests and our public officials. The Italians came and we put
them in our construction gangs. But their sons are our trouba-
dors and our makers of great music. The Slavs came and we put
them in our mines. But their sons fill our football stadiums on
Saturday afternoon. The Africans came—not by their own wish
—but by order of a people who had forgotten for a time the
worth and dignity of all men. We put them in our cotton fields
and our tobacco patches. But now their sons teach us to sing and
to dance and to have patience and to love even those who spite-

fully use them. Maybe Little Rock has troubled you, Archie, as it has disturbed others around the world. No, bayonets are not like us—that's all a phase in the realization of a dream. Give us a little more time and we shall prove by the very power of the democratic process that we can keep a just peace without resort to force. We are like so many others in the world, Archie, who while hating tyranny distrust freedom. Or while espousing freedom as an ideal are dismayed at its full application.

We are the world's composite here. The United Nations was no accident. We became in 1789 a test plot for a confraternity of nations. The American dream can expand into a world dream so that life can endure on the planet.

> *America, America! God mend thine every flaw,*
> *Confirm thy soul in self-control,*
> *Thy liberty in law!*

Have I said we are a superior people? No, we are a lucky people. How could we be superior to you and the brave countries about you—we are your sons and grandsons, we are your adventurous strain, your blood run warm with desire for a new creation under the sun. We are your belief, your dream, and if you choose to come to us, your land.

This is my day to give thanks, Archie. I can express it with more feeling than ever before. Not because we have so much but because we are capable of so much. Not because of the freedom we have but the freedoms that all the world can have if we just hold out and keep pure in the face of great adversity that our way of life can endure. Not because of our fulfillments but because of our ideals, kept alive here for all nations.

So I close, my bonnie Scot, with the black-and-red suit and bright silver buttons. If you should decide that my land shall be your land, then I shall pray more gratefully than before:

> *America, America! God shed His grace on thee,*
> *And crown thy good with brotherhood*
> *From sea to shining sea!*

The sermon doesn't seem like much of a rebuttal to the Baptist minister's inflammatory message on Little Rock. But many of those who were present that day knew that it was, that under the guise of Americanism and thanksgiving to God I had taken a stand opposed to that of my Baptist colleague. Perhaps it was not so much what I said but what I refrained from saying that made

the point. I got right up to federal bayonets and instead of a
ringing denunciation of them I eased off with an ambiguity. No
"true" Southerner would have missed the opportunity to condemn the haters of our section. But we who tried to be both
moral and sensible about the issue operated that way and, as
timorous as we might have sounded to non-Southerners, we held
the fort until reinforcements finally arrived.

Chapter Twelve

One day in early April of 1957 I was brooding over the devolution of my ministry from one of enthusiastic progress to a holding action. The first telltale sign of general unrest had been given at our last meeting of the Session. The financial report, that infallible barometer of the church's spiritual condition, was read. It was not good—the leveling off from the peak of two years previous was obvious. Whose fault was it? The answer to that was obvious, too. The comments were not positive but veiled and vague, not definite enough to be answered but insidious enough to spread discontentment and plant the seed of disaffection. And without even mentioning the race issue! Something was wrong, a few said. They didn't know what it was, but morale was falling off, disgruntlement was spreading. I knew the cause. So did they, but they wouldn't say it because their basic feelings were indefensible. They had to find enough secondary issues upon which to fight—like the financial report.

The telephone rang and it was a long-distance call from Atlanta. The caller introduced himself as Chester Morrison, an editor of *Look* magazine. He was looking for a Southern clergyman to write an article on the Klan to offset the many recent stories that had depicted the clergy as being in league with these night raiders. Would I be interested? I hardly believed him at the time, suspecting that this was some kind of hoax. I told him I would at least talk to him if he would come over the next day. This was a stall, of course. It would give me time to find out if there was such a person, and, if there were, to think up some legitimate reasons for not doing it.

In those twenty-four hours I investigated and found that Chester Morrison was legitimate, but I couldn't think of any valid reason for not writing the article except for the fear of repercussions in the church. I knew I could write the article because all my preparation in the last ten years had pointed toward just such an opportunity. I realized then that I was at the crossroads of my life. I had sworn to myself and God that I would not burden the church with another conventional ministry. The church was already overcrowded with soft-treading levites who did nothing but keep the temple fires burning, whose speaking was smooth and whose actions were cautious. Conventionality was stifling the church because it was giving answers to questions people were not asking, and it was assuring people that by the very act of playing down great issues they were adjusting to life as it really was. Writing an article on race in a magazine such as *Look* would not only be considered unconventional but brash, impudent, and even disloyal.

My mind flashed back to the restlessness in me when I entered the ministry, and especially those first few months in seminary. I remembered the first sermon I ever prepared and preached. It was delivered to my classmates and the professor of homiletics, who was also the seminary president. Though this was eighteen years later, my mood had not changed. I called the sermon "Complacency or Aggression," and used the text from Amos.

I was no prophet, neither was I a prophet's son; but I was an herdsman, and a gatherer of sycamore fruit: and the Lord took me as I followed the flock, and the Lord said unto me, "Go prophesy unto my people Israel."

By chance I found the sermon, though I had certainly intended to burn it along with several other previous mistakes. The conclusion of it was a poem by Henry Hitt Crane, one of the great battlers in Methodism for peace and justice, the man who told me in my senior year in college that there was a thousand-mile drop from the lowest pulpit to the highest pew if you are called. It was entitled "The Prayer Perilous."

> *Grant me a life that is forthright and daring,*
> *Full of adventures prodigious;*

Save me from seeking mere safety, or caring
For negative good dubbed religious.

Teach me to scorn with a holy contempt
Immunity, ease, and contentment.
Give me a world where none is exempt
From the duty of righteous resentment.

Make me uncomfortable, restless, defiant,
Hating injustice and weakness.
Fill me with faith that on love is reliant,
Aware of the might of true meekness.

Keep me from cowardice, compromise, quitting;
Force me to face every fact, God.
Fire me with courage and zeal unremitting,
Forever determined to act, God.

Jeanne and I discussed the matter briefly. We both knew that I was inclined, perhaps even compelled, to write the article; but how could I justify doing it when the consequences could be so disastrous? I reasoned that the local people really didn't know exactly how I felt on the race issue and this would give me the opportunity of telling them in such a way that they could read it, rather than have to be a captive audience to it some Sunday morning and have no text to refer to. I reasoned, too, that they would be agreeably surprised that I was less extreme than they thought. Most of all, however, I wanted to do something to bolster my fellow clergymen throughout the South, convincing them they could speak their convictions and still maintain their posts. I must freely admit, too, that I find deep satisfaction in writing. Douglas Steere said of Kierkegaard, "He found in his writing a form of worship of God, and in the exercise of his calling as a writer whose every page was composed as under the scrutiny of God, he found his healing."[1]

I find a distant kinship with the lonely Dane in this. I would like nothing better than to write every day, if I could do this and remain in the swirl of human affairs and thereby have something to write about.

1 Søren Kierkegaard, *Purity of Heart Is to Will One Thing* (Harper & Brothers, New York, 1938), p. 23.

So my answer would be affirmative if Chester Morrison did indeed show up at my door, which he did. We talked briefly, and he decided to alter the theme from a strictly Klan treatment to a more general article on the Southern minister's approach to the over-all problem. Just make a pass at the Klan, he advised, and move on from there.

"You realize that this could mean my neck," I parried.

"Yes," he said with a half smile. "You can back out of it if you want to, but I don't think you will."

I sensed he didn't like the South. At the airport he confessed that he had an eerie feeling about being in it, as though people were looking at him with suspicion. "These are basically friendly people here," I told him, "but you've got to admit you look pretty un-Southern. If they knew you were with *Look* magazine they would drop their suspicion and take up hostility. If I didn't feel that your outfit was going to help improve the image of the South through this article, I wouldn't be writing for you."

I didn't think he cared particularly for the church either. It was the same old story of the church censoring its own message and actually suppressing the good news it had to tell. To a veteran reporter this was unpardonable. He didn't say any of this, but it was all there in the tone of his voice. I don't think he felt that way about me. After being in my study for ten minutes he decided I was some sort of an ecclesiastical maverick. He gave me a week to write the story and flew out as quickly as he came, glad to be back to the anonymity of the Asphalt Canyon. My life took a right-angle turn for his coming.

I had expected hostile reaction to the story, but not as soon as it came. I had planned to announce its publication a couple of weeks before the magazine hit the newsstands. But the story leaked out a week before I could mention it publicly, and on Easter Sunday a friend called after the service to tell me an unbelievable thing was happening—I was being accused of having written an anti-Southern story for some magazine, and he wanted to know if it were true. I explained what I had done and that I had planned to be perfectly open about it, and that it wasn't anti-Southern at all. He went on to tell me that a group of officers had stood out on the sidewalk in front of the church during the service and engaged in an hour's vituperation.

"While you were talking about the cross inside they were plotting a crucifixion for you outside," he said.

That was the pattern for the next several weeks. The antagonists' anger was at white heat. Why didn't they wait and read the article before they passed judgment? They had no intention of reading the article. It was written in a South-killer magazine, wasn't it? They wouldn't dirty their hands by picking the thing up. The whole thing was a sellout, a betrayal of our section and our way of life. The chairman of the board of deacons later that day attempted to call an extraordinary meeting for the next night.

"For what purpose?" I asked him.

"To see if we can't get things straightened out," he replied.

"What could that mean?" I pressed.

"It could mean censureship of you," he answered.

He was talked out of it. I agreed to read the article to a joint meeting of elders and deacons, but without comment or discussion. I reminded him as agreeably as I could that what the minister spoke and wrote was not subject to the authority of either board, but that I wanted them to hear the article so that their fears of anything radical would be allayed.

Some few went away from the meeting admitting that they heard nothing for anybody to get excited about. The antagonists were the more angered because they heard so little that they could quote against me. A substantial group of church loyalists felt that what I had done was imprudent and against the best interest of the church. I think they resolved then that since I had acted independently of them in not consulting them about the article I would have to fend off the adversaries independently.

If I had consulted them the advice would have been in no uncertain terms to refrain from anything that would rock the boat. I knew that they would not make the race issue their fight. They were the gentle segregationists who had no stomach for disrupting social patterns. Their livelihood, social connections, personal stability, religious faith, everything, depended upon an atmosphere of tranquility. Therefore, they most admired the public man who worked for, even manipulated for, social concord. Deliberately to take the course of controversy was unthinkable, almost unforgivable. I don't believe most of them ever quite understood why I felt compelled to do this. It was so utterly contrary to their conception of what a minister should do and be. So for the next two years I kept the lonely vigil. I had to maintain my position and my point of view with little outspoken support.

The article itself was an attempt to divulge the step-by-step changes in my own thinking and to offer something viable for the present moment. The working plan was what I called "creative contact." I didn't invent the plan, I only coined a term to describe it. It was offered as an interim method of keeping up racial communication while federal and state authorities were in contention. As I read the article now it seems so mild and inoffensive. If it were written today it might be received as a deterrent to the progress of the Negro, and I would be accepted by my fellow Southerners as a friend of the section and a capable compromiser. How much can happen in a few short years! Here are a few salient excerpts from it.

Segregation on the basis of color alone implies inferiority, with the further implication that inferiority of nature permits inferiority of treatment. Segregation also legislates on the basis of group identification rather than individual accountability. This is at odds with regular democratic procedure.

The term integration has been weighted with meaning that did not originally belong to it. Now it implies the unnatural displacement of persons, abnormal gatherings of uncongenial people, awkward relationships, despoiling one group's culture by the encroachment of the other, sexual irregularities and intermarriage. If integration means this, then no one recommends it.

The term that best describes our mode of operation is *creative contact*. It means that even while the state and federal laws are in contention, there should be points of contact between the white and Negro people that are creative. This means representation of both groups on city councils, grand juries, school boards, medical societies, ministerial associations, and other public agencies. We have striven to reach a solution without even consulting the one around whom the controversy centers. We no longer understand him, his wishes and his needs. We have presumed to speak in his behalf on the basis of our knowledge of him as he was a generation ago, or as he is represented to be by a household servant.

Our contact with the Negro people can become creative if we sit with their leaders at the council table, listen to them with respect, and share with them the responsibilities as well as the privileges of living together. Then they will take the initiative in preventing those contacts that are not creative but, rather, are destructive. At least, they will join us in meeting crises before they arise.

It is inevitable that laws of racial reference will be abolished. If we now establish this free enterprise in human relations at the leadership level, a just, orderly, and contented society should result. . . .

Essentially, the Negro's struggle is for human dignity. The signs and the demeanor that bespeak his subordination oppress his soul. If tomorrow, he were given equal opportunities in all areas of life, he might not take advantage of them immediately, but victory would be his—an ungrudging salute to his human dignity. . . .

Our greatest concern is with good citizens who create the climate of opinion, in their service clubs, in their coffee-break talks, in business transactions, in political decisions, in church affairs, in the management of the home. The heavy pressure we ministers feel comes from them. They elect the state officials who vie with each other in proposing bizarre methods for strengthening segregation. They furnish a "Stars-and-Bars" backdrop against which we have to speak cross-centered words of reconciliation. They lay upon us the pressures they feel all the time, everywhere, in the regular concourse of life, as though we were the real disturbers of the peace. . . .

Why do we stay with it, why not leave the South that resists us? Well, we happen to love this land and we love the people who are offended with us. We are called to the section that nurtured us, knowing that only the Southern accent can speak intimately on the issue.

If the minister loses his sense of calling, he has nothing left to sustain him. The true prophet stays behind with his people, pleading, cajoling, lashing, soothing their wounded spirits, praying out their prejudices, taking their blows of resentment upon his own back, loving and forgiving them. Having spoken he must remain to bear the brunt of his own words. . . .

So having spoken I settled down to bear the brunt of my own words. I didn't go for the crucifixion bit that my friend had mentioned on Easter. I wasn't about to offer myself for martyrdom. I wasn't unconsciously sacrificing myself in order that I might emulate the Master—a kind of ministerial death wish. I was going to fend off all who would dislodge me if they could.

However, I was strictly on the defensive from then on. I had to maintain composure, never fight back, never strain to defend myself. The missiles were flying too fast now to duck. I had to rely upon a hard skull, a thick skin, a strong heart, and above all a sense of humor.

The opposition now had me out in the open. Four of the elders appealed to presbytery to intervene and straighten out the affairs of our church. The complaints were standard ones: people were being driven off; the money wasn't coming in; morale was low; new members were scarce; the sick and bereaved were not being visited. The *Look* article and my racial views had nothing to do with it, they claimed. It was the effects of these causes that they bore down on. If these same effects had resulted from a reading of the Sermon on the Mount or an invitation to the Apostle Paul to preach it would have made no difference. If people quit coming and quit giving that was my fault, not theirs. This was the tack they took because they knew it would be effective. The Christian church has maneuvered itself into just the position that requires this reversal of values.

After the complaint of these men the battle was on. There was never a moment's peace after that. Every conceivable technique was used to score points for the opposition and demerits for me. All recent complaints about my ministry, especially in the neglect of the sick and the hypersensitive, were injected in the proceedings. There was no defense against this because the clergyman has to rely upon his extrasensory perception to know of many cases of illness and sometimes it doesn't work very well. To admit that his spiritual radar has failed him is almost as serious a fault as to know and not go.

In the congregational meetings the favorite device was to snarl the parliamentary procedure and catch me on some faulty ruling. This would enable them to go out saying that I was arrogant, overbearing, and unfair.

The real killer, however, was gossip. Once the minister becomes the butt of it there is no limit to where it can go. The exaggerated veneration they give him at the outset because he is something set apart must now be balanced by exaggerated spite. Self-righteousness works like a seesaw—when the other man goes down you go up. When that other man is a clergyman, especially one who has needled the conscience of the people beyond the point of pleasant pain, the religious self-esteem of the "pious" layman soars out of sight. "How the mighty have fallen" is seldom said with a note of regret.

The combination of harassment and gossip was gradually picking off those who had tried to hold a position of neutrality. Without exception they disapproved of my racial views but they didn't feel there was enough at issue to merit their commitment. But issues could be concocted, issues over everything, no matter how infinitesimal. Keep pressing, keep your man off balance; he will eventually make some glaring mistake. So with the multiplication of issues there was a marked increase of occasions when I had to brush against somebody's personality. An officer might call or drop by the study to talk about some routine matter, knowing in advance how I would suggest handling it. I would sense by the tone of his voice that he was going to enlarge it into an issue. If I declined to express an opinion it would be reported that I was running scared. If I argued the point I would be accused of arrogance. I couldn't win.

The townspeople were giving me the treatment, too. There were no more invitations to speak to the countless civic and church organizations. The Kiwanis Club, of which I was a member, was conspicuously cooler now, especially since so many of their speakers were professional far-rightists who spewed clichés of hate and sedition. In these service organizations the minister is somewhat of a pet as long as he behaves himself. He is hailed, saluted, and made much of. There is competition among the tables over which one is to get the parson. The members can't wait to tell him some joke they heard, especially if it involves Jew, Catholic, and Protestant. He has heard all their stories a dozen times over, even the bawdy ones, but he always—repeat—always laughs appreciatively just as though he had never heard them before (which he has, usually at presbytery). I had been back-slapped for years, but now I could walk through the room of two hundred diners and get only a few nods of recognition. The president, who was the son of a Methodist minister, told me he made a point of speaking to me warmly in the presence of a cluster of members just to antagonize them. The general ostracism was a little more bearable than the phony adulation I had gotten back in my halcyon days.

Things were getting to be both ridiculous and unbearable. It was obvious that the obstructionists were going to continue their daily attacks on everything the church attempted to do for no other reason than that the minister was an undesirable. The loyalists of the church tolerated them, wincing at their antics, but refusing to take action against them. One reason was that the obstructionists had been with them as long as they could recall, some of them being members of old, established families. The other reason, of course, was that they couldn't pull them off my back without appearing to favor my point of view. They could endorse unequivocally neither my views nor my methods of circulating them.

The *Look* article was a timely one for Parson Jack. He was running out of rhetoric—he had castigated every adversary and had spewed bigotry in every way he could think of. He badly needed fresh material. I furnished it for him. When he read "creative contact" as an intermediate solution he scurried through his old files for pictures of matings between whites and blacks, most of which came out of the war years, as the uniforms indicated, and probably out of nations other than the United States. These he gleefully labeled "creative contact." Week after week he worked over the article bit by bit until I knew more about it from him than from my own memory. He hadn't had such an exposed and vulnerable victim in years. He boasted that several of our officers had contributed money to circulate his paper among the members of the congregation. He was truthful in this. One of the deacons shamefacedly admitted one day that he had contributed but that the man had gone too far in his diatribe.

It got to the place where I knew when to expect the anonymous calls in the dead of night. They would occur on the day that his paper was delivered. I complained once privately that I felt he had his scouts all around me. In the next issue he quoted my complaint and added, "We even know when you go to the bathroom." "No one pays any attention to this fellow," I was told frequently, but I heard respectable people repeat things as factual that came directly from his paper.

I remembered the advice never to contend with him but I was getting nowhere as a sitting duck. His two biggest advertisers were managers of two of the utility companies and members of our church. I decided to ask them why they would support this yellow sheet that was doing us so much damage. One of them turned livid when I posed the question. In an almost uncontrollable voice he told me that this paper got into homes that the two dailies never reached and then said accusingly, "You can't take it, can you? You want to suppress somebody who has an opposing point of view." Ironically, this man was from New England. He never came to church again after that.

The other manager and I were on much better terms and so could discuss the matter dispassionately. He had, in fact, been chairman of the pastor-seeking committee that had brought me to Columbus. His reason was that his central office had directed that advertising be taken indiscriminately in all weekly newspapers.

"Would you advertise in the *Daily Worker?*" I asked.

"No, of course not," was the answer.

I pointed out that regardless of our position on race this paper was under careful scrutiny at the post office, and its editor was under the surveillance of the F.B.I. The real reason for supporting it, as he and I both knew, was, "It's best to stay on the good side of Parson Jack."

My only hope for relief was to seek help from the outside, which meant the presbytery. I took the initiative away from my detractors by asking for a judicial commission myself. I had some confidence in the men who were to serve on it because we had often talked of our common problems and generally stood together on the race issue.

A judicial commission is like a blue ribbon grand jury. It comes into a church and takes evidence from the officers and gathers information from reliable sources. This one was made up of four ministers and four elders, coming from as far as two hundred miles away. I was to learn a lesson in ecclesiastical jurisprudence that I won't forget. There is something terrifyingly foreordained about the procedure. The system as it is applied is inept. Evidence was taken in one night. Witnesses were chosen by the commission itself. The minister has opportunity neither to hear the evidence, cross-examine the witnesses, nor to have counsel, that is, unless he is willing to submit to a formal trial. The court is made up not of his peers but of outsiders, who are not relieved of their local duties during the proceedings. They have to work in haste and for the most part at some distance.

The minister is presumed the defendant, because he is the only professional employee involved. Charges can be brought against officers or members but by the nature of the case the minister shrinks from doing this because his purpose is reconciliation rather than retaliation. Majority opinion does not prevail because of the recognition that the presence of a persistent vocal minority can be almost totally disruptive. The minister is presumed guilty of something or other by the very fact that the judicial commission is there. His guilt may be no greater than that of the ministers now judging him and there need be no definite charges confirmed. He can be removed for no other reason that that it is "imperative for the good of religion." The basic assumption is that the minister is expendable, but the church is not.

As for appeal, it would be to the synod, a church court that meets regularly only once a year and rarely on call. In the meantime, however, if the minister has been discharged by the first decision, he remains discharged until the decision of the higher court. Even if he should win the appeal he would already have found employment somewhere else and returning him to his pulpit would be a practical impossibility. The system could be brought partially into balance if the commission could simply transfer a minister to another parish, as a bishop can do or as a general might shift one of his officers. But the commission can only dissolve a relationship between minister and church—it cannot insure that the man will ever serve a church again in his own denomination.

After interviewing our elders the commission advised me that no charges had been made, that the race issue and the *Look* article were not admitted to be the causes of the contention, but that even my most loyal supporters agreed that I could not pull the church together again. Therefore, it would be a good thing if I could accept a call to another church in due time.

I freely admitted that I could not reconcile the hard-core opposition without total surrender of all that I stood for—and all the commission stood for, by the way—and that I felt obligated to try but not to succeed in this futile effort. They had to be required to face up to their accountability by someone or there would be no real church left for anybody to be concerned about. As for a call to another church, it was time that I considered that anyway since I was now in my seventh year in Columbus. I would put out feelers, but I thought I should not be rushed into it.

In November of 1958, the commission chairman appeared before our congregation and dropped the first depth charge. It dissolved the Session, the governing body of the church. This meant that all of the loyal and devoted men were washed out, with the fewer obstructionists. It meant that the church was to be governed by a small group of men scattered over south Georgia. This group would vest most of its authority in its chairman, who lived two hundred miles away.

This decision represented a temporary reprieve for me and was hailed by many as a signal victory. I no longer had to moderate meetings that made a mockery of Christian charity and fellowship and which threatened to become a kangaroo court at any time. I was freed from the organized chaos we had been experiencing, but none of us, commission, congregation, or myself, were prepared for what was to follow.

The opposition felt not at all chastened, only infuriated. So it shifted its pressure to the commission, which they bombarded with letters, calls, and personal visits. They continued to create issues which now required a decision from one man two hundred miles away. This was galling to me because in effect this man was acting as bishop over me and the church when he had neither the experience nor the credentials of a bishop. He was in an untenable position and I am sure would have done anything to escape it.

I could not escape my sense of uneasiness. The commission had warned me that I must fulfill my priestly as well as my prophetic functions, which meant speaking a little more comfortingly to the people and keeping my ecclesiastical shirttail in. So I concentrated on conventional diligence and thought I was doing rather well at it.

I also had entered into negotiations with two other churches. I had mixed feelings about this. I felt I should stay by my words, that I should prove that I could take the blacklash of abuse that forthrightness evokes and yet not hate the abusers, and that I should demonstrate that the Presbyterian system upholds a man if he attempts to proclaim the whole gospel. I did not plan to escape and yet I planned an escape route. This was not indecisiveness; this was preparation for whatever might happen. Much in the next few months would depend not so much on my initiative as on events that intruded upon the community and the church.

Chapter Thirteen

Life in the community and in the church was about to become peaceful again, despite the habitual grumbling of the opposition. But four events occurred that interrupted my routine existence and practically unhinged me. The first one developed around an invitation to Ralph McGill from the League of Women Voters to speak on the school situation. McGill had expressed his views through his front-page column in the *Atlanta Constitution* and was therefore a controversial figure.

There was no difficulty at first when the ladies asked for the use of the Coca-Cola Company's auditorium. Permission was granted, but later somebody woke up to what had been done. The Coca-Cola people called and said they were very sorry but the seats in the auditorium were going to be repaired on the very day that McGill was scheduled to speak. Next, the ladies asked for and received permission to use the Superior Court room of Muscogee County. But the county commissioners began to receive protest letters and so arranged for a hearing on the matter.

In the meantime, the League was having internal problems of its own. The officers were for the most part young army wives; the president was from Wisconsin. The older members, townsfolk who had practically let the League go by default, now came roaring out of their lairs, claiming that these outlanders were not only acting without authority but didn't even represent the legitimate League. So the Civil War erupted again among the women before the combatants reached the courthouse. Legitimate or not, the young women made their plea before the five county commissioners. They had asked my help on this since we were members of another subversive order called the Georgia Council of Human Relations.

Just a few months before this I had appeared before the city commission at a hearing on the question as to whether beer could be sold at the local baseball park. I didn't speak on that occasion: I didn't have to because there were dozens of fire-spitting prophets present who were to lift the lid of hell and show us that the inhabitants were literally boiling in beer. I had planned to say something mild to the effect that there were too many wolves at the ball park and I didn't advise lubricating their raucous voices with the suds. These fellows overpowered the commission and won their case. I looked around now for these champions of civic righteousness to do battle for free speech, free assembly, and racial justice. Not one of them was present. So I had to make a plea without any support from my fellow clergymen.

The county commission reversed itself, falling back on an old regulation that only the court itself could meet in its room. This threw out the bakers' union and the Boy Scout court of honor along with McGill.

The League president had the misfortune of having a Russian name. This fact was noted with relish by the commissioners. The fact that her husband was the son of White Russian immigrants and an officer in the United States Army was a mere detail with which these paragons of patriotism could not be bothered.

One of the commissioners was one of our deacons whom I had once encouraged to run for public office. He was sore as he showed me what he considered evidence that McGill had Communist connections. The evidence was that McGill had been a cofounder of an organization that allegedly had close connections with the Highlander Folk School in Monteagle, Tennessee. This school was a frequent meeting place for those who actively promoted civil rights and so had to face constantly the charge of Communism. The school was finally forced out of business in that area because they sold beer without a license, meaning that beer was kept in their cooler along with other drinks and a box was left nearby for deposit of money for the purchase of drinks on the honor system. The commissioner made McGill an accessory to everything the school did—or more accurately, was suspected of doing. I pointed out that a well-known Methodist bishop, solidly conservative and never having been known to have spoken an affirmative word for integration, was also a co-founder of the "red-tinged organization." This only made him more indignant. Needless to say, I lost him that day.

Out of nowhere came word that the manager of the big hotel, the Ralston, would be willing to take the meeting in his ball-room. A little dubious, I went by to talk to him about it, not really believing this Rotarian, N.A.M.-oriented fellow would take such a chance. But I had misread him. He set his jaw and said, "I don't require but two things: one, that they behave, and two, that they pay the fee."

"But there will be Negroes at the meeting," I reminded him.

He reiterated his position by holding up two fingers. However, the meeting didn't come off. McGill heard how much trouble the event was causing and canceled his appearance to take us off the hook.

The next event concerned a group of people who operated a communal farm named "Koinonia." The word is one of the two used to mean "church" in the Greek New Testament. This four-hundred-acre farm is outside Americus, Georgia, the town hard by Andersonville, the infamous prison and now burial ground of thirteen thousand or so Union prisoners. Several families went together and decided that they would pool their resources and labor and live by the standard set by the church as recorded in the early chapters of the book of Acts: "No one said any of the things which he possessed was his own, but they had everything in common." Their ministry would be to the surrounding farm-ers as they taught them the latest techniques in agriculture. Their charismatic leader, Clarence Jordan, was a graduate of an agricultural college and later a Baptist theological seminary. He is a native Georgian and talks and looks the part of a typical dirt farmer. He is well known in the East and Midwest as a lecturer and has appeared on national television panels. He is a thor-oughly competent and winsome man.

From 1942 until the 1954 Supreme Court decision this little colony of about fifty people was unmolested, even though the farm was known to be integrated. After that decision intimida-tion and destruction began in earnest. Their roadside store was burned to the ground. A fruit orchard of over two hundred trees was power-sawed down in one night. Barns and homes were set ablaze. Guns of every kind were fired into their houses in the dead of night. Two of their men were accused of stealing lime from a railroad siding and sentenced to imprisonment. Another was beaten on the street. In addition, a total boycott was thrown around them. They could neither buy nor sell anything in Sumter County. They couldn't get dental appointments for their children, or haircuts, or a loaf of bread. There was no use to plant crops because of the likelihood of their being destroyed before they could be harvested.

These people are pacifists, so they did not fight back. They refused even to call for the punishment of their tormentors by due process of law. They have appealed for federal protection but for some reason they haven't gotten it, certainly not enough of it. Local officials had no intention of protecting them, and went so far as to accuse them of committing these atrocities against themselves in order to elicit sympathy and money from outside the South. Once they appealed to President Eisenhower directly for help. He in turn passed the matter on to Senator Herman Talmadge, who channeled it to the attorney-general of Georgia with a grand jury investigation resulting. But the Koinonia farm was investigated, not the atrocities committed against it. The substance of the report was that these were thoroughly undesirable people of sinister background and motives. The suggestion was strong that these people were out-and-out Communists.

In 1963, nine demonstrators not connected with but friendly to Koinonia were arrested in Americus. They were badly beaten, imprisoned on a charge of attempting to overthrow the government based on an ancient sedition law, refused bail, and charged rental for lodging in the local jail. An awesome aspect of these arrests was that violators of this particular law could receive the death penalty. During the Albany crisis in that same year Martin Luther King was arrested, and because local jails were full was spirited away to Americus to be imprisoned. The Koinonians were alarmed at this, and Clarence Jordan called and asked if I knew anybody in Washington who had the ear of the Kennedys. I did, and the incident was promptly reported to the Justice Department. This removal of King to Americus looked like a perfect setup for a lynching, and I suppose nobody will ever know how close it came to that.

One day Clarence Jordan came to see me in my study. He had come before in an unmarked truck, but this visit to me was known about town within the hour. Because of the boycott he had to drive sixty miles to Columbus to make purchases for the farm that he was refused in his own county. Even now I can't mention what I helped him buy without fear of retaliation against the particular merchant. This time he needed fertilizer for the spring planting and he needed it desperately. He had four thousand dollars in cash to exchange for fertilizer and he would haul it himself. We went to a couple of places and he was turned down fast. Nobody in Columbus knew him by sight, so the fertilizer people in Sumter County must have passed the word to all the surrounding counties to watch for him. I told him I would keep trying and call him if we got any takers.

Later, I called on a distributor over the line in Alabama outside Phenix City. He agreed to sell me the fertilizer for cash and I would arrange to pick it up at his place. After I had notified Jordan that we had a collaborator who would sneak this contraband to us, I received a call from the brave soul. He asked if this fertilizer was going to those people over there in Sumter County. I admitted that this was so. Then he began to talk in lofty terms of business ethics and territorial rights. His company, he said, would not let him compete with its agent in this other county.

"They had their chance to make the sale," I argued, "and chose not to exert their territorial rights." I informed him that the F.B.I. had been requested to investigate this harassment of an innocent people and that certainly he would not want to be partner to this rank injustice. I got nowhere with him, of course. His excuses were lame but he wouldn't yield. I was disappointed, and thought the matter was ended. But I underestimated the hostility of the man I was dealing with.

Soon after this episode there was a meeting of the Board of Deacons. It went calmly enough until at the point of adjournment a young deacon got to his feet and began reading a letter he had received from our fertilizer dealer.

This deacon had the most belligerent nature I have ever known. Even on normal issues his tone was tinged with violence. If you didn't know him you would expect his next move in an argument to be to strip off his coat and lunge at his opponent. Way down in the depths of the unregenerate side of my nature I hoped that one day that would be his move toward me. He not only generated anger; he inspired it.

Now his reddish face was enflamed and his voice quivered with rage. In a way, I have to admit that he was the least complicated one of us all, and for this I had to begrudge him some respect. I never had any problem locating where he stood or how he would attack. At that moment he was at his irrational best. He read from the letter the account of my having attempted to buy fertilizer for the Koinonia farm. I was accused of having done this under false pretenses and of threatening to bring the F.B.I. in to investigate the dealer. When he finished the atmosphere was so electric that I said nothing except, "Let's stand and receive the benediction."

A word from me, in defiance or clarification, would have sent more tempers into orbit. I stood there and marveled at my alleged crime, and crime it was, as I read the faces of the men present. Ordering fertilizer for spring planting for some farmers; how could such a thing become so complicated as to be considered an act of subversion? Was I a traitor to my own people because I would not honor a boycott designed to strangle the economic life of a few conscientious farmers; because I believed in free enterprise for all people? Was all this real or was I standing in the middle of somebody's nightmare?

The Koinonia farm has continued to operate although the people there have been tempted often to fold up, sell out, and make their witness in some more effective but not necessarily less dangerous way. They wanted so much to be a part of community farm life, but their neighbors labeled them subversive and resorted to violence to drive them off. So their farm has become an embattled fortress under permanent siege. One special purpose it has served has been to be hospitable to groups from all over the country who have come down to see what the South is like. Clarence Jordan is a good teacher of the South. They learn from him no rancor, bitterness, or biting resentment toward his adversaries, only genuine affection and concern for all people, almost unearthly in its quality, as it would have to be to outlast the hate that is pitted against it.

The third event occurred within the church, an event as unbelievable as the others. Our church hostess and our minister of music, sometimes called choirmaster, had never gotten along well with each other. She thought him impudent and refused to take suggestions from him when he was in charge of certain phases of our program that required her cooperation. One day I returned from an out-of-town trip to learn that he had been arrested and charged with assault. I couldn't believe it—assault whom, why? They had had an argument, it seemed, and he had grasped her firmly by the arm and attempted to lead her out of the church, stating emphatically that she didn't belong there. It was a foolish act, as he admitted ruefully. It afforded too good an opportunity for the opposition to pass up. He was arrested and charged with assault on the basis of an old statute that had originally been directed against Negroes—to prevent them from so much as touching a white woman without her consent. She went to a leading law firm, of which two of our members were elders, and gave her deposition. She then secured another lawyer, not of that firm but recommended by one or more members of it. The lawyer secured was to be paid by several of our officers who chose to remain anonymous.

When I heard of the situation I simply couldn't believe that our officers would be party to the concoction of a criminal court trial involving nothing more than altercation between two of the church's employees. I called one of the elders of the big law firm, and he stated that they had done nothing but take her deposition and recommend another lawyer. Then he advised me point-blank to keep out of it, absolutely out of it. I told him I couldn't do that if I wanted to, that it was my job to prevent the case from coming to court if I could and to prevent a conviction if it did. I had the definite impression that he wanted the man punished and for me to give him up as a sacrifice to the opposition. He indicated later that a plea of guilty would be the most sensible thing. I also had the feeling that I would lose his wavering support if I intervened, for in a way it would reflect discredit on his firm if I contested the indictment.

Most amazing of all, however, was the way that the municipal court turned its facilities over to those who wanted to use it to settle a private affair. The city solicitor had no interest in the case and probably would have dropped the charge if left on his own. So he turned the prosecution over to the hostess's lawyer and took no part in the proceedings. The lady was to receive no compensation whatever, only the grim satisfaction—hers or somebody else's—of blind vengeance.

When I think back to a previous event five years earlier, I

shouldn't have been surprised that a court of law should be lent to a group of prominent citizens with an ax to grind. One of my first converts to the opposition began publicizing the fact that I was delinquent in my property taxes. Being relatively new in town I did not know there was such a tax, since I lived in the manse owned by the church. Upon investigation I learned that I was supposed to declare the value of my furniture and pay tax on it. But a clerk in the office informed me that I was not yet delinquent and that my declaration had been made. Somewhat embarrassed, he showed me my card and the amount declared and said in a confidential tone that a certain lawyer whose name he shouldn't repeat had dictated the figure himself. It was fifty per cent higher than the arbitrary value regularly assessed the other clergymen of the city. I marveled in some rather terse language that a private citizen had access to the files and could tamper with them as he chose. The clerk marveled, too, but with a shrug of helplessness.

Now a court of law was to be appropriated for a sham battle between two forces within a church. What could these fanatics want with the tender hide of a choirmaster? What purpose would a criminal conviction serve? It soon became apparent that the trial would serve to increase the tempo of the turmoil and force me to make another decision by taking sides. If I allowed the minister of music to be thrown to the wolves, I would disappoint all those in the several choirs who liked him. If I defended him, I would be guilty of condoning a wanton attack on a middle-aged woman who was recovering from a major operation when the incident occurred. I had only a choice of damnations.

The young musician was a fine person, accomplished in his field, and a faithful friend. I saw no justice in his being given a criminal record, even if the fine were small and the jail sentence suspended. An able lawyer, a member of his choir, volunteered to take the case, and couldn't have prepared for it more if the charge had been first degree murder. Again, I went to the courthouse feeling slightly incredulous. Surely this thing couldn't be happening, planned and executed by members of our official boards in good and regular standing! The courtroom was nearly filled, and for a case that required no more than a hundred-dollar bond from the defendant. I spotted several ill-wishers there who looked as though the herbs of bitterness they were tasting were quite satisfactory.

Fortunately, the bright young lawyer who took over the responsibilities of the prosecution tarnished quickly before the skillful maneuvering of the defense counsel. He was inept, it was no contest, and the jury brought in a verdict of not guilty after only thirty-five minutes of deliberation. But I had committed myself again, I had not taken the advice of the elder who had warned me to stay out of it, and a few more moved from neutral ground into the camp of the opposition.

The fourth event centered on the youthful Jewish reporter of the *Ledger*, Steve Lesher. After the excitement of the trial had died down a calm settled over the church and me. Some of us thought a state of permanent peace had been achieved. Lesher was impressed with this; he thought he was witnessing something unprecedented in the South, a spokesman for racial justice finally accepted by his community. His journalistic instinct told him there was a good story in this, a story with a happy ending, one that reflected credit on everyone. He got in touch with *Look* magazine and sold them on the idea of a sequel to my article of two years before. I had nothing to do with his story, never saw the manuscript, and knew only the general point of it from conversations with him. This time, I thought, I will announce the publication of the article myself through our church bulletin; then nobody will be shocked when rumor spreads the news, and nobody will be able to accuse me of collusion. Again, what would have been my crime even if I had collaborated in a saga that told of happy reconciliation? So I included a statement in the Sunday bulletin which explained how the story happened to be written and which pleaded for understanding and tolerance on the part of the membership:

Reserve your judgment until the article appears. . . . Above all, remember to do hurt to no one, neither to one who resists your opinion, nor to your church nor to yourself. . . . Someday, the one thing we shall marvel at is that it was ever necessary to have written the above lines.

But as before, it was not the message but the carrier of it that enflamed local minds. It was that damnable South-killing magazine again that no decent, self-respecting citizen would touch, much less read. I was not surprised at this reaction and I wanted to avoid evoking it. But to be consistent I had no right to urge the writer to suppress his article. I had the feeling that the temper of the people had passed the last point of control. I had tried not to incite them, but events forced decisions upon me and in every case it was a choice between damnations. I could not control events, I could only respond to them with what integrity I could muster at the moment.

Steve Lesher's article was bought and paid for, but it never appeared in *Look*. It turned out that our optimism was unfounded, or that the very printing of the optimistic note became my undoing. Instead, another article was published, written by Chester Morrison, which described how our hope had turned to despair.

Chapter Fourteen

Foreboding was a daily feeling now. I had counted on the presbytery's commission to deal firmly with the opposition in the local church, if for no other reason than that the presbytery itself was being hurt by their tactics. Its function was to assess difficulties in congregations, to advise, to arbitrate, and to take whatever action was necessary to stabilize the church. However, there were intimations that I had been overly optimistic about any further backing I might get from the commission. I was trying to comply with its wishes.

I had a call on my desk from a Charleston, West Virginia church to be its associate for a year and then succeed the minister who was planning to retire voluntarily. I had reservations about the wisdom of such a move. Men have second thoughts about voluntary retirement when they actually come to the moment of leaving. I didn't want to be there counting down the days of another man's ministry. I certainly didn't want to be there if he changed his mind or didn't want me. And West Virginia was so far away and so un-Southern. I also had an invitation to preach in a famous Washington church, and I held on to a slim hope that a pastor-seeking committee in that area could be persuaded to see me that day and start negotiations. Aside from these two lean prospects I had no way of honorable retreat.

But the panic button had been pressed. The sands of the hourglass were plunging downward. The members of the commission were noncommunicative now except in a very formal way.

Their demeanor was judicious and impersonal. All camara-

derie was gone, no more sympathetic counseling, no friendly exchange of problems and pleasures. I was a defendant in judicial
proceedings fighting for my professional life, not waging an
ideological battle of theirs any longer. This estrangement was
puzzling. Perhaps the strain had been as hard upon them as upon
me and they were sick of the conflict. Maybe they gathered that I
really had no intention of leaving and was not making sincere
efforts to be called elsewhere. Admittedly, I was reluctant to
leave and certainly not until a position opened to which I felt
truly called. I was anything but sought after in the South because
I was a racial disturber and under a cloud in my own church.
And yet with a little more time, just a little more. . . .

One afternoon in the first week of June the dreaded blow fell.
The commission chairman called me and stated that my pastoral
relationship would be dissolved effective the coming Sunday, and
he would be up to read the order.

"I don't see how you can do this," I countered desperately.

"It was unanimous," was his only answer.

So the long, bitter struggle was over, one in which I had
invested my very soul, and I had lost. I had lost an ideological
decision: I had pleaded for racial justice, and I had failed to gain
even a modicum of it for the Negro people. I had lost on another
front, in that I had failed to prove that a man could be aggressive for racial equality and keep his post. In fact I had now given
reason for my colleagues to be more cautious than ever.

And suddenly it occurred to me there was a personal loss in all
this. I would be driving home to a house that wouldn't be my
home in a few days. Five days from now I could not re-enter my
study without being a stranger to it. I was no longer a provider
for my family. My work had ceased, and I would be not only
unemployed, but unwanted either in a church or in business. A
clergyman is suspect in any other position just as if he were a
monk who had "climbed over the wall." At that moment I would
have welcomed secular employment, but by training and experience I was equipped only for personnel and public relations.
What industry would have wanted me for personnel when my
sympathies might favor Negro applicants, or for public relations
when I could not in good conscience preach the typical Horatio
Alger American way from banquet podiums?

My teen-age daughter would be wrenched from her little circle of friends. My ten-year-old boy would be taken off second base in his Little League team's drive for the pennant. My five-year-old boy wouldn't know what it was all about, but he would sense that something was dreadfully wrong. And my wife Jeanne—she had entered the ministry with me upon marriage, dedicated to service and self-giving. An accomplished organist, a good teacher, universally loved and respected, never one to arouse jealousy or resentment—how could she take this categorical rejection by an institution that had been mother to all her aspirations? Had I been guilty of dissipating my dear ones' happiness to foster some nebulous ideal that could never become reality? Had I allowed a society that didn't want my preachments to hurt those to whom I owed my first obligation? Was I the most unrealistic of all men? O God, what kind of man was I anyway!

That night Jeanne and I had to attend a banquet. I never remembered food ever tasting so unpalatable. In fact, it didn't taste at all. My salivary glands wouldn't work. My mouth was so dry that I couldn't make my words come out as I formed them. I told Jeanne about the telephone call and she, like me, became a wooden statue. She agreed to tell the children. Daughter Janet took it philosophically; she observed that we had been living dangerously for so long that it would seem unnatural if conditions were otherwise and shrugged it off by saying, "Mother, I have faith." Frank, the ten-year-old, took it manfully but would later cry in his sleep. Walt understood nothing, but he reflected our disturbance.

For the next few days we had to act as though we knew nothing would happen on the coming Sunday. Later, friends have harked back to those days and asked in unbelief, "You mean that when we saw you in the latter part of that week you knew what was going to happen?" In the meantime I had to finish a sermon—on the subject "Why I Believe in the Church."

I got through that final Sunday somehow. I had to show myself as a good loser and demonstrate that I had something left for a comeback somewhere. There could be no bitterness, grief, or recrimination. As I took off my Geneva robe for the last time the eminent elder came into the study and with tears in his eyes said that he hated this outcome, but it would make a better man of me. I was grateful for his love and loyalty and said so, but I thought to myself, I am tired of becoming a better man. I would like people to begin thinking about making a better society.

There would be no rest for me on the morrow nor the days after that. Neither the commission nor I wanted the melodrama that was to follow. I am sure that these men would not have blown the whistle on me in the way they did if they could have anticipated the publicity. We became hot copy all over the United States. The journalists simplified the complex by making the issue a straight black and white race story. The commissioners, especially the chairman, were cast in the roles of villains. Since the chairman's name was printed in the stories he was bombarded with calls from all over the country. My phone began to ring at two o'clock Monday morning with a crass-sounding New York newspaperman pounding me with questions as though he assumed I was rational enough to answer them. I don't recall what I said, but it was something to the effect that at that hour I didn't even believe in God, and who did he think he was anyway waking me out of a sound sleep—God?

The long-distance calls were countless during that day. I couldn't even eat a meal without interruption. Perhaps I should have left the city to escape the many well-wishers and friends whom I hadn't heard from in years. Besides, I was unemployed now; I needed a job, anything, anything at all. I got offers: two little churches in Kentucky might take me; an Alabama insurance man thought I might do well with him as a salesman; an area manager thought I could better my recent income by selling encyclopedias. Believe me, I was grateful; here were people who offered me a hand, not just sympathy. Several Northern radio stations wanted a taped telephone interview. A Negro magazine wanted an article. As for the newspapers, I just couldn't read them—it was like reading my name in the obituary column. It never did me any good to replay defeats or talk out my troubles. They only became etched more deeply in my mind. Now I wanted to forget, to let my bruises heal, and to assess what I had left. But I wasn't allowed to forget because I was thrust front and center in a human interest story, a drama of the ever-recurring conflict between racial ideologies, the most senseless and the most excruciating issue the nation has ever faced.

I hadn't taken time to think about my health, not because I was unselfish but because I thought I was indestructible. Occasionally I would congratulate myself because I hadn't cracked under the pressure and could sleep at night. I had seen other men fall ill under milder strains than I was facing, and I assumed I was made of sterner stuff. I had always been robust, had played every sport I could and thrived on the exertion. Just to be sure, I had a complete physical check-up every year.

But tension is a creeping thing and a real deceiver. I had been under it so long I hadn't realized how it had mounted, how tightly I was wound. With physical exercise a fatigue bell sounds and the body gratefully relaxes. But with this kind of tension, psychologically induced, warnings are ignored. The nerves grow taut, the muscles constrict, the jaws ache, the palms sweat, the stomach sours; but the mind races on, plummeting after some elusive solution to its problem. Concentration is rigid, and nothing can divert its attention. The mind is a projection room where scenes are played and replayed even when they are not called for. A film is repeated with the hope that the outcome will be different the next time. The mind is trapped by its own capacity to imagine. Under such stress something in the human body is going to give.

On Tuesday, two days after my discharge, as I was driving toward town I had a strange sensation. I felt as though I were being inflated with gas and that some kind of internal pressure was forcing it into every part of my body. I turned off into a parking lot, got out of the car, and walked around a bit. After ten minutes or so the feeling wore off and I was all right again. I made a mental note to check in with the doctor in a couple of days. I had been examined six weeks before and there couldn't be anything seriously wrong. How I wish some persuasive angel had coaxed me to the hospital at that moment, for it was then that a clot no bigger than the head of a match was playing fast and loose with my life.

One of the things I wanted to do that I had neglected was to play with my children. In our daily concern for our work, no matter whether it is fame-and-fortune hunting or selfless human service, we so easily forget that some of the deepest gratifications are the simplest, like the merriment of uninhibited children and a parent's rapport with them. At this point I needed desparately to forget about myself, the career I had just broken, and my uncertain future that at the moment I could do nothing about. I needed to convince these children of mine that I might fail in a few major or minor ventures here and there but never in the ultimate one, that of being a father. We would fish, travel, take in a few ball games. To begin with we would start bowling regularly. So the next afternoon, Wednesday, the children and I went over to the new lanes in the neighborhood. As I was getting my shoes at the counter the attendant, whom I didn't know, stuck out his hand and said, "I don't agree with you but I respect you for the stand you took."

"That's all I ask," I replied gratefully. But then I thought, I can't get away from this thing even in a bowling alley, can I?

I hadn't bowled in a long time, and I was throwing what's known in the game as a "dead ball," meaning that it wasn't scattering the pins as it should. When this happens the bowler leaves combinations of pins standing that are almost impossible to knock down on the next throw.

"I'm getting too many splits," I remarked disgustedly.

A voice from the next alley over said, "You're used to that, aren't you?"

I had never seen this bowler before and he introduced himself as a Roman Catholic who, like the attendant, had respect for anyone who made the big try no matter what the results might be. He was right—too many splits, too many impossible combinations to cope with.

After the first game I noticed that the ball was feeling unusually heavy, more than it should even considering the long layoff. My wrists and arms began to ache—not a muscular soreness. I told the children to keep bowling, that I would walk around and be back in a few minutes. Now the feeling moved into my shoulders and chest. It felt like a green-apple stomachache. My breathing became labored—I felt as if I were about to suffocate—sweat was standing out all over my face and neck. I walked outside, hoping the fresh air would bring relief, but the hot June air was stifling. I sat down on a bench and attempted to remove my bowling shoes—I stretched out on the bench and clawed at the air. Someone noticed me and asked who my doctor was and called him. Then the bowling alley attendant and another man I recognized as the high-school coach applied cold towels to my neck and face. When I saw who he was I said between clenched teeth, "Don't take me out, coach, the ball game's not over."

I ran into him several years later in Atlanta and he told me that he wasn't sure what I meant or that I was rational. I was praying when I said that, using him as a kind of a symbol of God as I squeezed his big brawny forearm for relief. He seemed as big and compassionate and life-giving as God at that moment.

The doctor arrived, gave me a shot of morphine, called for an ambulance, and took me to Memorial Hospital. I had visited this hospital a thousand times to give some comfort to the people of my church and of no church. I knew every room in it, all the doctors, and most of the nurses. Which room would be mine and for how long? What was wrong with me, in heaven's name, what was wrong? I was semiconscious now—the morphine had lessened the pain. Jeanne and the doctor were in the ambulance with me. I recall feeling the sheet being pulled over me and wondering if this was the final rite: if it were pulled up to my neck I was still alive, if over my face I was dead. My faith is that there is life beyond death; maybe now I would experience consciousness beyond the unconscious. I didn't panic when I felt the sheet drawn over me, I just wondered. It stopped short of my face so I was alive. This twilight zone was without pain and responsibility, but it was also without meaning. I had to move out of it but not then, not until I had found out what this last blow was that had struck me. When is the will to live dissipated? Perhaps at the time the resources to live, physical and spiritual, are exhausted. I have often wondered if either could outlast the other. I remembered how Saint-Exupéry put it; I refused to die out of respect for life. So if I was to live, then let's get on with it.

I was vaguely conscious of being wheeled into a room and an oxygen tube being fastened in my nose. This was the first hint to me of the seriousness of my trouble. I associated oxygen with extreme unction. Apparently I wouldn't be going home the next day or for a long time to come. The drugs they administered made me completely irrational. I kept rising in bed with the idea of getting out of there if I could find my pants. The nurse on duty took it upon herself to flop me back every time I tried to get up. In my irrational state I thought I was in the ring with a lady wrestler and was losing in straight falls. Between bouts I was trying to get out to the Little League ball park to hit to the Beaver infield before an important game.

That night it was diagnosed that I had had a massive heart attack, which meant that I was lucky not to have been cut off like a light. In addition, pneumonia had set in and lessened my chances considerably. I don't know when I learned all this—I might have been told directly or I might have picked it up in the whispered conversation around me by the doctors. Four days later I awoke to an unusually bright morning and looked up to see a peppery, redheaded nurse I recognized as Pat. She was the private nurse of a friend, then in ill-health, who had lent her to me because of a serious scarcity of private duty nurses. She was the first nurse I remember seeing clearly since entering the hospital. I must have been a pretty inert mass of protoplasm until the pneumonia ran its course.

"What day is this?" I asked.

"Sunday," she said, "but you ain't going anywhere."

Sunday to the minister is the day of awe and dread; awe because in formal ceremony he publicly confronts God as spokesman for his people, and dread because he might, through ineptness or conceit, fail the occasion. Sunday is that day of the week when his mind has to be so alert that he misses not a word or a phrase he intended to say. His voice must come through clear and uninhibited. He must think of himself as a kind of cable that extends from the heart of God to man, and it is important that the message be understood as something God is trying to say to man through the medium of man. This is an awesome presumption, but a necessary one.

The minister thinks of all the families that go through the routine of dressing the children, preparing the roast and setting the oven dial, counting out the change for the offering, finding a parking place, and making some effort to prepare themselves for an uplifting occasion. He cannot disappoint these people; he would literally sicken if he knew he were doing so. I envisioned the few hundred people who would be sitting in the pews and the few thousand who viewed the service by television, and something quickened in me. What was the message I had for the people today?

I didn't have one. Nurse Pat was right; it was Sunday but I wasn't going anywhere. I was no longer a cable. I had no message, voice, or pulpit; I had lost all these in those hazy, indistinctive hours between this morning and the previous Sabbath. That was a lot to lose all at once. But I had breath, I could raise my hands and move my fingers; so I had hope. Now I found myself not ministering but being ministered to. As a cable I was worn thin; the charges that had gone through me had taken their toll.

I was beginning to find out all that had happened. The night of the attack many concerned people came by to comfort Jeanne. Some of them were clergymen, but it was the Reformed rabbi whose presence meant the most to her. It was his prayers she asked for in the hospital chapel. His friendship was the most genuine because he had been unequivocal in his stand on racial justice; he had never left me stranded on any particular issue that pertained to that justice. The Jews know what it is to be an oppressed minority and generally have a sympathy for the Negro. But more than this, social justice is indigenous to their religion and is always given great stress. The Christian shares this heritage but has in many instances reduced his faith to a God cult so monumental and complex that his ethics are derived more from his culture than his theology. This has been the Christian heresy of twentieth-century America.

One of the very kind and sympathetic elders drove a hundred and fifty miles to Birmingham and returned with my mother. She came in to see me for a brief moment during that hazy time between the attack and the next Sunday morning when I began to take notice of life again. I remembered later how sorry I felt for her. She has lost her husband this way, then her first-born son, and now here was a third occasion, when she had to stand helplessly by and watch her only living son struggle to stay alive. And the painful irony was that the views she held on the social upheaval we were facing were more congenial with my antagonists' than with mine. The difference between her and them was that she never thought or acted punitively toward those who disagreed with her.

I also learned that a table had been placed outside my hospital room and a number of women took turns sitting there to receive visitors and to prevent so much as a knock on my door. Neither the attending nurse nor I was to be disturbed.

I had been around hospitals enough to learn what varieties of visitors there are. Besides the genuinely concerned who never force themselves on a patient or make him restless, there are at least three neurotic types. One is parasitic. He imagines himself as afflicted or oppressed and identifies almost completely with the patient, deriving some gratification from his exaggerated empathy. Another type likes to walk among the sick to be reminded of his own wholeness. It's a "glad it's you and not me" feeling. The third type subconsciously feels that there is some healing force in his personality and that he owes it to the sick to cast his shadow over them. These types were persistent and had to be handled sympathetically but firmly. Then there was the working press, which was interested in my case as long as I was on the critical list.

I had no idea what was being said and printed in the outside world. For the first couple of weeks I was not allowed to read a newspaper, hear a radio, or talk to anyone about recent events. Later I learned that the national press, radio, and television had picked up the story, and several columnists—and even Eleanor Roosevelt—had devoted space to it. There are many ways to lose your personality; becoming a symbol, even for a short time, is one of the ways. There is something abnormal about it. I didn't read these articles and stories until months after they were written. Not only did they wrench me back to a harrowing past, but they made me feel that my self had been borrowed from me and made to perform on the journalistic high wires—to act in another's plot or to speak someone else's lines. Let it be said that to become a symbol, purposely or inadvertently, is to experience a sense of foreboding—at least for me.

The Columbus newspapers, one covertly sympathetic to me and the other not, kept the story alive as long as possible by keeping hot the wires to the commission chairman and prodding him for angles. He obliged by giving them the kind of statements that kept the controversy alive. He wasn't practiced at this business. A local radio station, which its owner nicknamed Johnny Reb, had a field day blaring its editorials every hour on the conspiracy between me and the hated Northern press. After all, hadn't a *New York Times* reporter been in the congregation on the day of my discharge?

This news was the kind my doctors feared might get to me if I had any contact with the world outside hospital walls. Some of my detractors felt cheated by the illness, because out of propriety they had to bottle up their vitriol. They were unbelieving at first; they actually claimed I was faking the attack to prolong the drama. If I had had any sense of drama I wouldn't have picked a bowling alley for the setting.

One of the inevitable phases in the recovery period of a cardiac victim is depression. It comes with the regaining of strength, when the patient passes back across the line from complete dependence on others to a reawakening of a sense of responsibility. Lying in bed for four weeks allows much time for thinking, almost too much time. In between the pleasant and thankful thoughts some bitter herbs begin to grow. I was without a job, health, or reserve cash. I was also without immediate prospects of a position in what I called my country, the Deep South. Few churches are willing to take a chance on a deposed minister, and even fewer will call a man whose health is unsound. I was a bad risk.

A natural inclination in such circumstances is to blame somebody for one's condition. The eight men on presbytery's commission who sat in judgment on me might not be in any better frame of mind than I, but they could go to work every day, play golf on Thursdays, and romp with their children. They could rule that I should no longer serve my present church when the same pattern of resistance could form at any time in their own churches, not if they said the wrong thing, but the right thing. I knew them; their sense of insecurity was as great as mine, and if they should run into difficulty they would covet the unqualified support of their colleagues as I had. They could rule against me, and for the stated reason that "the good of religion imperatively demands it," which is the plea our Book of Church Order permits a commission to use in discharging a minister when no formal charges are pressed. And here I lay—for the good of religion.

This chain of thought ran through my mind, every link of it hurting. If I never knew it before I was learning it now—thinking can hurt. In this mental state the numbing pain in my arms and chest would return and I would begin to fear a repeat of the attack, which would probably close me out. I was damaging myself far beyond the capacity of anyone else to damage. I had to quit this kind of thinking, but how? I had used determination before—why not apply it to the raw problem of pain? So it was as simple as that—it took guts to forget. I had to force my imagination to switch off the projector and put on another reel. It was that or lie there in constant pain.

Then it occurred to me that forgetting might be a rather superficial solution after all. Shouldn't I find it in me to forgive? We are always being advised by doctor, psychiatrist, and minister that we must forgive those who have injured us, if not for their sake then for our own well-being, for one cannot maintain health in resentment. We are not promised that forgiveness will induce forgetfulness. We are given to believe that whether or not we forget really doesn't matter after that; in fact, we might do well to remember the experience and its aftermath as a kind of step forward spiritually.

But there is a perverse side even to this seemingly magnanimous gesture, this gracious act of forgiveness. The whole experience can turn into an occasion of self-congratulation for being so generous as to confer absolution on an enemy. The point is that to forgive may be a prerogative that is not ours. In some cases it might be, but in most cases it is probably not. Few issues are so clear cut that one party can be designated absolutely as the innocent and the offended and the other as the guilty offender. If a person thinks he has been offended by another he must realize that it is almost impossible for him to plead both sides of the issue. In his little mental drama he is both plaintiff and plaintiff's counsel, and if he will scrutinize the face of the judge he might see that it also is his own. In short, it is at this point that we are most subtly tempted to play God.

We may realize our lack of complete objectivity and yet insist that we were wrongfully treated. If the offender refuses to accept blame and to ask pardon, what can we do? If we forgive him overtly when he doesn't want it we insult him. If we forgive him in our own hearts we may be doing it just to rid ourselves of our own resentments. This is self-serving and so distorts the whole idea of forgiveness. The purpose of forgiveness should be reconciliation between two people, not the psychotherapy of one. If the alleged offender does acknowledge his fault and desires forgiveness there should be no problem; he should have it. Both parties should be gracious and grateful for this gesture of recon-

ciliation. But where the issue is not clear cut—and it seldom is—
the matter should be left in the hands of God. "Father forgive
them. . . ." And by offering this very prayer we concur with the
expected divine act of absolution.

Why can't we, in our own hearts, sincerely forgive an offender
for his own sake but just not communicate this to him? After all,
we are not priests whose service it is to confer pardon. And yet if
we are of Protestant persuasion we will assume the priestly responsibility of letting one know of our forgiveness of him. But if
it is undesired we insult him by conferring it, so we are right
back where we started. There is a better way.

There is a stratum beneath the layers of forgetting and forgiving. It is the refusal to indict, to accuse. The wrong done us
might be in retaliation of a wrong we had committed previously,
or it could have been done without evil intent, or even without
consciousness of our being hurt. In these cases it would be
equally as bad to extend forgiveness as to withhold it. The presumption on our part would be to set ourselves up as a grand
tribunal, pronounce sentence, and then offer reprieve. As my
mind dwelt upon those men who had radically changed my life I
realized that they and I had opposing perspectives of recent
events, but that they had not acted out of any motive to do hurt.
If they were shortsighted as to the magnitude of their decision it
was an error in judgment, not malice of heart. If I had exaggerated my importance to the community, the fault was mis-
guided dedication and not raw conceit. After all, I got a pretty
fair shake for that part of the country. Almost any other commission would have passed the same sentence upon me with less
sympathy and more dispatch.

I ask forgiveness for my fallible, even bumbling part in the
whole series of events, and for relief from neurotic remembrance
of them. I hope my temporary judges will ask and receive the
same for themselves.

Chapter Fifteen

Life began again, step by literal step. When after three weeks I was allowed to walk I had to look down at my feet to see if they were mine. I had the feeling not of putting my weight on the floor, but of the floor pushing up against me. I was a child again, learning to feed myself, to wash my face, and now to walk. With what great sense of achievement did I make it from the bed to the lavatory without the nurse's help, and sometimes without her knowledge! Gaining strength was important but regaining independence was paramount.

I was released from the hospital after twenty-six days. The manse never looked better to me, although I was required to vacate it as soon as I was strong enough to move. However, I refused to allow thoughts of the uncertain future to disconcert me. I was alive, my family was about me, friends dropped in for short visits, and I had no responsibility—except to live.

My schedule included walking a few minutes each day, increasing the yardage I covered according to my own pace. I counted the steps I took and occasionally vaulted over a footstool in slow motion to simulate a steeplechase. I was a child not only in strength but in imagination. Soon I strolled in the back yard and then on the golf course across the road. The manse was in a fairly new suburban section three miles from the center of town. The links were an ideal place because they were like an immense garden, and I knew the exact distances of the holes so I could pace myself accordingly. My circulation was below normal so the ninety-degree heat didn't bother me. My little boy, Walt, was my constant companion, taking very seriously his responsibility of watching me and running for help in case I grew faint.

Sunday was a special day for walking. I made a little ceremony out of going out at church time and returning at noon. My choir consisted of a few mockingbirds, flickers, robins, and meadow-larks. Occasionally I saw a field mouse gliding through the tall grass as though he knew that my big orange tomcat was stalking him. And he usually was. I have seen both types enter church in that fashion. This was the one disconcerting note, for it re-minded me that nature, apparently so at peace with itself, was essentially predatory. So is natural man, and all too few of us have removed ourselves from the parental grip of nature.

Now and then a foursome would pass me and look a little abashed at being caught on the golf course on the Sabbath, as though I were an ecclesiastical truant officer. I tried to put them at ease by reminding them that I was playing hooky too. In fact, I was now a kind of broken-down chaplain for the spiritually disinherited. On one of those Sundays a lawyer pulled out of his foursome, extended his hand, and said with real feeling, "I am for you, I believe in your cause—get well." He had never been outspoken—it would have been professional suicide—but here was a man in a strategic position who would yield willingly to the inevitable when the time came. I caught myself wishing he had said that in church, any church, but what he said on the golf course was more reverential than some aimless rite being per-formed at that hour within some stained-glass sanctuary.

I was playing truant. I could have been in church. I had sat through a couple of movies without ill effect. But where could I go? I couldn't return to my own church without extreme embar-rassment to the visiting preacher and a good number of people. I couldn't go to any other church without being a subject of whis-pered conversation both during and after the service. Of course there was always a choice of radio and television services, but after a couple of tries I found they were doing me no good. The fact that these ministers were in and I was out didn't bother me. It was the inanities that rankled; the use of throat noises to make nothing sound like something. The great issues of the day were all about them, the taunts of a secularized life challenged them, the manual of the ages was their text; but the only brilliance shown was in the avoidance of a clash of ideas. I could visualize

the people nodding contented approval. I wouldn't have traded
places with these clergymen at that moment—health for illness,
position for unemployment, respect for notoriety—if the option
was to be banal or begone. Perhaps they would not have ex-
changed places with me either; but they would have with the
persons they used to be when they first committed themselves to
be agents of salvation and change.

Out in the open on the Sabbath I began to sense some of the
negative feelings people have about churchgoing. One was that
the wide open universe provides a more beautiful cathedral than
anything man can construct. The argument that God's architecture is superior to man's is valid. Solomon said as much in his
dedication of the Jerusalem temple. Christians are guilty of a
serious heresy when "The Lord is in His holy temple" implies
only His temple. The ill effect of this is the impression left that
nice people go downtown on Sunday to reach God, Who with-
holds Himself from all others who do not make the effort; and
that if God is to be found only in the churches, then religion for
the most part is practiced within the confines of the church. No
Christian would say as much, but many act as much. Perhaps this
feeling is the foundation for the resistance to putting one's religious faith to work in the complex social order. If the Presence
is experienced mainly in church sanctuaries, then maybe this
means that God Himself would rather retreat there and be relieved of the annoying quarrels between classes, races, and nations.

Out in the open air a sense of freedom is added to one's awe of
beauty; freedom from schedule, from being guided, from the
boredom of shallow minds, from the venom of evil tongues, from
attempts to pound truth and beauty into exact doctrines, from
pretenses of piety, from bigotry pleading for sanction. All this I
missed—gratefully.

There is a real temptation to keep religion strictly personal
and entirely individualistic because of a degree of freedom we
lose when we commit ourselves to a church and accept its discipline. I would not deny that one can be privately religious,
with no public acknowledgment or social practice of his faith.
This is religion, but not the Christian religion. Christianity from
its earliest Hebraic origins has proclaimed that love of God and
love of mankind are a single emotion. Therefore, I knew this

delicious indulgence of mine was only temporary and that it would soon lose its taste if it were more. I resolved that when the time came for me to commit myself to another people, we would be such a glad-hearted, mutually concerned people that no one would miss the fragment of freedom given up.

The natural world is a great creation. Yet a greater one is he who observes and enjoys it. But that one is greater only as he exchanges vitality with those of his kind. For this reason the Christian faith needs the church, despite its frequent and awful derelictions. I had been taught this fact before, but now I had learned it by experience. For this reason my Sabbath truancy had to come to an end.

Now that I was on my feet again I could be told some things that had happened that concerned my future. One Sunday morning at the Mt. Lebanon Presbyterian Church in Pittsburgh, John Calvin Reid, the minister and a predecessor of mine at Columbus, told the Columbus story to the people, and right then and there they subscribed twelve thousand dollars to have me serve on their staff for a year and then accept a call wherever I pleased. My duties would be anything I wanted to make them.

The call to Charleston, West Virginia, at my insistence was returned to the congregation for reconsideration in light of recent developments. The Charleston people reiterated their desire to have me. In a four-way telephone conversation one of their elders cut in with, "What kind of people do you think we are, that would let you down now?" I had not heard words like that in years. This was my first experience with a trait that I was to see a great deal of later: a stubborn loyalty that these people had brought down with them from the Appalachian hills. I accepted their call despite my misgivings about moving in on another minister. Though in a border state, I would be in a Southern church, and though I had no fight left in me then, I had a feeling that the contest was not quite over and I might fire a few more salvos before the issue was resolved.

Considerable mail had come and I was now allowed to read it. There were several hundred letters—and from every part of the country. I heard from neighborhood playmates whom I hadn't seen in thirty years and college friends whom I had forgotten and had assumed they had forgotten me, too. Kinsmen wrote who had never written me before, always leaving family news to the wives to disseminate. College and seminary professors added their words, and I still blush when I remember what an indifferent student I was. I heard from my hot-plate side-kick at Dinty's Diner where we were short-order cooks while attending the University of Alabama. He is an Episcopal rector now.

Many of the notes were from people who had been stationed at Fort Benning and had come into town for Sunday services. These letters began something like, "You don't know me but I attended your church for several months while I was stationed at Benning." Some in particular I did remember, like one agreeable young fellow who had played on the United States Olympic hockey team, who is today in the state legislature in Minnesota and should mature into one of the country's outstanding statesmen. Other letters began, "I am a transplanted Southerner living in the North and I just want to say . . ." Some letters were resolutions officially passed by various organizations. Several contained money to help me through my financial straits. I nearly cried when I saw a dollar from a young seminary student, who probably couldn't afford it. Roman Catholic and Anglican priests whom I had never heard of sent word that they were holding special Masses in my behalf.

Some few well-meaning zealots wanted to convert me to their faith. I received such overtures from a Roman Catholic, a Unitarian, a Mormon, and a Jehovah's Witness. This just about runs the ecumenical gamut. Of course, there were several offers to relocate me in the United Presbyterian Church to the north, where I would be acclaimed as something of an abolitionist champion.

There were even notes of sympathy from men who I was pretty sure were quietly disdainful of my efforts and considered me brash and stubborn. Maybe they did and still do. But fighting to live is primordial, and other issues are forgotten temporarily until this elemental contest is won or lost. Some wrote who were avowed enemies of all I stood for and still are. I could not even call them friends because we had so little in common. We like to see each other beaten fairly, but few of us, even secretly, wish the demise of our most bitter opponent.

The afternoon spent in reading the letters was a rather overwhelming experience. The affection and support shown was moving, of course, but more than anything else I was impressed by the tone of these letters. They seemed to come from deep down in the soul where feelings are stored that seldom come to the surface. Their writing seemed to be an act of purification. There was so little encouragement given to bitterness, recrimination, and self-pity. It was not in them to nurture any seedlings of hostility or resentment in me, knowing that this would mean death not only to my body but my spirit. What I derived from their messages that day was an indomitable faith that though I had stumbled, been trapped, and halted, I had found the path of integrity and must press on. In my darker moments I had not been sure of this; I needed their confirmation. A friend from Texas wrote, "I earnestly hope you will avoid the twin dangers of compromising your own integrity and deliberately seeking martyrdom." Another quoted a prayer which he said applied to me: "May God deny you peace and give you strength."

One day one of my correspondents, a good clergyman friend from Atlanta, drove down to tell me he had collected fifty-five hundred dollars in pledges to get me through the next year. "You have courage," he said straightforwardly.

"Not courage, Tom," I replied; "I have lived in dread for a long time. Instead, I have faith, faith in the predestined outcome of this issue and that our efforts are not wasted. I can't take much credit for a faith that was implanted by God and nourished by all you who are in this thing with me."

These friends had confirmed integrity for me, and I knew somehow that I would have another season to serve its requirements.

It was September, 1959, and the time was drawing near for us to leave the city and take up a new life in the strange and distant place, Charleston, West Virginia.

What about farewells? how would they be expressed? Churches always have receptions for their departing ministers, give them silver, and say the usual complimentary things about them. Of course my case was exceptional: I had been impeached. But the congregation wanted to have one anyway if I was up to it physically. I was reminded of Lincoln's story of a man who, on being ridden out of town on a rail, commented that if it weren't for the

honor of it, it would be a mite uncomfortable. I recognized this
as an earnest and beautiful gesture on their part; they wanted to
show how deep was their respect and affection. They needed this
occasion more than I did. They needed to make public their
good will and to show defiance toward the dissident faction that
had brought on this calamity. The lady in charge said, "Please
come, please come for our sake." I knew what she meant and was
grateful for it. So I came and sat out the reception, a seemingly
normal one, for apparently we had all disciplined ourselves
against any display of emotion. This was the only reception I
ever heard of for a loser.

A few days later Mike, a most unusual fellow, called and said
that a few of the "disciples" wanted to eat lunch with me in a
private room at the hotel. The disciples—his term—consisted of
some from the evening social group and some from the Knights
of the Round Table. My name for them and those of their temperament was "apostles of agnosticism."

I had something in common with most of these men. I had
worked on community projects with Mike and his side-kick
Johnny, had conducted the funeral service for Bill's father and
the wedding for Brent, and Pete and I had sons on the trium-
phant Beavers.

There was much we didn't have in common. These men for
the most part were wealthy, compared to my modest income.
They entertained frequently. They were interested in race
horses, even financially, and would travel hundreds of miles for
an afternoon at the track. They took their wives to places like
Bermuda and Nassau. They sent their sons and daughters to
expensive summer camps. Strong drink in moderate proportions
was a regular feature of their routine of living. Some of these
things I liked but couldn't do; some I could do but didn't like.
But among them all there was not a man who attended church,
even on Easter.

The real binder among us was that we liked each other, regardless of philosophy, habits, or status. I think we liked each
other because each of us loved the quest for truth, for more than
just the little bit of it we had cornered.

Three of the men were physicians, all extremely well trained in
their specialty and all very successful in practice. They had been

trained as scientists and so they had a healthy regard for facts; facts established by exhaustive experiment. They were quick to despise dogmatism in any field, especially where the scientific method could not be applied.

Mike, who had a philosophical turn of mind, owned and managed a high-toned clothing store which was more a base for conversation than a livelihood. He was a hounds, fly-rod, and nut-brown-ale type of fellow to whom time was nothing but the lull between exciting ventures. He conferred respectability upon his wild ideas by opening an office which he called Unlimited Enterprises, Inc. Mike's quest for truth was like the hunting of a deer; he was equally as fascinated by its escape as by its capture. He was the fellow who promoted Pete Radamacher, who had never had a professional fight, into the ring with Floyd Patterson, the heavyweight boxing champion. Pete spent the evening of the fight dusting resin from the seat of his pants. Mike also picked up a snuff salesman named Lucky McDaniel, wrote a book about his marksmanship, got him on several television shows, and convinced a couple of Major League baseball teams that he could improve the batting eye of the hitters. Lucky was a trick rifle shooter who used no sights. He called it instinct shooting. He could teach people with an hour's practice how to shoot coins and red balls flipped in the air. His luck and skill were remarkable, but his penchant for exaggeration was astounding. Unlimited Enterprise's most exciting adventure was chasing down Lucky and covering his boasts, his promises, and his debts. Mike's befriending me could have been based on his recognition that I was playing the long odds, as he was.

So these apostles of agnosticism and I had a final meal together. They needed a ministry and it was unlikely that they would ever come into church to find it, even if I were the man behind the pulpit, and even if I infallibly predicted the winners at Hialeah every Sunday as a part of the service. The church held out nothing to them that they felt like appropriating; it did not command their profound respect. This was partly their fault, but the church must share the blame for being so deadly conventional and irrelevant. They were typical skeptics in that their initial attitude toward the minister was one of suspicion—suspicion that he was either psychologically abnormal or intellectually dogmatic. But they were also typical in that once they discovered that he was "of like passions with them," they began to explore every nook and cranny of his thinking and to prod him with every doubt or complaint they ever had about religion. These were not unbelievers. They suspected there was a God; they just didn't think we could know much about Him. They knew religion was valid; they were appalled at some of its claims and its excesses. They knew that the church was a good thing; they blanched at being caught in the swirl of it if it proved to be as pedestrian as they expected it to be. They admitted that a real Christian was a fine human; they were disappointed that the average Christian was indistinguishable from a pagan. That's why they liked to have a minister in their midst for a time who understood their misgivings and shared a good many of them.

Some of my colleagues whose orthodoxy is more tightly wound than mine might accuse me of being promiscuous with the keys to the kingdom, handing them to those who have met none of the requirements of salvation, and of being overcome with sentimentality toward those who could possibly be appropriating me as a priest for their cult of gentility. This is not likely. The keys to the kingdom were never in question. They were not mine to offer or withhold. I must fall back on what is often considered the most austere doctrine of orthodoxy, which is that the Lord Himself in His own good time and by His own standards elects whom He shall call unto Himself. If salvation were mine to dispense I would lose numberless souls in my filing system. If a minister offers a formula of salvation he must do so at his own peril, for he is making salvation conditional and he is making himself the judge as to whether the conditions have been met. He can afford a little agnosticism at this point, or he will be guilty of one of the gravest of all crimes, that of soul-tinkering.

The celebration of my departure was not quite over. The Knights of the Round Table wanted me back for one more round of argumentation. They conducted themselves as usual with complete absence of decorum; they passed insults as easily as the salt, but this day their approach to me was different. They commented on how well I looked, how pleased they were with my "promotion," and then asked my opinion as to the future of race relations, which was a way of nudging me into a farewell speech. Then they conferred on me the traditional farewell gift.

Whenever one of the group moved away or got married, the other men pitched in and bought him a piece of silver. The publisher of the *Ledger* was usually the ringleader in this, and inevitably the gift was a tureen. The routine was always the same: the surprised recipient opened the box, fought through the tissue, and exclaimed, "It's beautiful—what is it?" Our savant would explain loftily that it was a tureen. Then the punch line of the dialogue, always the same: "What in hell is a tureen?" So when the gift was presented to me we went through the same delightful routine; with a slight modification of language. As I look at the tureen now in the old china closet that came down to me from ante-bellum South Carolina, I count it as one of my finest trophies, a prize of uninhibited friendship.

I shall never forget these friends who showed me their affection and respect in the face of a public that considered me a marked man. I hope I shall always be able to show them that the Christian faith is not a finality but a quality of life. Certainly there is a quality in them that the Christian faith longs to use for its propagation.

The Negro people in the Carver Heights church and in the community whom I had tried to help could not in any open or social way bid me good-by. Occasionally there was a note or a timid telephone call expressing concern and appreciation, but we lived in a two-storied world. Segregation had done this, and I am not sure that integration will change it. They felt that their gestures toward me should be guarded, for their own sakes, but especially for mine. I sensed their love and respect, and the sensing of it was more precious than a formal farewell.

The final day came, all good-bys had been said, and we as a family were left alone for a few hours in a manse stripped of everything that had made it our home. That September day was cold and drizzly, befitting my somber mood. I was weak and disheartened. I had watched the movers transform my place of security into emptiness; I had seen familiar places and people slide by for the last time. Now I realized how provincial I was, how attached to the land and the people of my origin.

Chapter Sixteen

In the fall of 1959, three months after my discharge from the Columbus church, we settled in the vastly different state of West Virginia: different in climate, terrain, and personality. It belongs to no particular region; it is a ground of neutrality between South, East, and Midwest. It claims no kinship to other states, least of all to proud Virginia, from which it seceded in 1863. It makes no claims for itself, either. Its people not only refrain from boasting but vie with each other in running down the state. Perhaps these essentially mountain people look with suspicion upon all social organizations as a threat not only to their solitude but their independence. Though I am in Charleston, the capital of the state, I sense that cosmopolitanism has never quite covered over the primal temperament of the people.

The acceptance of this call meant, of course, that I had to decline the magnanimous gestures of the Pittsburgh church and of my friend, Tom, who had raised the money for my "sabbatical." Their concrete offers of assistance had their profound effect on me, however; they strengthened my faith that there were still some people left who would do the impossible for someone in whom they believed.

We moved into a fine manse that the congregation bought for us and proceeded to the business of adjusting to a new life. Perhaps each of us in the family became misty eyed at times and ached for the familiar faces and sounds and scenes. What made our adjustment more difficult was that, unlike families that are transferred from one part of the country to another for business reasons, we were in a sense a family in exile, a family no longer considered acceptable in its own country because it held an alien social philosophy. But we were stoical about it. No one would allow his mood to show and depress the rest of us. And after all, adaptation to a new environment was a minor problem compared to our struggle to survive in the previous one.

I convalesced here for four months, as was the agreement, and then went to work on a part-time basis. It was evident at the outset that the senior minister did not like my association with him and that he had no firm idea about retiring. In the ensuing months efforts were made to nudge me on, and for no valid reason. I hadn't been here long enough or said enough to offend anyone. But my colleague, though talking about retirement, was fighting for his position, and I was a threat to it. So the battle was on again. The past was disinterred: excerpts from Columbus papers were duplicated and sent anonymously to the congregation. Rumor ran wild, even reporting that I had served a term in the federal penitentiary. This time I tried to run: I didn't want the other man's job; I didn't want to fight where there was no issue. But there was no place to go; I was already backed against the border. No church of my denomination that could support me and my family wanted me. I had to stay and endure an internecine conflict for which I had no stomach.

Presbytery's commission was called in—O Lord, how I had hoped that I would never have to see one in action again, especially involving itself in my life! Innumerable meetings and caucuses were held, hostility crackled, and I was reliving a nightmare. But this time the troops were on my side and the other man resigned. Some of his followers attempted to force me to go out with him by clamoring for that now abhorrent method of compromise, and almost succeeded. Presbytery debated the issue three hours before I was declared in, but with a third of the votes going against me—a dubious victory.

What a way to begin a new ministry! This stupid and bitter conflict had wound me tight again, and for the next three months I had no rest, having no professional help in ministering to a church which reportedly had twenty-two hundred members. In February of 1961, after a particularly hard Sunday, around midnight, I felt that dreaded smothering feeling come over me

again and was taken to the hospital to remain there six weeks—
another heart attack. I wondered if I would ever return to the
outside world, and if I could ever be the least bit useful. Once
when I was in a lighter mood I remarked to a droll friend that I
had had one attack because of my enemies and another for my
friends, so I was through with it. "Don't be too sure," he cautioned, "you ain't heard from the neutrals yet."

Nearly four years have passed since the second attack, and I am
securely settled in these Appalachian hills. I have made friends
with the mountains, no longer resent the grim winters, and have
come to appreciate the traits peculiar to this state. Most unusual,
I think, is the assemblage of clergy on the staff of this church.
Dunbar Ogden came here as an associate and John Payne as
minister of education. Ogden had come out of the Little Rock
crisis in 1957. When the nine Negro children walked toward
Central High School to enroll there he was one of four white
clergymen who walked with them, acting as their spokesman before the commander of the National Guard. Within weeks he was
forced to resign his pastorate of a Little Rock church. Payne was
minister to students on the University of Tennessee campus at
Knoxville where local John Birch people blitzed him for making
available pamphlets that opposed the House Un-American Activities Committee film *Operation Abolition*. He had to resign
soon afterward with no place to go.

That three of us of similar experience could collect at one
church bespeaks the remarkable tolerance and loyalty of these
people. Payne has since become minister of another church.
There is not an abolitionist temperament in the whole congregation: they just don't like to see people pushed around or forced
to conform to conventional standards. There are several more in
the Kanawha River valley who have come here as a result of
their stand on the race issue, so we call this the Ecclesiastical
Siberia of the church, but concede that it is a lovely place in
which to be exiled.

The wounds of the brief schism have healed, and there is
tranquility among us. The church has recently integrated. I have
complete freedom of speech and movement, and there are no
spirit-killing issues that threaten the existence of the church or
myself. Jeanne obtained her Master's degree and is associated

with West Virginia State College just outside town, one of the few all-Negro colleges which integrated in reverse. I realize now that my entire adult life and the lives of my wife and children have been seriously affected by the race issue. If there had been no issue, or if I had refused to face it, the course of my life would have been drastically different. My mind would not have expanded, I would have been a religious hack if religious at all, and my children would have had a conventional glob for a father. So with freedom and with time to reflect I try to put things in perspective again. What have I become because of and in relation to the issue, and why?

I have become known as a white Southern liberal. If this is what I am, I became so not by heritage or by any severity of logic, but by submitting myself to experiences that slowly sweated prejudice from my pores. I don't believe the Negro or the Northern liberal will ever quite understand how the Southern white could conceive of a two-storied civilization in which one race was innately superior to the other and must protect itself from assimilation with the other. Recently a Negro college student asked me if I had ever thought his race inferior and stared at me incredulously when I told him that I had.

To him and the Northern liberal the matter is academic, and this is fortunate; but it does not convert the South. The Southerner who has been liberated feels called to liberate his own people, because such freedom will not come from the Negro or the Northerner. They may achieve elemental justice for the black man, but not freedom for the white man of the South. Without this freedom he will continue to resist the Negro as though he were captive to him.

I would not claim that the approach of the white Southern liberal is the most effective. Others must do it their own way. The Southerner's is the most excruciating, the loneliest, and the least successful. Sometimes he is envious of a Martin Luther King who inspires his people with revivalistic joy when he speaks to them, or the many clergymen from the North who went singing to jail in Albany, Georgia and returned to their parishes new-made heroes. (Albany was the town, by the way, where presbytery's judicial commission met when I was called to appear to plead for my ministerial life.) And yet the Southern liberal has a role to play even though he be the loser for it. The concomitant of the Negro's justice is the white man's liberation, and even more, his salvation.

The Southern white moderate (the moderate being a few degrees to the right of the liberal) is often annoyed at both the Negro and the Northerner; their tactics seem so roughshod, so oblivious to his more personal and conciliatory approach. Ramrod methods may accomplish immediate results, he reasons, but will leave much of the South as resistant as ever and deplete what little affection there is left between the races. What good is justice, he asks, if love goes down the drain in the process? It was this feeling that prompted eight white Birmingham clergymen to write Martin Luther King in the city jail, complaining of the intensity of his demonstrations and questioning their value.

What we of the white community must get used to is the fact that the Negro, while desiring our good will, is no longer dependent upon it and no longer willing to accept it in lieu of elemental justice. The typical Negro wants the removal of stigma first and friendship with whites second. He is more interested in having his children in qualified schools than in association with white pupils. He prefers moving freely in all public accommodations to moving self-consciously in the white man's private clubs. He will take his equality begrudged him now, even with its social ostracism, in preference to promissory equality to be conferred in the distant future. To him, love without justice is a rather sickening kind of sentimentality.

The Southern moderate must understand this or he will be gravely disillusioned. If he insists on the Negro doing things his way and operating by his timetable he will be bypassed, counted as a deterrent to the cause. He must recognize that the leadership has passed from his hands; that his is a secondary role, as it should be. Let him honor and even assist the Negro in his methods of nonviolent resistance with its religious overtones, but let him concentrate on saving himself and his own people from the poisons of prejudice and racial arrogance.

I suppose at this point I ought to profess what I am, liberal or moderate or what? The truth is, I don't know. It's no good to call myself a moderate because this is perhaps the broadest term we have in the lexicon on race relations. Moderate is the safest identification in that so many of such varying points of view call themselves that. Frankly, the philosophy of moderation as I have experienced it is so much compromise, equivocation, and indecision.

I don't call myself a liberal because in theological circles, as a Presbyterian, I am in the conservative camp. I might be called liberal by my fellow pastors, but not *a* liberal or I might have to face one of those commissions again, and this time for creedal heresy. All that I can say of myself in regard to the race issue is that I try to be unequivocal in my beliefs, temperate in my expression of them, and tactical in putting them into action. What I am called depends upon the company I keep at the time. In one circle I might be considered a wild-eyed radical, in another I might be called a phony liberal.

I am convinced that the Negro will remain segregated as long as he is willing to be, and no longer. The white man by moral persuasion among his own people has not been able to accomplish many immediate objectives for the Negro. Sad to say with such a grave social issue, appeal to morality has had little effect.

The Negro has found his technique now. He has all but abandoned the civil courts and the white churches. The courts are too ponderous and the white churches are too fraught with indecision to offer immediate and substantial assistance. The Negro's approach is political where he has the votes and economic where he has the money. He has not adopted a policy of force because there is no way he can win thereby. With the exception of several wildcat riots in the summer of 1964 the Negro has used not force but nonviolent resistance to accomplish his purposes. But the more volatile are watching and timing this method now, and it had better settle the issue soon or it will yield to methods of physical force. Already the more belligerent are saying that nonviolent resistance is simply a method and not a philosophy. The segregationist might smarten up and find a method that will checkmate nonviolent resistance. If he does he will do so to his own hurt because open rebellion could be the next step. Fortunately, the segregationist's prejudice has stupefied him in most instances, so that with him as a foil nonviolence is still an effective method. But if the segregationist should learn to defeat this method, he would invoke another one more unpalatable than before. This is the fatalism of his cause.

Where do we stand at this juncture in race relations? We are in the penultimate stage. Adolescence might be a proper term, except for the possibility that it might be interpreted as immaturity in the Negro as well as in the relationship between him and the white man. Among those who are working for integration complete objectivity is suspended for a time; the Negro can do little wrong and if he does the cause of it is often traced to the white man's treatment of him. If a white man should insist on moral responsibility on all sides or urge a conciliatory attitude or counsel deceleration in a particular movement he exposes himself to the possibility of being called a phony liberal. The Negro becomes a little heady at times and attempts some bizarre things, such as demanding preferential treatment because earlier discrimination retarded his development. This is equality made retroactive. Aside from the morality of it, the practical application of such an opinion is impossible. At times a Negro pushes his intimacy upon his white colleagues and blames their rejection of him on his color alone, when the real reason may be that he is a bore who is readily rejected by his own people for the same reason. Once at a conference a white man said to another, "I dislike that person even if he is a Negro." This was a sign of maturity and of genuine integration.

The cause of integration has attracted to itself some rare specimens of human eccentricity. So many temperamental eccentrics, quasi-intellectuals, social rejects, and dead-beatniks have found status in Negro groups simply because they are white and dislike most other whites. Fortunately the wise among the Negroes have recognized them for what they are and have refused to be duped by them. Nevertheless, they infiltrate many integrated groups and draw suspicion upon the whole Negro movement.

The quota system of employment is unnatural. That three out of ten secretaries in a particular office should be Negroes because they represent thirty per cent of the population in that area seems ridiculous on the face of it, and Governor George Wallace made capital of this in states outside the South in the election year 1964. He reduced it to absurdity by claiming that the system should also apply to Methodists among Baptists. But this abnormality applies to the white man as well. In employment we stand in limbo between discrimination and antidiscrimination, practicing what is so exasperating to the Negro, token integration. Art Buchwald wrote a penetrating satire in his syndicated column about a highly intelligent Negro who was competed for by several industries, but all they wanted him to do was sit near the office door to show that they were integrated. How else can the Negro gain a substantial break-through in employment unless he insists on this intermediate but angular quota system?

The Negro's fierce desire to win the top rungs, especially on the sports and entertainment ladder, seems to be more than personal ambition. There is probably more than a little ethnic pride in their successes. At least, their newpapers and magazines reflect this feeling. It calls to mind the competition among college fraternities for athletic captaincies and student body offices with which to impress prospective pledges each rush season. But the Negro has been galled for a hundred years by the claim that, man for man, his people will never be the equal of the white man. Harry Golden reminds us that the Irish were doing the same thing just a half century ago and have gained full recognition now as American citizens with the late president John F. Kennedy, grandson of an Irish immigrant, making it all the way to the White House. Now the rejoinder that these Negro successes are exceptions to the rule is offered, but without any real conviction behind it.

The awkwardness of the stage is reflected in the very things the Negro has to do to win his point. One can't help feeling a little ridiculous when he sits at a lunch counter and has ketchup poured on his head, or gets hosed down by policemen, or gets shocked by a cattle prodder. He is bound to feel a little foolish as he submits to these indignities, but he knows that this is a stage that must be passed but not skipped. He would feel more heroic if he were shot at or beaten. So many causes are either lost or never launched because its advocates would not yield for a time to a loss of personal dignity. No cause ever reaches fulfillment unless its advocates are willing to suffer through an awkward stage. This is not to say the stage is all angularity. Many fine relationships and lasting friendships have been formed among those who have worked together for social justice, and those who have worked against it find themselves on the defensive, having to begrudge respect to these sons of slaves who have not yet reached their promised land.

What of the future in race relations? When Negroes no longer have to demonstrate against injustice "race relations" is going to recede as a term. The Negro is going to ask less of the white man because he will produce more for himself, and because of his deeply imbedded bitterness he might well reverse the ostracism on the other. He might cease to be concerned about how he is related to him. When the white man sees this new independence in the Negro his respect for him will increase and he will be much less conscious of race or of a need to discuss the matter.

The rest of the twentieth century and the twenty-first century, if there be one, will belong to the dark-skinned people of the world in Africa and Asia and in the United States. The Negro now has the momentum, the fierce passion to prove himself, the hunger in his vitals to excel, the impatience to see the shocked recognition in the eyes of the whites that he is not their lackey but their peer. The dark race will furnish the heroes of tomorrow, for it is molding them now in the streets of Albany and the jails of Birmingham. Their champions will be forged by the heat of the white man's anger and tempered by the tears of their own anguish. *Time* magazine made Martin Luther King its Man of the Year for 1963, but *Time* was late; King was made that man while still in his twenties by the contempt of the Montgomery citizenry for a humble plea for human dignity. Those who succeed him in leadership will come from those tiny marching school children who went to jail with him in Birmingham. The white man has had his position of ascendancy, but his very success portends his decline. He will not again for centuries muster the ethnic passion that it takes to catapult to the top of the human heap. It is hoped that catapulting to the top and struggling, even fighting, for racial or national supremacy will be a thing of the past, and that all groups will struggle for excellence but not for dominance.

As the Negro gains equal status he might find the going tougher than it was while he was fighting for that position. When the ground rules are uniform, then his responsibilities will be brought into balance with his privileges. This, of course, is exactly what he is asking for, but the competition will be fierce, the rivalries keen, and the social ostracism demeaning. No concessions will be made because of his color, no suspending of high standards because he was late in catching up. The Negro will be moving into a white man's world, and there may be features of it to which he can never adjust or which he will heartily despise. In all likelihood he will be right in despising and not adjusting, but this does not remove the internal conflict.

Perhaps the most subtle erosion of his selfhood will result from his being gauged by his ability to convert himself into a white personality. He may conclude that he will never get anywhere unless he thinks, talks, laughs, dresses, and acts like the whites of his association. He must be himself; he cannot bleach his soul. And yet the stereotype of his race haunts and enrages him. How can he be himself without sounding like somebody out of an Amos and Andy script? Yet, how can he be himself and sound like Cary Grant? The freedom he is gaining is most precious at this point, for it contains the right to let one's personality grow as it will without having to conform to an image a whole race has attempted to impose upon him.

But back to responsibility. I well remember when the color line in professional baseball was broken by Jackie Robinson when he won a position at second base for the Dodgers, then in Brooklyn (where all true Dodgers ought to be). Branch Rickey, his sponsor, schooled him carefully in the proper demeanor on and off the field. He must be a gentleman at all times in order to dispel any doubt that his race could be big league in conduct as well as ability. Above all, he must never question an umpire's decision. So he played his first game, and major league baseball was integrated, I thought.

Several years later, after Robinson was no longer a novelty, he turned around one day and challenged the umpire's call of a pitch. Then I realized that Jackie hadn't really been integrated before, because he had been denied the ball player's prerogative of a few choice words in rebuttal to the umpire's decision. But now he had had his way like any white man and had gotten away with it. This was integration, I thought; but it wasn't. Genuine integration occurred some time later, when Jackie repeated the performance with a little more spleen and the umpire poked his thumb in the air, which in baseball means that the verbose gentleman is no longer welcome on the premises for the rest of the day. So Robinson was given the privilege and charged with the responsibility of its use. This finished the integration process and probably made Robinson feel like a complete person for the first time in his baseball career.

But I am concerned more about my own completeness and that of those whom I directly serve. I am almost envious of the Negro. He assembles himself around his fierce passion to gain freedom and respect. There may be a desire in the white man to see him attain these and to rid his own soul of the racial arrogance that might prevent it. But that desire is not passion! Passion might drive a person to extremities of feeling and action, but it engenders a singleness of purpose which dispels indecision and self-doubt. The term "integration" was used to indicate a well-organized personality before it was adopted to describe an amalgamated society. The Negro, then, who resists the inequalities in society with all his might, can at least take comfort in the fact that the opposite of his integration is segregation, whereas the opposite of the bigoted white man's is personal disintegration.

Chapter Seventeen

In the late winter of 1963 my mother lay dying in the University Hospital of Birmingham. At eighty-two she had suffered a massive brain hemorrhage and had been in a coma for two months. Now she was scarcely recognizable. The nurse, who had never seen or known her before unconsciousness, said wistfully, "She was a lady." She did not realize the full extent of her pronouncement. Mother's passing was more than the passing of the one who had given me birth; it was the passing of an era. As long as she was with me the Old South was with me, calling to me out of the past to understand it and to represent it proudly.

Now that she had gone, was I prepared to accept and transmit to others the philosophy she had so consistently lived? I realized how far short I had fallen of the aspirations she had had for me and I felt penitent, as any son would feel. Her indoctrination on personal honesty, integrity, humility, charity, industry, I had readily accepted and had tried, not too successfully, to fulfill. But what the theologians call her doctrine of man and the social scientists call anthropology, I could no longer accept. A rift had occurred between us over this, not great enough to break the filial tie, but serious enough to require us to suspend all reference to the race issue in our conversations. In my mature years I could not even talk to her about the Old South, for the part of it she knew had gained its distinctiveness from the presence of slavery. I could not talk dispassionately with her over the relative effects upon a person of heredity and environment, because her views were shaped at a time when the permanent inferiority of the Negro was a corollary to her hereditary determinism. I recoiled at her frequent references to aristocracy, which implied a studied classification of people, the lowest of which, by reason of color, was the Negro. I hated the race issue because it divided us by generations, whereas without it we were close. I hated it because it even divided us geographically, for I was forced to leave the region of my rearing. The race issue is life's issue, and there is no escape from it.

The Old South had become a mythology offered to the twentieth century. I had been cast under its spell and had reveled in it. It had been the love poem of my romantic nature. But now I had to say inaudibly to my departed mother: "Our love shall last but not the myth; I cannot, I dare not believe it nor repeat it to my children. Go now in peace to the place where all our myths and speculations and fumbling ways shall yield to the truth as God alone knows it."

So my mother died and with her the symbol of the Old South in my ambivalent nature.

The funeral was to be conducted in the church of my younger years, the First Presbyterian of Birmingham, called "Old First" because it was moved from the outskirts to the center of town in the year of the city's origin, 1872, and so was considered the first of any church to become a part of the Magic City. This is where I was baptized and received my early training in religion. I heard many famous preachers in that pulpit, including Gypsy Smith, an old time evangelist, George Buttrick, one of the outstanding ministers and scholars of the twentieth century, and Peter Marshall, who became a member of this church when he came to this country from Scotland.

The church is noted for its carillons, which were given by one of the first families to settle in Birmingham. One of its sons, an elder in the church and one of the city's financiers, might be said to have had a penchant for bells. He also installed a set of chimes on the fifteen-story Protective Life Building, just four blocks away from the church. He has arranged for the chimes to play "Dixie," among other tunes, at intervals throughout the day. So office people and shoppers are caught in a cross fire between. "In Christ there is no East or West, in Him no South or North" from the church and "I wish I was in the land of cotton" from the insurance company.

All the subclans of my mother's family from South Carolina sent representatives to the funeral. What a fine appearance they made, what a comfort they were, and they seemed to be willing to suspend their memory that I was a maverick both to the family and to the section.

As we entered the sanctuary I made sure that Lucinda Garnett, our cook for so long, was with Jeanne and me and would sit with my family. This was my way of saying that in this time of sorrow this was a privilege I was taking whether anybody liked it or not. But the people there looked at me with my hand on Lucinda's arm as if to say this was a concession they were gladly granting. We might return to our ideological war tomorrow, but today all of us would share our common grief. Actually it wasn't a concession, for the Southerner has always looked with favor upon such a gesture. The presence of Negro servants at the funerals and weddings of their white folks was considered a compliment to the relationship between them and even an approval on the part of the Negroes of the system.

As the service began, the chimes from the Protective Life building struck three and some tune was to come next. I thought, O Lord, don't let it be "Dixie." Mother was proud and stubborn but she was not rebellious. She is only departing from the earth, not seceding from it.

We laid her away in the family plot in Elmwood Cemetery, where I had often gone with her to trim the shrubbery and water the pansies she had planted over the graves of my father and my brother. Now that she was placed there with them I was the last living of that small family, a little boy again for a few brief moments, looking about for some familiar person who would lend me his strength. The moments were quickly over, and I slipped on my mask of maturity and back into the practiced role of taking everything in stride. She was gone now, her human dwelling crumbling back into the Southern soil of which it was made and in which lay her mystic devotion. And now I had neither her nor her South to nurture me. How orphaned I was!

"Old First" is now in turmoil. A month after the funeral the all-out demonstrations of 1963 began in Birmingham. On Easter Sunday two Negroes attended worship at this church and the

minister spoke a word of welcome to them, backed by an order of
the Session that they would be received. Two more appeared the
next Sunday and the Session began having some second thoughts
about it. Once was an incident. But twice was a habit, and the
people became both apprehensive and disgruntled. The minister
began getting anonymous calls and his automobile tires were
slashed. He now belongs to the grand fraternity of the harassed.
This treatment he endured with good nature. Those who have
taken this sort of punishment can laugh and make jokes about it.

But he, like the rest of us, had a point of vulnerability. He
could not endure to see his people fall out of communion with
each other and with him. Their tie had been one of love; when
this is broken there is little left to call a church. Newspapermen
and politicians often take this kind of abuse, but the relationship
they have with their constituency is not necessarily one of affection. Often it is one of veiled contempt. They may even conclude
that "the people is a great beast" and still remain secure in their
positions. But not so with the minister; if he does not love and
receive love he has nothing. So his agony is acute and real—how
far can a minister go in proclaiming a Christian principle at the
risk of alienating his people and breaking the unity of the
church? It is painfully obvious that the church and the gospel are
at loggerheads. A folk religion cannot resolve the conflict, in fact,
cannot see it. When, in agony over the issue, the elders gathered
at a special meeting, the minister patiently pointed out that
unity was coveted but a Christian principle was involved. To
which the insurance company president rejoindered, "To hell
with Christian principles—we've got to save the church!"

This insurance executive had been my Sunday School teacher
when I was a teen-ager, and my admiration for him had been
boundless. He had helped pull me through a period when I was
slipping into disillusionment over a tragic schism that had occurred in the church about that time. He held me to the church
by sheer devotion and intelligence. How insidious racism is that
would change all that! If I could answer him now it would be
with a question: "Save the church for what, a family shrine?"

This is the city that Martin Luther King chose as his starting
point for a national movement. King needed a Birmingham, and

a Bull Connor-led Birmingham. He needed to dramatize to the nation the grotesque side of segregation. He knew he could count on Bull for the dogs and fire hoses. He knew that the police department would accommodate him by filling the jails with Negroes and providing just enough rough stuff to be called brutal. He knew he could get his people aroused against the Bull because their resentment toward him had smoldered as long as some could remember. A gentle segregationist wouldn't do. Moderation would dissipate the passions of the Negroes and the whole cause would lose its sense of urgency. This King and his colleagues will not let happen. This was 1963, the centennial of the Emancipation Proclamation. The year 1963 was the announced target date by the NAACP several years ago for full integration.

King needed a city whose clergy had not bolstered their people with the whole gospel of the Christian faith, so that the church could be shown for what it was, inept and indecisive. He was waiting for some churchman to clarify the issue with brutal candor—"To hell with Christian principles, we've got to save the church." But King has not waited for the church to throw itself into the breach and become the solvent. He has said that the issue will be settled not by the tolling of the church bell but by the ringing of the cash register. This is the saddest fact of the hour. The agency of reconciliation is not even reconciled to its own body of truth. Churchmen lament loudly that the church would fall apart if required to face the issue squarely. The very fact that we use the term "church" to refer only to white congregations indicates that the church fell apart long ago. The Negro churches are the headquarters of the integration movement. The white churches are bastions of resistance and reactionism. It is harder for Negro and white churchmen to negotiate on the basis of principles of the Christian faith alone than for racial demonstrators to get together with downtown merchants. Generally, white churchmen don't realize that the church has already split, because it has never really dawned on them what the church is.

Before I left the city to return to my border state home I went back again to the old neighborhood of my boyhood days. Jeanne

and the children had flown back ahead of me. My home stood
out starkly, the trees that had sheltered it were gone, and the
fresh white paint with red trim did not conceal its age. The
Beecher house was gone altogether, mysteriously burned to the
ground. It had been bought by a real estate company formed by
the neighbors to prevent its being sold to Negroes. It was vacant
at the time it was burned. The cause of the fire was combustion
from some old painting rags left around, the neighbors say. The
spacious yard, back and front, which had been my domain was
now an ugly jungle of weeds. And my fir tree was gone; but even if
it had been there, what a sorry scene I would have surveyed from
the pinnacle of it. When John Beecher, now in California, heard
of the destruction of his house he wrote this angry poem:

"If I Forget Thee, O Birmingham!"

I
Like Florence from your mountain.
Both cast your poets out
for speaking plain.

II
You bowl your bombs down aisles
where black folks kneel
to pray for your blacker souls.

III
Dog-torn children bled
A, B, O, AB as you.
Christ's blood not more red.

IV
Burning my house to keep
them out, you sowed wind. Hear it blow!
Soon you reap.

Even now the white neighbors are fighting, though neat little
brick homes for Negroes have been built within five hundred feet
of my house at the very point where I used to launch my kites.
The whites formed themselves into a corporation to buy every
house that was about to be offered for sale to a Negro. Theirs is a
losing battle. The system is self-defeating. Those white families

who want to get out and don't mind being labeled traitors realize that they can get competing bids from Negroes and the corporation. So they play one against the other, with the result that real estate values have increased considerably. The corporation in turn finds it harder and harder to obtain capital to match the going prices.

The head of the corporation is my old coach Ben, who is now in charge of development for the very fine Birmingham-Southern College. I spent a couple of hours with him one day before I returned home, good-naturedly discussing the race issue. There are only a few left who can still maintain a sense of humor when they talk of it. Thank heaven, he can. I asked him why he and the other neighbors persisted when the ball game was lost. He, like the rest of my Southern friends, is indomitable to the point of fatalism. "You might be right," he said, "but we are going to fight on anyway."

It's the old Confederate spirit still alive and struggling, holding on irrationally but proudly, hoping to wear down the opposition by stalemate. Though bred upon this spirit, I am still amazed at it.

"What about your Methodist minister," I asked Ben. "What does he think about all this?" The one I was referring to I didn't know by name, but he was in charge of the church that served the college and the predominantly Methodist neighborhood.

"He looks at it this way," Coach Ben said. "The bishop sent him here to hold together a church that is losing members because the neighbors are moving away to avoid integration. The church comes first with him; he is for whatever holds the church together."

"I believe I've heard that story before," I concluded a little wistfully, and bade him, my neighborhood, my college, and my city good-by.

I am often asked, if I had to do it over, would I have done what I did. The answer is that I don't see how I could have done otherwise. In retrospect, the details and the daily decisions seem small and inconsequential, though at the time they weren't. There were great forces at work and my adversaries and I were caught up in them and thrown against each other. We were like

flotsam and jetsam bobbing on the surface, whose movements
were determined by the strong undercurrents. There was a force
that accumulated from the fears of a people that to extend justice and equality to another people would be the end of what
they were and stood for. There was a countervailing force that
arose from the anguished and angry souls of a people who had
been oppressed too long. I was caught up in this latter force and,
considering my background, heaven knows why. If ever predestination meant anything to me, it does now.

I am the servant of the church, but it gradually became clear
to me that I owe a higher service to the *message* of the church
that we call the gospel. The agony of the minister begins when
he recognizes that the two, church and gospel, are at odds with
each other. To put it another way, it is structure versus function.
I had to decide which had primacy. The church at large was
preoccupied with its structure and overly jealous of its unity. My
decision was the lonely one: I had to take my chances with the
gospel, the whole gospel.

I feel some degree of satisfaction in sensing that my old Southern acquaintances are thawing out in their attitude toward me.
Recently, the *Columbus Ledger* carried pictures of thirteen former citizens under the caption, "Say, Whatever Happened
to . . . ?" There were a few generals, a former city manager, a
couple of governors, the two men indicted for the murder of
Albert Patterson; and there I was among them. This was the
second time in a month the paper seemed to have gone out of its
way to evoke memories of my turbulent years in Columbus. The
manager of one of the local television stations read my "Archie"
sermon for his program one day. The Human Relations Council,
which I had helped to organize and which was so pitifully weak
when I left, has come above ground, and now numbers some of
the town's leading citizens as members. According to its headquarters in Atlanta, Columbus is the "success story" in race relations. On May Fellowship Day for the United Church Women,
one of the members of our subversive group, serving as program
chairman, arranged to have a Negro woman as a speaker and
several other Negroes to attend. And this was done in the First
Presbyterian Church! And not an eyebrow was arched!

Occasionally I run into a citizen of Columbus who will urge

me to come back for a visit. This shouldn't be too difficult. The cause I espoused is firmly entrenched. The people there, like those over most of the South, have seen integration come in their time. The whites' attitude toward this is better described as acquiescence than acceptance, but the wall has been breached. Should I return, I would probably be regarded as a rather harmless fellow now. When I do go back it will be a pleasure to greet friend and antagonist alike, recalling not the agony and the strife, but only that we were all a fallible people more often being driven than driving to an unsure destiny. True, it is a place where I nearly lost my life, but it is also the place where I found my integrity.

I keep wondering if the *Look* article of Steve Lesher, the young Jewish reporter, could not be published now and be readily received.

There are many more ministers in the South who are being subjected to siege over the race issue. So many, in fact, that an organization has been formed in our denomination, the Fellowship of the Concerned, consisting of some of the best known clergy and laity, for the purpose of giving not only moral support but financial assistance to these beleaguered men. This is an organization, and a large one, made up of Southerners living in the South. It may never have to use the money it has collected, because its very existence is such a serious indictment of the churches that opposition to their forthright clergymen will no longer be respectable. No such help was available to me in 1959, but I am now enjoying the thought of it in looking back. I sent the organization a check and told its leader I will never want its help—just say a requiem for me.

The process of thaw continues. The 1963 General Assembly, meeting in Huntington, West Virginia, passed by voice vote a report written by a Negro, Irvin Elligan, and myself which read in part:

Although our Southern region basically clings to the philosophy of racial separation, strong evidence of its failure is seen in its almost universal rejection by darker skinned people and an increasing disapproval among the whites. Unfortunately the church has the reputation of being a bulwark among major institutions practicing segregation, in spite of its profession of the fatherhood of God and the brotherhood of man. Continuing efforts by Christians to justify separation policies are incurring serious disdain, especially among young people who belong to the very congregations where segregation is approved. This racial policy, supported neither by our theology nor our scripture, is reflecting disrespect upon those churches that condone it.

Forthright statements have been made by our church through its higher courts, but they become weaker the nearer they draw to the point of practical application. In time of racial crisis local sessions, ministers, and even presbyteries have generally been silent, or if speaking at all have only counselled against violence and in favor of law and order. In the face of crisis our churches practice insularity which they have mistaken for spirituality. They have sacrificed the forthrightness of the gospel for the peace of the congregation, preferring local unities to community solidarity. The churches are intact but the gospel has been split. The Christ who considered Himself expendable is followed by churches which count themselves indispensable. The church now finds itself not leading but being led, being the conservator but not the prophet, confessing its sins of ineptness and omission, but preferring to continue the confessional rather than to take the more agonizing course of eradicating the wrong. Our default of leadership in this time of racial strife has been one of the grave disappointments of twentieth century Christendom.

Three of its recommendations were:

That every Presbyterian institution, whether church, school, orphanage, home for the aged, or conference center, as well as boards and agencies of the church, abolish all racial barriers and references, and that this nondiscriminatory policy be made known to the public.

That Presbyterian churchmen, Negro and white, in their local communities, seek to establish a realistic communication between the two racial groups, to re-establish a relationship of mutual trust and affection, and together prepare to prevent such episodes as have shamed our region, not waiting for equality and justice to be accomplished by force or the passions of people to be goaded to violence; and that Negro and white churchmen assume proportionate responsibility for racial evils in society and for the solution of such problems which we face together in these rapidly changing times.

That Presbyterian churchmen in local communities, while rec-

ognizing the right to criticize their leadership, protest in their
own way defamatory statements and vindictive acts from public
officials directed against the President of the United States, the
Supreme Court, and other officers, state and federal, whose decisions and actions are for the purpose of upholding the law and
keeping the peace.

Anything I had ever said before this was timid by comparison,
and yet the highest court of the church accepted it in 1963 with
only a few scattered negative votes. Attitudes do change, not just
by the passage of time, but by the persistence of those who utilize
every moment of it to good advantage.

I have had some second thoughts on whether it is too late for
the white churches of the South to aid the cause of social justice.
It is true that the cash register had rung more loudly than the
church bell, that economic pressure had gained for the Negro
more concessions than moral persuasion, and perhaps even more
than the passage of laws. These churches defaulted on the issue
because they feared and hated it. They had their opportunity to
use the mighty weapon of moral persuasion, but they themselves
were not persuaded.

This seems to remove the white churches at least two stages
from being of any use to the cause. But it doesn't. They can move
into the demonstrations themselves and make their witness. The
demonstrative method can fail the cause if it is not both wisely
and graciously used. It is used wisely when it is both nonviolent
and relevant. James Farmer, national director of CORE, speaks
of a "relevant confrontation," and he condemned the intended
stall-ins at the 1964 World's Fair in New York because they were
not. Demonstrations that have no more than nuisance value and
that inconvenience the wrong people, that is, white sympathizers, are not relevant.

Even nonviolence by itself is not enough. As such it is a
method dictated by prudence and nothing else. Generally, the
Negroes know that physical violence will invite strong retaliation. There is too much destructive power in the hands of the
whites. As long as nonviolence is a method and not a philosophy,
it will be subject to change when violence promises to accomplish
more. Therefore, demonstrations must not only be wise but gracious. Graciousness doesn't mean that the thrust will be any less

persistent or aggressive, but it does mean that the demonstrators will manifest a certain amount of tolerance and sympathy toward their antagonists and especially toward their sympathizers, who either will not or cannot join them in this particular method. Graciousness cannot be extemporized; it must come from a down-in-the-soul recognition of the collectivity of our guilt, the ambiguity of both black and white nature, the mutuality of faults, and the ultimate triumph of love over animosity. It was my Negro friend, Irvin Elligan, who taught me this. The church has always and continues to teach this grace because it considers itself the heir of the grace of life.

The trouble is that the church has not felt deeply enough about the issues of life to know how and where to make the application of graciousness. The white churches can suggest guidelines for demonstrations and can furnish demonstrators who will, in the face of the fiercest showdowns on human justice, supplant veiled contempt with compassion, resentment with good humor, impatience with friendly persistence, and suppressed hatred with open tolerance. If our churches continue to hold themselves aloof to the issue, they do so at the risk of much blood and an unbridgeable gap between two races. For they will forfeit the issue to opportunists, whose appeal is not to reconciliation but retaliation. After equality and justice are finally achieved, the rewards will be cheap and short-lived if they are gotten at the expense of total racial estrangement. It is becoming plainer every day that the Christian way is the practical way.

The white people would do well to analyze the several groups within the Negro movement and their attitudes. Martin Luther King and his Southern Christian Leadership Conference learned their tactics from Gandhi, but owe their disposition to the Sermon on the Mount. Their dreams of freedom occurred in their churches; their strategy sessions were held there, their marching orders rang from their pulpits. Through ordeals that would turn cynical the sweetest saint, King has held on to his Bible and has riveted the hearts of his followers with love.

His opposite is the Black Muslim, waiting for King's cheek-turning tactics to fail. The Black Muslims are restrained from the use of force neither by prudence nor ideology. One gets the impression that they are spoiling for a fight and waiting impatiently for provocation. Somewhere between these two are the Congress of Racial Equality and the Student Nonviolent Coordinating Committee. Their attitude seems to say that nonviolence is simply a method and not an ideology, and that they couldn't care less for such a fuzzy and sentimental idea as reconciliation of the races as long as equality and justice are achieved. Then there are those such as the Harlem rioters, who belong to no major organization and feel that nobody outside their own precinct is speaking for them. In fact, the summer riots of 1964 in several Northern cities seem to indicate that large elements of the Negro population feel that the talking stage is past, that the rational approach is but a delay of justice.

The white element in the integration movement is encountering a problem that it could not have anticipated, say, twenty years ago. It is the addition of several other organizations to the major one, NAACP. The problem is now two-fold. First, Negro leaders of these organizations occasionally display some professional jealousy and white sympathizers are caught in the cross fire of rival ambitions. And second, it is becoming obvious that these organizations differ with each other both in ideology and in procedure. The white person, in attempting to serve the cause of justice in an organized way, is now forced to consider which of the major groups he is in sympathy with before he commits himself. It can almost be said that the movement for racial justice has become sectarian. This fact does not help the cause, but human nature being what it is, I don't see how it could have been averted.

The white community had better hope that the King disposition prevails, and the white churches had better recognize it as a unifying spirit within the larger Christian family, match it with a gracious concern of their own, and implement it with concrete forms of justice.

What about civil disobedience? The Christian from the first century on has been exhorted to respect civil government and obey its laws, so long as conscience is not violated. As Paul put it in his Roman letter, "Let every person be subject to the governing authorities." Yet when two of the disciples were preaching on the street (unlawful assembly and dissemination of forbidden propaganda), they defied the local authorities by declaring "that they must obey God rather than men." So the Christian faces a dilemma when higher and lower authorities are in conflict or when a particular human authority, if obeyed, forces one to violate his own conscience.

The solution seems to be civil disobedience. Again, the Christian churchman can go to work at the point where disobedience could become civil or uncivil. To be civil (and therefore a legitimate method) four things are required: one, that the particular law be openly and purposely violated; two, that the violation of the law entail no physical hurt to anyone; three, that the lawbreaker willingly and peacefully accept the prescribed punishment for his infraction; four, that the particular law if repealed would increase not the license but the liberties of the people. Civil disobedience will always be a possible method of the Christian as long as he can distinguish between human and divine law and between convention and conscience. He has no ultimate allegiance unless he reserves the right to declare at some point in his life when the human system threatens to consume his soul, "I must obey God rather than men." The church is never too late as long as it can recover the nerve to say just that.

I have heard many of my colleagues say that they love the church they serve. I often ask myself if I do. I have had few peaceful years in it. I have had three battles over the race issue and two bouts with presbytery. I have no trophies of success, such as important appointments and honorary degrees. I have never done more than break even on my income. My life has been jeopardized and probably shortened by being an integral part of the church. In other centuries, when the church was fighting some assailant outside itself, I would have loved it all the more for what it would have cost me. But today's church as an *institution* I cannot love. I cannot love that which loves itself, which considers itself indispensable and yet will not be itself. I cannot love its ingrownness, its measurements of success, its suppression of its own message, its compromise of its mission. I cannot love the credulousness that passes for faith, the literalness that stifles inquiry, the social compatibility that poses as fellowship, the peevishness that aspires to martyrdom, the dogmatism that intimidates, the salvational formulas that do not save, the piousness that conceals spite, the conventionalism that stunts originality, the respectability that thinks itself moral, the unction that is accepted as spiritual. This does not describe the church; it describes what we have to cut through to find the church, or what we are offered in lieu of the church.

Perhaps I sound disillusioned. Not at all—I belong to a breed that might be called the happy malcontents, a type that works overtime within the church, loving and enjoying its people, but never equating the church with the Kingdom of Heaven, its membership's consensus with the will of God, nor its smooth sayings with the gospel. This type feels called to be critical of itself and discontented with the church until both are, not totally good, but totally committed to something and someone beyond the human among us.

Let me put it this way. There is something imponderably elusive, indescribable about life, that I love—the quest of it, the charm of it, the reward of it, though it draws the grail beyond one's grasp. The artist attempts to capture it in forms and combinations of colors. The singer would find it after he has learned the score and the proper placements of his tones. The philosopher hopes that it shines through his reasoning. The theologian aspires to it after his precise creeds are in place. Each hopes that his skill has the glow of it, for it is what he would transmit, would communicate to some other soul as eager as he to embrace it. It is not in his native or acquired skill; it is in his person, in that unique combination that makes up the self that is his. What shall we call it? The preternatural, the supersensible, the ultimate dimension, the overplus, faith, the spirit of God? Whatever it is, it separates men from beasts and a man from his bestiality. It is a spirit that motivates and identifies the clod, it is eternity inseminating time, perfection permeating obliqueness, meaning infiltrating despair, the unfathomable penetrating the commonplace, the incarnation in the midst of the carnal, resurrection quickening mortality.

Whatever it is, we can find it in that malaise we call the institutional church, for where it is there is the church in all its pristine purity. About it will be gathered those who, with eyes open, walk by faith and not by sight, and who seek each other out and become communal with each other; because whatever this overplus of life is, it is preserved not by contemplation but by relationship. Life's superlative artistry is found not in combinations of colors but in combinations of persons. In their concourse alone is God comprehended as a person. So those perceptive ones who sense more of existence than is seen, who are already tinged with eternity, form a host within the mass and become the heartbeat of the church—in fact, they are the church.

This I love, to this I commit my life, for this I will die and be forgotten. I have and want no other fascination.